P9-AFY-189

Contents

◄◄ Liberation monument ◄ Széchenyi Lánchíd

Introduction to

Budapest

With a wonderful natural setting straddling the River Danube, beautiful architecture and its excellent Magyar cuisine, Budapest is one of the most rewarding cities in Europe to visit. Its magnificent waterfront and boulevards invite comparisons with Paris, Prague and Vienna – as do many features of its cultural life, from coffee houses and a love of opera to its wine-producing tradition. However, the city is also distinctively Hungarian, its inhabitants displaying fierce pride in their Magyar ancestry. Their language, too, whose nearest European relative is Finnish, underlines the difference.

▲ Architectural detail, Várhegy

Ironically, provincial Hungarians have long regarded Budapest as a hotbed of alien values and loose morals – a charge that misses the point. Foreigners have played a major role in the city since its inception, and the Chinese and Arab communities established since the end of Communism simply bring Budapest up to date as an international city. Even the sex trade that has earned it the reputation of the "Bangkok of Europe" is nothing new, having been a feature of life during Habsburg times. In politics, art and much else, Budapest is not only the capital but a catalyst for the country, without which Hungary would be a far duller place.

Fundamental to the city's layout and history, the **River Danube** (Duna) – which is seldom blue – separates **Buda** on the hilly west bank from **Pest** on the eastern plain. Until 1873 these were separate cities, and they still retain a different feel. Buda is older and more dignified: dominated by Várhegy (Castle Hill), a mile-long long plateau overlooking the Danube, it was the capital of medieval monarchs and the seat of power for successive occupying powers. Laid out during the city's golden age in the late nineteenth century,

4
■

with boulevards of Haussmann-like apartment blocks sweeping out from the old medieval centre, **Pest** holds the city's magnificent Art Nouveau edifices and has a noisy, bustling feel. Following construction of the first permanent bridge between the two cities in 1845, power gradually moved across the river, culminating in the building of the grandiose Parliament on the Pest side. The two halves of the city still retain their differences, but as a whole Budapest is a vibrant city today, never in danger of being overwhelmed by tourism but nonetheless offering plenty for visitors to enjoy.

One of Budapest's strongest suits is its **restaurants**, with places to suit all budgets and a huge range of cuisines on offer. As well as the richly sauced meat and fish dishes of Hungarian food, you'll find Indian, Chinese, Italian and Middle Eastern cooking alongside plenty of options for vegetarians. And though it's often overlooked abroad, Hungarian **wine** makes a delightful accompaniment to any meal. Catering for a wide range of tastes, Budapest's **nightlife** is also very much of a draw. Generally trouble-free and welcoming, the scene boasts a whole network of events that are surprisingly accessible. This is especially true of the *táncház* (dance house) scene, where Hungarians of all ages perform wild stamping movements to the rhythms of darkest Transylvania, and internationally renowned artists such as Márta Sebestyén appear in an informal setting.

There's plenty to offer in terms of **classical music and opera**, too: world-class ensembles and soloists can be enjoyed in the Palace of Arts' state-of-the-art concert hall or the grander, older settings of the Music Academy and State Opera House. For fans of **pop**, **rock** and **world music**, the two big events are the Budapesti Bucsú, first held to celebrate the departure of Soviet troops in 1991, and the huge **Sziget Festival**, which attracts many international stars.

What to see

▼ Coronation regalia, Parliament

Pest is where you're likely to spend most of your time, enjoying the streetlife, bars and shops within the **Belváros** (Inner City) and the surrounding districts. These surrounding areas are defined by two semicircular boulevards – the **Kiskörút** (Small Boulevard) and the **Nagykörút** (Great Boulevard) – and radial avenues such as Andrássy út and Rákóczi út. Exploring the area between them can easily occupy you for several days. In the financial and government centre of **Lipótváros**, interest lies in St Stephen's Basilica and the monumental Parliament building, which rivals the grand structures across the Danube. In **Terézváros**, Andrássy út leads out past the grandiose Opera House and the House of Terror to Hősök tere (Heroes' Square), a magnificent imperial set-piece where the Fine Arts Museum displays a fine collection of old European masters. Beyond, the **Városliget** (City Park) holds one of the finest zoos in Europe, both in terms of its animals and its architecture, as well as the hugely popular Széchenyi Baths, served by its own thermal springs.

Of Pest's remaining inner-city districts, **Erzsébetváros** and **Józsefváros** hold the most appeal. The former is Budapest's old Jewish quarter, with a rich and tragic history that's still palpable in the atmospheric and eminently explorable backstreets. The great synagogue on Dohány utca provides more historical background. From here, it's not far to the National Museum, a well-presented introduction to Hungarian history, and to the Great Market Hall, further round in **Ferencváros**.

Várhegy (Castle Hill) on the **Buda** side was once the seat of Hungary's monarchs, and its palace, museums, churches and Baroque streets offer some absorbing sightseeing. The historic Turkish baths along the banks of the Danube are also well worth experiencing. In fine weather people flock to **Margit sziget**, the large and verdant island between Buda and Pest, to swim and sunbathe at enormous lidos. Encircling the city to the west, the **Buda Hills** have a different kind if allure, with enjoyable rides on the Cogwheel and Children's railways, and intriguing caves to be visited. **Further out**, the steam trains of the Rail History Park and the redundant Communist monuments within the Statue Park rate as major attractions.

The **Rough Guide** to

Budapest

written and researched by

Charles Hebbert and Dan Richardson

**ROUGH
GUIDES**

NEW YORK • LONDON • DELHI

www.roughguides.com

Hungarian Art Nouveau

Bedecked with distinctive green and yellow tiles and beehive decorations, the former Post Office Savings Bank, just off Szabadság tér in Lipótváros, is a particularly exuberant example of the stunning Art Nouveau buildings that so enliven the streets of Budapest. As the trend for Art Nouveau design swept across Europe at the end of the nineteenth century, Hungary was in a state of high national confidence, enjoying a period of rapid economic growth, celebrating the thousandth anniversary of the arrival of the Magyar tribes in Europe and yearning for independence from Austria. The prevailing architectural style had produced neo-Gothic wedding cakes like the Parliament, but Art Nouveau rejected this approach – here, as in Vienna, it was known as "Secessionism". Often cited as Budapest's Gaudi, and one of Art Nouveau's leading lights, the Hungarian architect Ödön Lechner said he sought to "shape a new age in art, to give birth to a new style" – and he wanted that style to be distinctively Hungarian. He covered his buildings in brightly coloured ornamentation, drawing on folk motifs and using new materials such as reinforced concrete and the glazed Zsolnay tiles that adorn roofs such as that of the Applied Arts Museum. Though Lechner's designs caused uproar when unveiled, they have since become a major influence on Hungarian architects, and today are rightly considered national treasures, evoking nothing but pride in Budapestis' hearts.

▲ Roof detail, former Post Office Savings Bank

When to go

The best times to visit Budapest are **spring** (late March to the end of May) and **autumn** (Sept–Oct), when the weather is mild and there are fewer tourists (though things tend to get busy during the **Budapest Spring Festival** in late March/early April). The majority of tourists come in the summer, when many residents decamp to Lake Balaton and those who remain flock to the city's pools and parks to escape the heat and dust. Though some concert halls are closed over summer, there are all kinds of outdoor events to compensate – especially in August, when the **Budapest Plázs** (Budapest Beach) turns one side of the Danube into a sandy resort, and the Sziget Festival and Formula One Grand Prix take place. Winter is cold and may be snowy, but you can still enjoy all the city's sights and cultural attractions (as well as trying roasted chestnuts from street vendors), while the thermal baths take on an extra allure. It's wise to book accommodation in advance for Christmas, New Year, the Spring Festival and Grand Prix.

Average daytime temperature, and average monthly rainfall

	Jan	Feb	Mar	Apr	May	June	July	Aug	Sept	Oct	Nov	Dec
°F	29	32	42	53	61	68	72	70	63	52	42	34
°C	-2	0	6	12	16	20	22	21	17	11	6	1
mm	37	44	38	45	72	69	56	47	33	57	70	46

▲ Nyugati Station

25

things not to miss

It's not possible to see everything that Budapest has to offer in one trip – and we don't suggest you try. What follows is a selective taste of the region's highlights: magnificent Art Nouveau treasures, unique thermal baths, and world-class concerts and festivals. They're arranged in five colour-coded categories, which you can browse through to find the very best things to see and experience. All highlights have a page reference to take you straight into the guide, where you can find out more.

01 Thermal baths Page **182** • Bathe in splendour at the city's spas, fed by hot natural springs.

02 Coffee houses Page 163 • Ponder the world over a coffee and cake – after all, it's an old Central European tradition.

03
No. 2 tram ride Page **31** • No.2's route along the banks of the Danube provides stunning views of Buda.

04
Food markets Page **189** • Stock up on paprika and salami at the city's busy markets and market halls.

05 Gresham Palace

Page **55** • Enjoy an apéritif or cake in the elegant surroundings of this landmark Art Nouveau hotel, now immaculately restored to its former splendour.

06 House of Terror

Page **68** • Grim yet gripping, this is a moving monument to those who suffered in the terror that afflicted the country during and after World War II.

07 Libegő chairlift

Page **125** • A beautifully silent and swift way to ride up to the top of the Buda Hills, from where there are great views over the whole city.

08
Margit sziget
Page **121** • A car-free refuge from the bustle of the city: go for a swim, hire a bike or a pedalo or just laze around on the vast expanses of grass.

09 **Children's Railway** Page **123** • Rattle through the scenic woodlands for a leisurely day out in the Buda Hills.

10
Budapest Zoo Page
81 • Feed the giraffes, tickle the rhinos and marvel at the magnificent Art Nouveau buildings – the Elephant and Palm houses are particularly impressive.

11 Applied Arts Museum Page **89** • Budapest boasts some splendid Art Nouveau buildings, and this museum is one of the finest examples, with an interior that rivals a Moghul palace.

12 Fishermen's Bastion Page **96** • Enjoy great views over the city from this extraordinary mock battlement in the Castle district.

13 Hungarian National Gallery Page **101** • Showcased in the imposing Buda Palace, this is Hungary's best collection of home-grown art, from medieval altar-pieces to works by young contemporary painters.

14 Budapest's cemeteries

Page **87, 88, 126 & 128** • A wander round the cemeteries offer a fascinating historical overview, with monuments ranging from the vast Pantheon of the Working Class to the elaborate turquoise Schmidl tomb.

16 Jewish quarter

Page **70** • The Dohány utca synagogue is the high point of a visit to the ghetto area, with its old streets, monuments and bars.

15 Museum of Fine Arts

Page **75** • This excellent display of European old masters includes a Spanish collection that's unrivalled outside Spain.

17

Statue Park
Page **128** • A fascinating gathering of monuments from the communist past, now preserved in this park on the edge of town.

18 **Rail History Museum** Page **127** • Both children and adults will enjoy this extensive collection of steam trains, carriages and paraphernalia – you can even get to drive a steam engine.

19 **National Film Theatre** Page **177** • Worth a visit for the fabulous Venetian-Moorish decorations – and it also has an excellent selection of Hungarian and foreign films.

20 **Classical concerts** Page **173** • The Budapest Festival Orchestra, under the baton of Iván Fischer, is one of the city's many outstanding classical ensembles.

21

Castle District Page **92** • Dominated by the Buda Palace and peppered with museums and historic buildings, the Castle District is the capital's defining feature.

22 Wine Page 157 • Hungarian
wines are a voyage of discovery for visitors to Budapest. Forget Bull's Blood and enjoy the rich reds from Villány and the fine whites from Badacsony.

24 Sikló funicular Page
92 • Take the scenic way up to the Castle District and watch the views unfold as you rise above the rooftops.

23 Budapest Spring Festival
Page 37 • The biggest arts event of the year includes music, dancing and theatre, as well as a grand parade.

25 Folk music Page 175 • Catch the
irrepressible sounds of Muzsikás and other top bands on Budapest's dynamic folk circuit.

Basics

Basics

Getting there

Several airlines fly to Budapest from airports in the UK and Ireland, while there are nonstop flights from the US and Canada with the Hungarian national carrier Malév. Travelling overland from the UK takes around a day by train and a day and a half by bus.

Airfares always depend on the **season**, with the highest fares from June to August, when the weather is best. You'll get the best prices during the low season, November to February (excluding Christmas and New Year when prices are hiked up and seats are at a premium).

You can often cut costs by going through a **specialist flight agent** – either a consolidator, who buys up blocks of tickets from the airlines and sells them at a discount, or a **discount agent**, who in addition to dealing with discounted flights may also offer special student and youth fares and a range of other travel-related services such as travel insurance, rail passes, car rentals, tours and the like.

Budapest is now an extremely popular **city-break** destination and this is reflected in the growing number of operators offering the city as a destination in itself; it's also included on some two- or three-centre itineraries.

Booking flights online

Many airlines and discount travel websites give you the opportunity to book your tickets, hotels and holiday packages **online**. These are worth going for, though note that the best deals may be non-refundable and non-changeable.

Online booking agents

ⓦ **www.cheapflights.co.uk** (UK & Ireland), ⓦ **www.cheapflights.com** (US), ⓦ **www. cheapflights.ca** (Canada), ⓦ **www.cheapflights. com.au** (Australia & NZ). Flight deals, travel agents, plus links to other travel sites.
ⓦ **www.cheaptickets.com** (US). Discount flight specialists.
ⓦ **www.ebookers.com** (UK), ⓦ **www.ebookers. ie** (Republic of Ireland). Efficient, easy-to-use flight finder, with competitive fares.

ⓦ **www.etn.nl/discount** A hub of consolidator and discount agent links, maintained by the non-profit European Travel Network.
ⓦ **www.expedia.co.uk** (UK), ⓦ **www.expedia. com** (US), ⓦ **www.expedia.ca** (Canada). Discount airfares, all-airline search engine and daily deals.
ⓦ **www.flyaow.com** "Airlines of the Web" – online air travel info and reservations.
ⓦ **www.flynow.com** Simple-to-use independent travel site offering good-value fares.
ⓦ **www.lastminute.com** (UK)
ⓦ **www.lastminute.com.au** (Australia)
ⓦ **www.lastminute.co.nz** (NZ). Comprehensive site with last-minute offers for flights, accommodation and car hire.
ⓦ **www.opodo.co.uk** (UK). Popular source of low airfares, owned by nine major European airlines.
ⓦ **www.skyauction.com** (US). Bookings from the US only. Auctions tickets and travel packages to destinations worldwide.
ⓦ **www.travelocity.co.uk** (UK).
ⓦ **www.travelocity.com** (US).
ⓦ **www.travelocity.ca** (Canada). Destination guides, hot web fares and best deals for car hire, accommodation and lodging as well as fares.
ⓦ **www.travelshop.com.au** (Australia). Australian site offering discounted flights, packages, insurance, and online bookings. Also on ☎ 1800 108 108.
ⓦ **www.zuji.com.au** (Australia). Destination guides, hot fares and deals for car rental, accommodation and lodging.

Flights from the UK and Ireland

The cost of flying to Budapest **from the UK** has been sharply reduced by the appearance of several **low-cost operators** – at the time of writing, these included easyJet, SkyEurope, Wizz Air and Jet 2. Tickets on these airilnes go for as little as £50 return, including tax. These flights do fill up quickly, and you should think about booking a couple of months ahead for the summer; moreover, the earlier you book, the cheaper the flight is likely to be. As for scheduled fares, these start from around £180 in high season and £100 in low season, or from €180 in low season if you're travelling from the **Republic of Ireland**.

Airlines

Aer Lingus UK ☎0845 084 4444, Republic of Ireland ☎0818/365 000, ⊛ www.aerlingus.ie. Dublin to Budapest.

Air Berlin UK ☎0870/738 8880, ⊛ www.airberlin.com. London Stansted to Budapest.

British Airways UK ☎0870 850 9850, Republic of Ireland ☎1800 626 747, ⊛ www.ba.com. Daily flights from London Heathrow to Budapest, as well as from London Gatwick during the summer.

easyJet UK ☎0871 750 0100, ⊛ www.easyjet.com. Budget flights to Budapest from Bristol, London Gatwick, Luton and Newcastle.

Jet2 UK ☎0871 226 1 737, Ireland ☎0818 20001, ⊛ www.jet2.com. Low-cost summer-only flights to Budapest from Manchester.

KLM (Royal Dutch Airlines) UK ☎0870/507 4074, ⊛ www.klm.com. To Budapest via Amsterdam, with convenient departures from regional airports in the UK and Republic of Ireland.

Lufthansa UK ☎0845/773 7747, Republic of Ireland ☎01/844 5544, ⊛ www.lufthansa.com. Departures from city and regional airports in the UK and Republic of Ireland to Budapest, via Frankfurt.

Malév Hungarian Airlines UK ☎0870 909 0577, Republic of Ireland ☎01/844 4303, ⊛ www.malev.hu. Budapest from London Heathrow, London Stansted and Dublin.

SkyEurope UK ☎020/7365 0365, ⊛ www.skyeurope.com. Budget flights from London Stansted to Budapest.

Wizz Alr ⊛ www.wizzair.com. Polish budget operator with Budapest flights from Liverpool and Luton.

Travel agents

Co-op Travel Care UK ☎0870 112 0085, ⊛ www.travelcareonline.com. Flights and holidays from one of the larger independent travel agents.

Flightcentre UK ☎0870 890 8099, ⊛ www.flightcentre.co.uk. Rock-bottom fares.

Joe Walsh Tours Republic of Ireland ☎01/676 0991, ⊛ www.joewalshtours.ie. Long-established general budget fares and holidays agent.

McCarthys Travel Republic of Ireland ☎021/427 0127, ⊛ www.mccarthystravel.ie. Established Irish travel agent.

North South Travel UK ☎01245 608 291, ⊛ www.northsouthtravel.co.uk. Discounted fares; profits are used to support projects in the developing world.

Premier Travel UK ☎028 7126 3333, ⊛ www.premiertravel.uk.com. Discount flight specialists based in Belfast.

STA Travel UK ☎0870 160 0599, ⊛ www.statravel.co.uk. Specialists in low-cost flights and holiday deals. Good discounts for students and under-26s.

Top Deck UK ☎020 8879 6789, ⊛ www.topdecktravel.co.uk. Long-established agent dealing in discount flights and tours.

Trailfinders UK ☎0845 0585 858, ⊛ www.trailfinders.com, Republic of Ireland ☎01/677 7888, ⊛ www.trailfinders.ie. Well-informed agent geared up to independent travellers.

Travel Bag UK ☎0800 082 5000, ⊛ www.travelbag.co.uk. Discount deals on flights, accommodation and car rental.

Travel Care UK ☎0870 112 0085, ⊛ www.travelcare.co.uk. Flights, holiday deals and city breaks.

usit NOW Republic of Ireland ☎01/602 1600, Northern Ireland ☎028 9032 7111; ⊛ www.usitnow.ie. Student and youth specialists for flights and trains.

Tour operators and agents

Bridgewater Travel ☎0161 703 3000, ⊛ www.bridgewater-travel.co.uk. Budapest city breaks and accommodation.

CME Travel ☎0870 128 0636, ⊛ www.cmefortravel.co.uk. Hungarian specialists offering Budapest city breaks, spa and therapy packages, and an extensive range of tailor-made tours such as bird-watching, fishing, horse-riding and gastronomic trips, as well as fly/drive holidays.

Martin Randall Travel ☎020 8742 3355, ⊛ www.martinrandall.com. Upmarket art, architecture and music tours on specific dates with expert guides and speakers. Packages include one focused on the Budapest Spring Festival, which starts at £1200.

Prospect Tours ☎020 7486 5704, ⊛ www.prospecttours.com. Spring Festival breaks in Budapest (from £900) and a four-night Christmas break in a five-star hotel.

Regent Holidays ☎0117 921 1711, ⊛ www.regent-holidays.co.uk. Eastern European specialists offering Budapest city breaks (£260) and tailor-made itineraries.

Saga Holidays ☎0800 414525, ⊛ www.saga.co.uk. Two-day city breaks in one of the *Hilton* hotels; caters to senior travellers.

St Albans Travel Service ☏ 01727 840244, ⓦ www.theatrebreaks.com. Two-night opera breaks in Budapest for £185 excluding flights, plus tailor-made breaks.
Thermalia Travel ☏ 020 7586 7725, ⓦ www.thermalia.co.uk. Spa holiday specialists offering stays at four-star thermal resorts in Budapest from around £720 for seven nights, plus beauty, fitness and slimming courses, tennis for beginners, golf and sailing.

Overland from the UK

Travelling by **train** is likely to be considerably more expensive than flying, and the shortest journey from London's Victoria Station to Budapest takes around 25 hours, not much quicker than the bus. A standard second-class London to Budapest rail **return ticket**, incorporating Eurostar, costs around £300; prices are more attractive if you're a student, under 26 or over 60. Tickets have two to three months' return validity, and stopovers are allowed as long as you stick to the prescribed route. Arriving in Paris, you can continue the journey to Budapest from Gare de l'Est via Munich or Vienna, both of which take around 19 hours. Having an Inter-Rail (ⓦ www.interrail.net) or Eurail (ⓦ www.eurail.com) **train pass** makes it convenient to take in Hungary as part of a wider rail trip around Europe.

The **bus** journey to Budapest from London takes around 27 hours. A standard return fare costs around £110 (valid for six months), but regular promotional offers can bring this down to as low as £70.

Driving to Hungary can be a pleasant proposition, though it's really only worth considering if you want to take advantage of stopovers en route. Once across the channel, the most direct route to Budapest is from Ostend, travelling via Brussels, Aachen, Cologne, Frankfurt, Nürnberg, Linz and Vienna. It's a distance of 1500km, which can be covered in 24 hours nonstop, but you shouldn't bank on driving it in under 36. To avoid the long queues at Hegyeshalom and other main border crossings over summer, consider entering Hungary from Deutsch-Kreutz, just south of Eisenstadt, instead. See p.33 for information about licences, insurance and driving in Budapest.

Rail and bus tickets

Eurolines UK ☏ 0870 580 8808, ⓦ www.eurolines.co.uk; Republic of Ireland ☏ 01/836 6111, ⓦ www.eurolines.ie. From London's Victoria Coach Station direct to Budapest.
Eurostar UK ☏ 0870 160 6600, ⓦ www.eurostar.com.
International Rail UK ☏ 0870 751 5000, ⓦ www.international-rail.com. Offers a wide variety of rail options, including Eurostar, all European passes and tickets, international sleepers, ferry crossings and more.
Rail Europe UK ☏ 0870 584 8848, ⓦ www.raileurope.co.uk. Broad range of mainstream rail options, including Eurostar, and tickets for major destinations in Europe. Also Inter-Rail and Eurodomino passes.
Trainseurope UK ☏ 0900 195 0101 (60p/min, refundable against a booking), ⓦ www.trainseurope.co.uk. Tickets, passes, Eurotunnel, Inter-Rail, Eurodomino, and more.

From the US and Canada

The Hungarian national carrier Malév is the only airline with **nonstop** Budapest flights from North America, operating from New York and Toronto, with flights lasting around eight hours. Other European carriers will get you to Budapest via their hub city, and many work in tandem with North American carriers, making it easy to book your Budapest flight together with any connections within the US or Canada that you might need.
Fares from the **US** to Budapest are typically US$600 from New York and US$850 from West Coast cities in low season, rising by $400 during high season. From **Canada**, fares are around Can$1000 in low season, rising to Can$1300–1600 in high season.

Airlines

Air Canada ☏ 1-888/247-2262, ⓦ www.aircanada.com.
Air France ☏ 1-800/237-2747, Canada ☏ 1-800/667-2747, ⓦ www.airfrance.com.
American Airlines ☏ 1-800/624-6262, ⓦ www.aa.com.
Austrian Airlines ☏ 1-800/843-0002, ⓦ www.aua.com.
British Airways ☏ 1-800/AIRWAYS, ⓦ www.ba.com.
Northwest/KLM ☏ 1-800/447-4747, ⓦ www.nwa.com, ⓦ www.klm.com.

Lufthansa ☎1-800/645-3880, Canada ☎1-800/563-5954, ⓦwww.lufthansa.com.
Malév Hungarian Airlines ☎1-800/223-6884 or 212/566-9944, ⓦwww.malev.hu.
United Airlines ☎1-800/538-2929, ⓦwww.united.com.

Travel agents

Airtech ☎212/219-7000, ⓦwww.airtech.com. Standby seat broker; also deals in consolidator fares.
Educational Travel Center ☎1-800/747-5551 or 608/256-5551, ⓦwww.edtrav.com. Low-cost fares worldwide, student/youth discount offers, and Eurail passes, car rental and tours.
Flightcentre US ☎1-866/WORLD-51, ⓦwww.flightcentre.us, Canada ☎1-888/WORLD-55, ⓦwww.flightcentre.ca. Low fares worldwide.
New Frontiers US ☎1-800/677-0720, ⓦwww.newfrontiers.com. Discount firm specializing in travel from the US to Europe, with hotels and package deals.
STA Travel US ☎1-800/329-9537, Canada ☎1-888/427-5639, ⓦwww.statravel.com. Worldwide specialists in independent travel; also student IDs, travel insurance, car rental, rail passes, and more.
Student Flights ☎1-800/255-8000 or 480/951-1177, ⓦwww.isecard.com/studentflights. Student/youth fares, plus student IDs and European rail and bus passes.
TFI Tours ☎1-800/745-8000 or 212/736-1140, ⓦwww.lowestairprice.com. Well-established consolidator with a wide variety of global fares.
Travel Avenue ☎1-800/333-3335, ⓦwww.travelavenue.com. Full-service travel agent that offers discounts in the form of rebates.
Travel Cuts US ☎1-800/592-CUTS, Canada ☎1-888/246-9762, ⓦwww.travelcuts.com. Popular, long-established student-travel organization, with worldwide offers.
Travelers Advantage ☎1-877/259-2691, ⓦwww.travelersadvantage.com. Discount travel club; membership required.
Travelosophy US ☎1-800/332-2687, ⓦwww.itravelosophy.com. Good range of discounted and student fares worldwide.
Worldtek Travel ☎1-800/243-1723, ⓦwww.worldtek.com. Discount travel agency for worldwide travel.

H3/Tour operators

Adventures Abroad ☎1-800/665-3998 or 604/303-1099, ⓦwww.adventures-abroad.com. Adventure specialists. Budapest tours as well as multi-city (eg with Prague and Vienna) tours.

Classic Journeys ☎1-800/200-3887, ⓦwww.classicjourneys.com. Eight-day, two-city tours, starting in Prague and finishing in Budapest, from around US$2900.
Forum International Travel ☎1-800/252-4475, ⓦwww.foruminternational.com. Easy seven-day self-guided cycling tours from Vienna to Budapest staying in family pensions and hotels (from $655 including bicycle rental), and a Danube Bike and River Cruise (Passau–Vienna–Budapest; from US$630). April/May to September.
Saga Holidays ☎1-877/265-6862, ⓦwww.sagaholidays.com. Group and educational travel, including Budapest city breaks and Danube cruises, for senior travellers.

From Australia and New Zealand

There are no direct flights to Hungary from Australia or New Zealand so you'll have to change planes, either in Asia or Europe; the best option is to fly to a Western European gateway and get a connecting flight from there. A standard return **fare** to Budapest from eastern **Australia**, via London, with the Australian carrier Qantas, is around Aus$2000 in low season, rising to Aus$2800 in high season. From **New Zealand**, a standard return ticket with Air New Zealand costs around NZ$2200 in low season, NZ$3000 in high season.

Airlines

Air France Australia ☎1300 361 400, New Zealand ☎09/308 3352, ⓦwww.airfrance.com.
Air New Zealand Australia ☎13 24 76, ⓦwww.airnz.com.au; New Zealand ☎0800 737 000, ⓦwww.airnz.co.nz.
Austrian Airlines Australia ☎1800 642 438 or 02/9251 6155, New Zealand ☎09/522 5948, ⓦwww.aua.com.
British Airways Australia ☎1300 767 177, New Zealand ☎09/966 9777, ⓦwww.ba.com.
Malév Hungarian Airlines Australia ☎02/9244 2111, New Zealand ☎09/379 4455, ⓦwww.malev.hu.
Lufthansa Australia ☎1300 655 727, New Zealand ☎09/303 1529 or 008/945 220, ⓦwww.lufthansa.com.
Qantas Australia ☎13 13 13, New Zealand ☎0800 808 767 or 09/357 8900, ⓦwww.qantas.com.

Travel agents

Flight Centre Australia ☎13 31 33, ⓦwww
.flightcentre.com.au; New Zealand ☎0800 243
544, ⓦwww.flightcentre.co.nz. Low fares worldwide.
Holiday Shoppe New Zealand ☎0800 808 480,
ⓦwww.holidayshoppe.co.nz. Great deals on flights,
hotels and holidays.
STA Travel Australia ☎1300 733 035, ⓦwww.
statravel.com.au; New Zealand ☎0508/782 872,
ⓦwww.statravel.co.nz. Worldwide specialists in
low-cost flights, overlands and holiday deals. Good
discounts for students and under-26s.
Trailfinders Australia ☎02/9247 7666 or
☎1300/780 212, ⓦwww.trailfinders.com.au. One
of the best-informed and most efficient agents for
independent travellers.

travel.com.au and **travel.co.nz** Australia
☎1300/130 482 or 02/9249 5444, ⓦwww.travel
.com.au, New Zealand ☎0800/468 332, ⓦwww
.travel.co.nz. Comprehensive online travel company,
with discounted fares.

Tour operators

Danube Travel Australia ☎03/9530 0888. Danube
river cruises and specialist tours.
Eastern Eurotours Australia ☎1800 242 353 or
07/5526 2855, ⓦwww.easterneurotours.com
.au. Package tours to Budapest and multi-city tours
including Vienna and Prague.
Explore Holidays Australia ☎1300/731 000 or
02/9857 6200, ⓦwww.exploreholidays.com.au.
Package tours to Budapest.

Red tape and visas

Citizens of the EU, US, Canada, Australia and New Zealand, and most other
European countries, can enter Hungary with just a passport and may stay in the
country for up to ninety days.

If you happen to **lose your passport**, you
must report this to the local police station.
You then take the police report to your
embassy or consulate, who will issue a new
passport or sort out your papers to leave
the country. Note that you may need to go
back to the police for an exit stamp in order
to leave the country. Your consulate should
be notified by the police if your passport is
found.

Hungarian embassies and consulates

Australia Embassy: 17 Beale Crescent, Deakin,
Canberra, ACT 2600 ☎02/6282 3226 or 6285
3484; consulate: Suite 405 Edgecliffe Centre,
203–233 New South Head Rd, Edgecliffe, Sydney,
NSW 2027 ☎02/9328 7859 or 7860.
Canada Embassy: 299 Waverley St, Ottawa,
Ontario, K2P 0V9 ☎613/230-2717; consulates:
1200 McGill College Ave, Suite 2040, Montreal,
Quebec H3B 4G7 ☎514/393-3510; 121 Bloor St,
East Suite 1115, Toronto M4W 3M5 ☎416/923-
8981.

Ireland Embassy: 2 Fitzwilliam Place, Dublin 2
☎01/661 2902.
UK Embassy 35b Eaton Place, London SW1 8BY
☎020/7235 2664.
US Embassy: 3910 Shoemakers St NW, Washington
DC 20008 ☎202/362-6730; visa enquiries
☎202/362-6737. Consulates: 223 East 52nd St,
New York, NY 10022 ☎212/752-0209; 11766
Wilshire Blvd, Suite 410, Los Angeles, CA 90025
☎310/473-9344.

Customs

Visitors over the age of 16 are allowed to
bring 200 cigarettes (or 250g of tobacco or
fifty cigars), one litre of wine and one litre of
spirits into Hungary. There is no **import duty**
on personal effects, though items like laptop
computers and video cameras, which are
judged to have a high resale value, are liable
to customs duty and 25 percent VAT unless
you can prove that they are for personal use.
Duty-free export limits for tobacco and alcohol are the same as the import limits. These

customs regulations change fairly frequently, so it's worth checking the latest rules at a Hungarian consulate or tourist office before leaving home.

Insurance and health

You'd do well to take out an insurance policy before travelling to cover against theft, loss and illness or injury. Before paying for a new policy, however, it's worth checking whether you are already covered: EU health care privileges apply in Hungary, some all-risks home insurance policies may cover your possessions when overseas, and many private medical schemes include cover when abroad. In Canada, provincial health plans usually provide partial cover for medical mishaps overseas, while holders of official student/teacher/youth cards in Canada and the US are entitled to (meagre) accident coverage and hospital in-patient benefits. Students will often find that their student health coverage extends during the vacations and for one term beyond the date of last enrolment.

After checking out the possibilities above, you might want to contact a specialist travel insurance company, or consider the travel insurance deal we offer (see box below). A typical travel insurance policy usually provides cover for the loss of baggage, tickets and – up to a certain limit – cash or cheques, as well as cancellation or curtailment of your journey. Many policies can be chopped and changed to exclude coverage you don't need; for example, sickness and accident benefits can often be excluded or included at will. If you do take medical coverage, ascertain whether benefits will be paid as treatment proceeds or only after you return home, and if there is a 24-hour medical emergency number. When securing baggage cover, make sure that the per-article limit will cover your most valuable possession.

If you need to make a **claim**, you should keep receipts for medicines and medical treatment, and in the event you have anything stolen, you must obtain an official statement from the police.

Rough Guides travel insurance

Rough Guides has teamed up with Columbus Direct to offer you travel insurance that can be tailored to suit your needs. Readers can choose from many different travel insurance products, including a low-cost backpacker option for long stays; a short-break option for city getaways; a typical holiday package option; and many others. There are also annual multi-trip policies for those who travel regularly, with variable levels of cover available. Different sports and activities (trekking, skiing, etc) can be covered if required on most policies.

Rough Guides travel insurance is available to the residents of 36 different countries via ⓦ www.roughguidesinsurance.com, with different language options to choose from. Alternatively, UK residents should call ☎0800 083 9507, US citizens ☎1-800 749-4922 and Australians ☎1 300 669 999. All other nationalities should call ☎+44 870 890 2843.

Health

No inoculations are required for Hungary. Standards of public health are good, and tap water is safe to drink. All towns and some villages have a **pharmacy** (*gyógyszertár* or *patika*) authorized to issue a wide range of drugs. Pharmacies are normally open Monday to Friday from 9am to 6pm, and on Saturday from 9am until noon or 1pm; signs in the window give the location or telephone number of the nearest all-night (*éjjeli* or *ügyeleti szolgálat*) pharmacy.

In **emergencies**, dial ☎104 for the Mentők ambulance service, or catch a taxi to the nearest **hospital** (*kórház*). Hungary's national health service (**OTBF**) provides free emergency treatment in any hospital or doctor's office for citizens of the EU and most other European countries, but there is a charge for drugs and non-emergency care. Unfortunately, the standard of hospitals varies enormously. Low morale among medical staff and shortages of hospital beds testify to poor wages and the general underfunding of the health service.

For non-urgent treatment, tourist offices can direct you to a local **medical centre** or doctors' surgery (*orvosi rendelő*), and your embassy in Budapest will have the addresses of foreign-language-speaking **doctors** and **dentists** (see also the listing on p.196), who will probably be in private (*magán*) practice. Private medicine is much cheaper than in the West, as attested by the thousands of Austrians who come here for treatment. For muscular, skin or gynaecological complaints, doctors often prescribe a soak at one of Hungary's numerous **medicinal baths** (*gyógyfürdő*).

Sunburn (*napszúrás*) and insect bites (*rovarcsípés*) are the most common **minor complaints** for travellers. Suntan lotion is sold in supermarkets, and pharmacists stock bite ointment. Mosquitoes are pesky, but the bug to beware of in forests around Budapest is the *kullancs*, a tick which bites and then burrows into human skin, causing inflammation of the brain. The risk is fairly small, but if you get a bite which seems particularly painful, or are suffering from a high temperature and stiff neck following a bite, it's worth having it checked out as quickly as possible.

Information, websites and maps

Leaving aside the business of finding accommodation, perhaps the best source of tourist information in Budapest is Tourinform (☺www.tourinform.hu), with offices at several locations. The one at V, Sütő utca 2, just around the corner from Deák tér metro (daily 8am–8pm; ☎1/438-8080), is run by the National Tourist Office, and the polyglot staff can answer just about any question on Budapest or travel elsewhere in Hungary.

However, this office is often packed and the staff are overstretched, so you might get more attention at the friendly, privately run **Yellow Zebra** at V, Sütő utca 2 – inside the courtyard behind Tourinform – which can help with all kinds of practical information (daily 9.30am–6.30pm; ☎1/266-8777 ☺www .discoverhungary.com). Alternatively, head for the Tourinform offices run by the Budapest Tourist Office (☺www.budapestinfo.hu) at VI, Liszt Ferenc tér 11 (daily: May–Sept 10am– 10pm; Oct–April 10am–6pm; ☎1/322-4098); and in the Vár on Szentháromság tér (daily 8am–8pm; ☎1/488-0453). There are also Tourinform offices at the airport in terminals 2A and 2B.

A large number of free brochures, maps and special-interest leaflets are produced by the Hungarian National Tourist Office, and distributed by their offices abroad and by Tourinform in Budapest. As well as the booklets on hotels and campsites, there are also useful brochures on cultural events and festivals, gastronomy and wine, health tourism, riding, cycling and activity holidays.

There are several sources of English-language **listings information**: the weekly *Budapest Sun* and the *Budapest Times*, the free monthly magazine *Where Budapest* (available in hotels), and a handful of web-sites, listed below. While not in English, *Pesti Est* is a useful free weekly listings pamphlet, and widely available – you'll find it at tourist offices, hotels, restaurants and entertainment venues.

Hungarian tourist offices abroad

UK Hungarian National Tourist Office, 46 Eaton Place, London SW1 8AL ☏ 020/7823 1032. ⓦ www.hungarywelcomesbritain.com.
US Hungarian National Tourist Office, c/o Embassy of the Republic of Hungary, Commercial Counsellor's Office, 150 E 58th St, 33rd Floor, New York, NY 10155-3398 ☏ 212/355-0240, ⓦ www.gotohungary.com.

Websites

Usefully, plenty of Hungarian sights and tourist amenities make it a point to have an English version of their website. The list above right features websites of general interest; websites on specific themes, such as accommodation or gay life, are covered in the appropriate section of this book.

Useful websites

ⓦ **www.budapestinfo.com** The best site for information on the capital, as well as online hotel and services bookings.
ⓦ **www.budapestweek.com** A comprehensive online arts and entertainments weekly, with excellent listings sections as well as a useful classifieds section.
ⓦ **www.festivalcity.hu** Complete programme listings and ticket-ordering service for the Budapest Spring and Autumn Festivals, the Bridge Festival and the Budapest Bucsú.
ⓦ **www.insidehungary.com** Comprehensive national news site.
ⓦ **www.inyourpocket.com** The Budapest section of this website is an informative and up-to-date source of listings information for the city.
ⓦ **www.met.hu** Daily weather bulletins and forecasts.
ⓦ **www.pestiside.hu** Irreverent but informed website with a wide range of useful information on bars, events and films.
ⓦ **www.travelport.hu** Excellent general Hungarian travel site.
ⓦ **www.winesofhungary.com** Interesting site with information on Hungarian wine and wine regions, with links to dozens of wineries.

Maps

It's a good idea to get hold of a proper map of the city at the earliest opportunity. The small freebies supplied by tourist offices give an idea of Budapest's layout and principal monuments, but lack detail. Larger folding maps are sold all over the place, but their size makes them cumbersome. For total coverage you can't beat the wirebound **Budapest Atlasz**, available in bookshops for 1700Ft, which shows every street, bus and tram route, and the location of restaurants, museums and such like. It also contains enlarged maps of the Vár, central Pest, Margit sziget and the Városliget, plus a comprehensive index.

Costs, money and banks

Hungary's unit of currency is the forint (Ft or HUF), which comprises 100 fillér, though you'll rarely encounter these any more. The forint comes in notes of 200, 500, 1000, 2000, 5000, 10,000 and 20,000Ft, with 1, 2, 5, 10, 20, 50 and 100Ft coins. At the time of writing the exchange rate was around 350Ft to the pound sterling and around 200Ft to the US dollar.

Although Hungary is not quite the bargain destination it once was, it's still good value on the whole. If you need to work to a pretty tight **budget**, you could get by on 8000Ft (around £23/$40) a day, staying in a hostel, eating in cheap diners and using public transport. More generously, a daily budget of 30,000Ft (around £85/$150) would allow you to stay in a three-star hotel, eat in restaurants and take the odd taxi ride. Five-star accommodation, dining in the slickest restaurants and getting around exclusively by taxi will take you up to the 100,000Ft (£285/$500) mark or beyond.

The **Budapest Card** (see p.32) offers a good range of discounts, including reductions at certain hotels and restaurants, museum entrances, public transport and special events. Full-time students are eligible for the inexpensive International Student ID Card (ISIC; www.isiccard.com), which entitles the bearer to discounts at museums, theatres and other attractions.

Cash and traveller's cheques

If you're taking **cash**, note that **euros** are the most widely accepted foreign currency in shops and restaurants, though banks will change most hard currencies. By far the most recognized **traveller's cheques** are American Express, either sterling or dollars. The usual fee for traveller's cheque sales is one or two percent, though this fee may be waived if you buy the cheques through a bank where you have an account. It pays to get a selection of denominations. Make sure to keep the purchase agreement and a record of cheque serial numbers safe and separate from the cheques themselves.

In the event that your traveller's cheques are lost or stolen in Budapest, report the loss forthwith to the issuing company's office. Lost or stolen cheques can usually be replaced within 24 hours.

Banks and exchange

As a rule you're best off changing money in **banks**, which are generally open Monday to Friday between 9am and 3pm or 4pm. There are also an increasing number of **Automatic Currency Exchange Machines** outside banks, into which you insert foreign currency in return for forints; the exchange rate is usually the same as that offered in the bank itself. It's not advisable to change money at the private exchange offices in Váci utca and Vörösmarty tér, as they offer poor rates. Changing **traveller's cheques** is a relatively painless operation, and can be done at any bank or at the majority of large hotels and campsites. The advantages of changing money on the illegal **black market** are negligible and, in any case, scalpers are skilled at cheating. Make sure you get rid of any unwanted forints before you leave the country, as it's unlikely you'll be able to change them once outside Hungary.

Credit and debit cards

Mastercard, Visa and American Express are accepted just about everywhere in Hungary, but other cards may not be recognized. As for withdrawals from cash machines **(ATMs)**, remember that all cash advances on credit cards are treated as loans, with interest accruing daily from the date of withdrawal; there may be a transaction fee on top of this. Withdrawals from ATMs using a debit card incur a flat transaction fee, usually quite small – your bank will be able to advise on this.

A compromise between traveller's cheques and plastic is **Visa TravelMoney**, a disposable prepaid debit card with a PIN, which works in all ATMs that take Visa cards. You load up your account with funds before leaving home, and when they run out, you simply throw the card away. For more details, check ⓦ international.visa.com/ps/products/vtravelmoney.

Wiring money

Having money **wired** from home using one of the companies listed here is never convenient or cheap, and should be considered a last resort. It's possible to have money wired directly from a bank in your home country to a bank in Hungary, although this is somewhat less reliable because it involves two separate institutions. If you go this route, your home bank will need the address of the branch bank where you want to pick up the money and the address and telex number of the Budapest head office, which will act as the clearing house; money wired this way normally takes two working days to arrive, and costs around £25/$40 per transaction.

Money-wiring companies

Travelers Express/MoneyGram UK, Ireland and New Zealand ☎ 0800 6663 9472, US ☎ 1-800/444-3010, Canada ☎ 1-800/933-3278, Australia ☎ 1800 6663 9472, ⓦ www.moneygram.com. **Western Union** UK ☎ 0800 833 833, Republic of Ireland ☎ 66/947 5603, US and Canada ☎ 1-800/CALL-CASH, Australia ☎ 1800 501 500, New Zealand ☎ 0800 005 253, ⓦ www.westernunion.com. Customers in the US and Canada can send money online.

Arrival and transport

Other than the airport, all points of arrival are fairly central; most are within walking distance or just a few stops by metro from downtown Pest. There are accommodation-booking services at the airport and the Keleti train station.

Budapest's excellent **public transport** system ensures that few parts of the city are more than thirty minutes' journey from the centre; many places can be reached in half that time. The city's three metro lines and three main roads meet at the major junction of Deák tér in Pest, making this the main transport hub of the city (a **transport map** appears at the back of this book).

Arriving by air

Ferihegy Airport, 20km from the centre, has three passenger terminals. Ferihegy 2A serves Malév and Malév's joint flights with other airlines, while Ferihegy 2B is used by the other scheduled airlines. The older Ferihegy 1, which is the other side of the airport – ten minutes' drive away – has been renovated and now serves as the terminal for no-frills airlines. There are **ATMs** in all the terminal buildings. When **leaving**, it is worth checking which terminal you're flying from, as some airlines have had their departures shifted between terminals to ease congestion.

The easiest and most expensive option for heading into the centre is by taxi. The **airport taxis** that wait at the exits charge way above the odds, with fixed rates of 5200–7000Ft depending on your destination, though they will charge unsuspecting foreigners far more. Ask for help in booking an ordinary city cab (around 4000Ft) at Ferihegy's Tourinform offices (daily 8am–11pm).

A cheaper option – especially if you are travelling alone – is the **Airport Minibus**, which will take you directly to your destination. Tickets (2300Ft single, 3900Ft return;

Buduapest addresses

Finding your way around Budapest is easier than the welter of names might suggest. Districts and streets are well signposted, and those in Pest conform to an overall plan based on radial avenues and semicircular boulevards.

Budapest is divided into 23 districts, numbered using Roman numerals. Except when addressing letters, a Budapest **address** always begins with the district number, a system used throughout this book. On letters, a four-digit **postal code** is used instead, the middle two digits indicating the district (so that 1054 refers to a place in the V district). For ease of reference, we list below the district numbers you're most likely to encounter, along with some of the areas within those districts, the ones which you're most likely to be visiting:

I	Várhegy and Viziváros	IX	Ferencváros
II	Rózsadomb and Hűvösvölgy	X	Kőbánya
		XI	The area south and east of Gellért-hegy
III	Óbuda and Aquincum		
IV	Újpest	XII	The area from Várhegy west into the Buda hills
V	Belváros and Lipótváros		
VI	Terézváros	XIII	Újlipótváros and Angyalföld
VII	Erzsébetváros	XIV	Városliget and Zugló
VIII	Józsefváros	XXII	Budafok and Nagytétény

As a rule of thumb, **street numbers** ascend away from the north–south axis of the River Danube and the east–west axis of Rákóczi út/Kossuth utca/Hegyalja út. Even numbers are generally on the left-hand side as you head outwards from these axes, odd numbers on the right. One number may refer to several premises or an entire apartment building, while an additional combination of numerals denotes the floor and number of individual **apartments** (eg Kossuth utca 14/III/24). Confusingly, some old buildings in Pest are designated as having a half-floor (*félemelet*) or upper ground floor (*magas földszint*) between the ground (*földszint*) and first floor (*elsőemelet*) proper – so that what the British would call the second floor, and Americans the third, Hungarians might describe as the first. This stems from a nineteenth-century taxation fiddle, whereby landlords avoided the higher tax on buildings with more than three floors.

discounts on single tickets with the Budapest Card – see p.32) can be bought in the luggage claim hall while you are waiting for your bags, or in the main concourse; you give the address you're heading to and then have to wait five to twenty minutes until the driver calls your destination. **Public transport** might be more inconvenient but it's not much slower, and it's certainly cheaper: take one of the Reptér-busz, which leave every fifteen minutes from the stop between terminals 2A and 2B, and stay aboard until the final stop at the faded, red-and-yellow metro station at Kőbánya-Kispest; here you can switch to the blue metro line for the centre. It all takes about 45 minutes and costs 170Ft for each of the two tickets. Tickets are available at the newsagents in the terminals or from the machine by the bus stop – buying

one from the driver on board will cost you 200Ft.

Arriving by train

The Hungarian word *pályaudvar* (abbreviated "pu." in writing) is used to designate a **train station**, of which there are seven in Budapest, only three of which are on the metro and of any use to tourists. Note that their names, which are sometimes translated into English, refer to the direction of services handled rather than their location.

Most international trains terminate at Pest's **Keleti Station** on Baross tér in the VIII district. This station is something of a hangout for thieves and hustlers, and there are plenty of police about checking people's ID. There are usually plenty of people offering accom-

29

modation as international trains arrive. The most reliable of several hostel-booking agencies here is Mellow Mood, whose offices are to the right of the big glass doorways at the far end of the Station. They will also organize transport to hostels, and should be able to offer other city information, too. Otherwise, head for the Tourinform office at Deák tér. Unmarked **taxis** lining the road outside the doors of the Keleti station are worth avoiding, despite their drivers wearing badges saying "official taxi". Instead, look out for taxis from the companies listed on p.33, such as Fótaxi, which you can find by going out of the main doors and turning right. In summer there are long queues at the 24-hour left-luggage office by platform 6 (300Ft or 600Ft for 24hr depending on size, half that amount for six hours) – the lockers (300Ft for 24hr) are a better bet if they are in operation.

Nyugati Station, on the northern edge of Pest's Nagykörut, has a 24-hour left-luggage office (300Ft or 600Ft for 24hr) next to the ticket office beside platform 13. The Budapest Tourist Information Office (Mon–Fri 9am–6pm, Sat–Sun 9am–3pm; ☎1/302-8580), by the police office (*rendőrség*) to the left of the main entrance to the station, is a reliable source of information on the city. To reach Deák tér, take the blue metro line two stops in the direction of Kőbánya-Kispest.

Déli Station, 500m behind the Vár in Buda, has left-luggage facilities but no tourist office. It's four stops from Deák tér on the red metro line.

Arriving by bus or hydrofoil

International bus services wind up at the **Népliget Bus Station** in the IX district, southeast of the centre, which also handles buses from the Great Plain and Transdanubia. The bus station is six stops from Deák tér on the blue metro line. The same warning applies here on **taxis** as to the airport – it's best to ask the staff to help you order a regular taxi, which will cost 1000–1500Ft to the centre.

Of the other bus stations, the **Árpád híd Bus Station** in the XIII district (on the blue metro line) is the jumping-off point for buses to and from Szentendre and the Danube Bend, the **Stadion Bus Station** in the XIV

district (on the red metro line) serves the Northern Uplands and the **Etele tér Bus Station** in the XI district (take buses #173 or #7 to the centre) serves the Buda hinterland. None of the four has any tourist facilities.

Hydrofoils from Vienna (April–Oct) dock at the **international landing stage**, on the Belgrád rakpart (embankment), near downtown Pest.

City transport

Budapest's **metro trains**, **buses** and **trams** reach most areas of interest to tourists, while the outer suburbs are well served by the overground **HÉV** rail network. There's a whole array of **tickets** available on public transport, but since validating your ticket can be complex and is easy to forget, the best advice if you are staying for more than half a day is to get a **pass**. The website of the **Budapest Transport Company** (BKV; ⓦwww.bkv.hu) has comprehensive information on routes and prices.

A word of warning: there's an active **pickpocket** battalion on both the metro (especially the yellow line) and the city buses. Gangs distract their victims by pushing them or blocking their way, and empty their pockets or bags at the same time. Also beware of bogus ticket inspectors (see p.40).

The metro

The Budapest **metro** has three lines, usually referred to by their colour (see the map at the end of the book), and intersecting at Deák tér in downtown Pest. Trains run at two- to twelve-minute intervals between 4.30am and 11.10pm. There's little risk of going astray once you've learned to recognize the signs *bejárat* (entrance), *kijárat* (exit), *vonal* (line) and *felé* (towards). Drivers announce the next stop between stations and the train's direction is indicated by the name of the station at the end of the line.

Buses, trams and trolleybuses

Buses (*autóbusz*) are especially useful around Buda, where Moszkva tér (on the red metro line) and Móricz Zsigmond körtér (southwest of Gellért-hegy) are the main bus terminals. Bus stops are marked by a blue sign with the

Buses

#7 Bosnyák tér–Keleti Station–Móricz Zsigmond körtér (via Rákóczi út, Ferenciek tere, *Gellért Hotel*, Rác and Rudas Baths).
#16 Erzsébet tér–Dísz tér (Castle District).
#26 Nyugati tér–Szent István körút–Margit sziget–Árpád híd metro Station.
#27 Móricz Zsigmond körtér–Gellért-hegy.
#56 Moszkva tér–Szilágyi Erzsébet fasor–Hűvösvölgy, with the #56E going almost without stopping.
#65 Kolosy tér–Pálvölgyi Caves–Hármashatár-hegy.
#86 Southern Buda–Gellért tér–the Víziváros–Flórián tér (Óbuda).
#105 Apor Vilmos tér–Lanchíd–Deák tér.
Várbusz Moszkva tér– Dísz tér (Castle District) and back.

Night buses

#6É Moszkva tér–Margit sziget–Nyugati Station–Great Boulevard–Móricz Zsigmond körtér.
#78É Örs vezér tere–Bosnyák tér–Keleti Station–Erzsébet Bridge (Buda side).
#14É and **#50É** Kispest (Határ út metro Station)–Deák tér–Lehel tér, along the route of the blue metro and on to the north and south.
#49É Moszkva tér–Erzsébet híd–*Gellért Hotel*–Móricz Zsigmond körtér.

Trams

#2 Margit Bridge–Petőfi híd (along embankment)–HÉV Station at Közvágóhíd.
#4 Moszkva tér–Margit sziget–Nyugati Station–Nagykörut–Petőfi Bridge–Október 23 utca.
#6 Moszkva tér–Margit sziget–Nyugati Station–Great Boulevard–Petőfi híd–Móricz Zsigmond körtér.
#19 Batthyány tér–Víziváros–Kelenföld Station.
#47 Deák tér–Szabadság híd–*Hotel Gellért*–Móricz Zsigmond körtér–Budafok.
#49 Deák tér–Szabadság híd–*Hotel Gellért*–Móricz Zsigmond körtér–Kelenföld Station.
#56 Moszkva tér–Hűvösvölgy.

Trolleybuses

#72 Arany János utca metro Station–Nyugati Station–Zoo–Széchenyi Baths–Petőfi Csarnok–Thököly út.
#74 Dohány utca (outside the Main Synagogue)–Városliget.

label "*autóbusz*" or with a picture of a bus in the centre, and have timetables underneath; most buses run every ten to twenty minutes from 5am to 11pm (*Utolsó kocsi indul . . .* means "the last one leaves . . ."). Regular services are numbered in black, while buses with red numbers make fewer stops en route, and those with a red "E" suffix run nonstop between terminals. To get the bus to stop, push the button above the door or on the handrail beside the door. Busy routes are also served by **night buses** (up to four every hour), with black numbers and an "É" suffix.

Yellow **trams** (*villamos*) are chiefly good for travelling around the Nagykörút or along the embankments. Services run from early in the morning to 11pm. **Trolleybuses** (*trolibusz*) mostly operate northeast of the centre near the Városliget. The reason their route numbers start at 70 is that the first trolleybus line was inaugurated on Stalin's 70th birthday in 1949. Trolleybus #83 was started in 1961, when Stalin would have been 83.

HÉV trains

The green overground **HÉV trains** provide easy access to Budapest's suburbs, running at least four times an hour between 6.30am and 11pm. As far as tourists are concerned, the most useful line is the one from **Batthyány tér** (on the red metro line) out to **Szentendre**, which passes through Óbuda, Aquincum and Rómaifürdő. The other lines originate in Pest, with one running northeast from **Örs vezér tere** (also on the red metro line) to **Gödöllő** via the Formula One racing track at Mogyoród; another southwards from Boráros tér at the Pest end of Petőfi Bridge to Csepel; and the third from **Közvagohíd** (bus #23 or #54 from Boráros tér) to **Ráckeve**.

Tickets and passes

Single **tickets** valid for the metro, buses, trams, trolleybuses, the Cogwheel Railway (see p.123) and suburban HÉV lines (up to the edge of the city) cost 170Ft and are sold at metro stations, newspaper kiosks and tobacconists. Tickets valid only on the **metro** come in a variety of types, depending on how many lines you want to use, and how many stops you want to go: a metro section ticket (120Ft) takes you three stops on the same line; a metro transfer ticket (270Ft) is valid for as many stops as you like with one line change; and a metro section transfer ticket (185Ft) takes you five stops with one line change. Tickets bought on **buses** and **trolleybuses** cost 200Ft. You can get **weekend family tickets** (2040Ft), and **books** of ten and twenty tickets (1450Ft and 2800Ft) are also available – but note that if a ticket is separated from the book it becomes invalid.

Tickets must be **validated** when you use them. On the metro and HÉV you punch them in the machines at the entrance (remember to validate a new ticket if you change lines); on trams, buses and trolleybuses you punch the tickets on board in the small red or orange machines.

Day passes (*napijegy*) cost 1350Ft and are valid for unlimited travel – on the metro, buses, trams, trolleybuses, the Cogwheel Railway and suburban HÉV lines – until midnight; three-day passes cost 2700Ft and weekly passes 2700Ft. **Season tickets** cost 4050Ft for two weeks and 6250Ft for a month, and are available from metro stations, but you'll need a passport photo for the accompanying photocard, available from the BKV office, VII, Akácfa utca 22 (Mon–Fri 6am–8pm, Sat 8am–1.45pm), near Blaha Lujza tér metro, or from the ticket office at Kálvin tér.

There is a 2000Ft **fine** for travelling without a valid ticket and inspectors (identifiable by their red armbands) are very strict. If you have a season ticket but are not carrying it, the fine is higher, though most of it is refunded upon presentation of the season ticket within three days at the BKV office. **Children** up to the age of 6 travel free.

Ferries and other rides

Although **ferries** play little useful part in the transport system, they do offer an enjoyable ride. From May to September there are boats between Boráros tér (by Petőfi híd) and Batthyány tér up to Jászai Mari tér and Rómaifürdő. These run every fifteen to thirty minutes between 7am and 7pm, and cost between 200Ft (for going from Pest across to the Margit sziget) and 600Ft. Ferry tickets can be obtained from kiosks (where timetables are posted) or machines at the docks.

The Budapest card

If you're doing a lot of sightseeing you might be tempted to buy a **Budapest Card**. For 4700Ft (48hr) or 5900Ft (72 hr), you get free travel in most of the city, free entry to over sixty museums, and discounts of up to fifty percent in some shops and restaurants, and on some sightseeing programmes and cultural and folklore events. The card is available from tourist offices, hotels, central metro stations and at the airport, and comes with a booklet explaining where it can be used. However, the price means you'll have to work hard to save money on it, especially since the card is not valid for the funicular that goes up to the castle or for tours of Parliament, and because 21 national museums in Budapest – including the Hungarian National Museum and the National Gallery – don't charge admission for their permanent displays.

City tours

If you're hard-pressed for time you might appreciate a two- to three-hour **city bus tour**. These usually cost 5000–6000Ft (or 10,000Ft if combined with a visit to the Parliament building) and can be booked through Ibusz (tickets from their office at V, Ferenciek tere 10 in the centre; ℡www.ibusz.hu) or Buda Tours (℡1/374-7070, ℡www.budatours.hu; VI, Andrássy út 2).

Most of Budapest's backstreets and historic quarters are eminently suited to walking – and this is much the best way to appreciate their character. Traffic is restricted in downtown Pest and around the Vár in Buda, and fairly light in the residential backstreets off the main boulevards, which are the nicest areas to wander around. For a range of **walking tours**, including some which take in less obvious attractions, such as around Communist Budapest or the city's bars, try the friendly Absolute Walking Tours (℡06-30/211-8861, ℡www.absolutetours.com), who also handle **bike tours** of the capital (4000–5000Ft; ℡www.yellowzebrabikes.com). For information on being guided round the old Jewish area behind the Dohány utca synagogue, see p.70.

Other pleasure rides can be found in the Buda Hills (see chapter 9 for details), on the **Cogwheel Railway** (Fogaskerekű vasút), the **Children's Railway** (Gyermekvasút) – largely staffed by kids – and the **chairlift** (libegő) between Zugliget and János-hegy. Note that BKV tickets and passes aren't valid for the ferries, Chairlift or Children's Railway, so you'll need to buy tickets at the point of departure or on board.

Taxis

Budapest's **taxis** have gained themselves a reputation for ripping off foreigners. The best advice is to use one of the established companies: Főtaxi (℡1/222-2222), Citytaxi (℡1/211-1111), Tele-5-taxi (℡1/355-5555) and Volántaxi (℡1/466-6666); the first two are the most likely to have English-speaking operators. Avoid unmarked private cars and those hanging around the stations and airport – the latter often charge far higher rates than the firms listed above. There are also a few fake Fő- and Citytaxis, sporting poor copies of the red-and-white chequerboard or yellow shield logos, which charge a vastly inflated price; a genuine taxi will have the tariff displayed on the dashboard.

Taxis can be flagged down on the street or, for a cheaper rate, ordered by phone. There are **ranks** throughout the city and you can hop into whichever cab you choose – don't feel you have to opt for the one at the front of the line if it looks at all dodgy.

Be sure your taxi has a meter that is visible, that it is switched on when you get in, and that the rates are clearly displayed. **Fares** begin at 300Ft, and the price per kilometre is around 200Ft. Főtaxi do a fixed-price fare between the centre and the airport of 3500–4000Ft.

Driving and cycling

All things considered, **driving** in Budapest can't be recommended. Road manners are nonexistent, parking spaces are scarce and traffic jams are frequent. The Pest side of the Lánchíd (Chain Bridge) and the roundabout before the tunnel under the Vár are notorious for collisions. Careering trams, bumpy cobbles and unexpected one-way systems make things worse. If you do have a car, you might be better off parking it somewhere outside the centre and using public transport to get in and out.

Renting a car is easy provided you're 21 or older and hold a valid driving licence that's at least one year old. Rental **costs** are not particularly cheap; expect to pay around 12,500Ft upwards for a day's hire (unlimited mileage) and 80,000Ft for a week, though, as anywhere, it becomes cheaper the longer the rental period. You might find that local outlets offer better deals than the major international rental firms. Credit cards are usually required for a deposit. Before signing, check on any mileage limits or other restrictions or extras, as well as what you're covered for in the event of an accident.

Though cyclists are banned from most major thoroughfares, **cycle routes** are now appearing, for example, up Andrássy út and along the Buda bank of the Danube to Szentendre and beyond, and the number of cyclists has shot up. Tourinform has free cycling maps of Budapest, or you can buy them in map shops. Cyclists must contend with the same hazards as drivers, as well as sunken tram-lines. Bicycles can be carried on HÉV trains and the Cogwheel Railway for the price of a single ticket, but not on buses or trams.

For the addresses of car rental agencies and bike shops in Budapest, see p.195.

Communications

Both the Hungarian postal and telecommunications services are as efficient as anywhere else in Europe. All the major courier companies, including DHL, Fedex and TNT, have offices in Budapest, and Internet cafés are fairly ubiquitous.

Mail

Post offices (*posta*) in Budapest are usually open Monday to Friday 8am to 6pm and Saturday 8am to noon. The city's main post office at V, Petőfi Sándor utca 13, stays open a little later than this (Mon–Fri 8am–8pm, Sat 8am–2pm), and there are several post offices open even longer hours; one is by Keleti Station at VIII, Baross tér 11c (Mon–Fri 7am–9pm, Sat 8am–2pm), another by Nyugati Station at VI, Teréz körút 51 (Mon–Sat 7am–9pm, Sun 10am–5pm). **Stamps** (*bélyeg*) can be bought at tobacconists or post offices, though the latter are usually pretty crowded and very few staff speak English. Note that letters and postcards have different rates, so don't buy a job lot of stamps.

Poste restante mail from abroad goes to the branch next to Nyugati Station, and should be addressed "poste restante, posta Budapest". Tell your friends to write your surname first, Hungarian-style, and underline it. Even this may not prevent your mail being misfiled, so ask them to check under all your names. When collecting letters, show your passport and ask "*Van posta a részemre?*"

Telephones

Cardphones are far more common than coin-operated public phones (the latter have a minimum charge of 20Ft and take 10, 20, 50 and 100Ft coins). You can buy a phonecard (*telefonkártya*; 800Ft and 1800Ft) from post offices, tobacconists and some hotels. The best card for international calls is the Barangaló card (2000Ft and 5000Ft), but eTel and Ezphone cards are also good. All offer good rates to countries worldwide, and are available from post offices, newsagents and tobacconists. To call to a part of Hungary outside the area you're in, dial ☎06 (which gives a burring tone), followed by the area code and the subscriber's number.

One of the most convenient ways of phoning home from abroad is via a **telephone charge card** from your phone company back home. Using a PIN number, you can make calls charged to your account from most hotel, public and private phones. Most major charge cards are free to obtain, though you should enquire whether Hungary is covered.

Mobile phones

Hungarian **mobile phone** numbers begin with ☎06-20, ☎06-30, ☎06-60 or ☎06-70, followed by seven digits. Calling a mobile from a public or private phone, you have to dial all the numbers; calling from a phone on the same network, drop the first four digits;

Telephone codes

When **calling Hungary** from abroad, dial your international access code, then 36 for Hungary, then the area code (omitting the initial zero where present) and the number. If the Hungarian number begins with 06, omit these two digits.
Within Hungary, directory enquiries is on ☎198, international directory enquiries on ☎199. When making international calls from Hungary, dial ☎00, then the country code (some useful ones appear below), then the number, omitting any initial zero.

UK	44
Republic of Ireland	353
USA and Canada	1
Australia	61
New Zealand	64

and calling from mobile phones on different networks, dial all the digits.

If you want to use your home cell phone in Budapest, check with your phone provider if your mobile will work in Hungary, and what the call charges will be; US cell phones need to be triband to work. If you want to buy a Hungarian SIM card, try the outlets of the local mobile providers, such as T-Mobile, Vodaphone and Pannon.

Internet access

There are **Internet cafés** all over Budapest, though connections are generally pretty slow, and only some have keyboards labelled in English. Expect to pay around 500Ft per hour online, more in central locations such as Váci utca. More and more cafés and hotels have **wireless** connections, many of them free, making access to the Internet on a laptop very easy. The website ⓦwww.pestiside.hu has a list of places with Wi-Fi access, as does the free *Dining Guide* pub-

lication you'll find in cafés and restaurants. Matáv shops, too, usually have at least a couple of terminals.

Internet cafés

Ami V, Váci utca 40. Some English keyboards; fifty terminals, plus games available. Daily 9am–2am.
C&Trade VII, Kazinczy utca 4. Daily 10am–midnight.
Castro IX, Ráday utca 35. Mon–Fri 10am–midnight, Sat & Sun 2pm–midnight.
CEU Net V, Október 6 utca 14. All English keyboards. Daily 11am–10pm.
Electric Café VII, Dohány utca 37. Some English keyboards. Daily 9am–midnight.
Internet Ráday IX, Mátyás utca 17. Some English keyboards. Daily 10am–11pm.
Millenaris Park C Building, near Moszkva tér. Free for up to 1hr.
Szabó Ervin Library VIII, Reviczky utca. Register at the desk in reception. Mon–Fri 10am–8pm, Sat 10am–4pm.
T-pont V, Petőfi utca 17–19. Also has outlets in many large shopping malls. Daily 9am–8pm.

The media

There are several main broadsheets available in Hungary, in addition to, of course, plenty of tabloids doing the daily rounds of sensationalism, plus a handful of English-language papers. Television differs little from that in other European countries, with foreign cable and satellite television having made huge inroads in recent years.

The largest circulation **broadsheet newspaper** is the formerly Communist *Népszabadság* (still left-wing, but firmly repudiating the old regime); competing with it is the centre-right *Magyar Nemzet*. There are several Budapest-based **English-language weeklies**, including the *Budapest Sun* (ⓦ www.budapestsun .com), a rather lightweight, newsy rag with entertainment and events listings, and the *Budapest Business Journal* (ⓦ www.bbj.hu), which covers mainly business and politics. Many **foreign broadsheet** papers are available in Budapest's classier hotels, and from some newsagents and street kiosks. For details of listings magazines and websites, see p.26.

TV and radio

Generally speaking, Hungarian **television** is pretty dismal, with state TV (MTV) screening a dreary diet of gameshows and low-budget soaps from morning to night. In addition, there are numerous commercial channels such as TV2, the German-Belgian owned RTK Klub and Duna TV, a state-supported channel geared to Hungarian minorities abroad, though these are little better. For this reason many Hungarians subscribe to satellite channels, with whole apartment blocks sharing the cost of installation. Most half-decent hotels have access to foreign channels, though in some cases they will be German channels only, while the better hotels will have the full satellite package.

The **BBC** can be heard on 92.1FM in Budapest, broadcasting in English and Hungarian during the evening and early morning.

Opening hours, holidays and festivals

Shops are generally open Monday to Friday from 10am to 6pm, and on Saturdays from 9am to 1pm, with the larger shopping centres open for a few hours on Sundays. Supermarkets and grocery stores open daily from 7 or 8am to 7 or 8pm. There are also a growing number of 24-hour shops (signed "non-stop", "0–24" or "éjjel-nappali"). For the opening times of banks and pharmacies, see p.27 and p.25 respectively.

Most things in Hungary shut down on the following **public holidays**. When these fall on a Tuesday or Thursday, the Monday before or the Friday after may also become a holiday, and the previous or next Saturday a working day to make up the lost day.

Hungarian holidays

January 1 New Year's Day
March 15 Independence Day
Easter Monday
May 1 Labour Day
August 20 St Stephen's Day
October 23 National holiday
November 1 All Saints' Day
December 25 Christmas. (Since celebrations start on Christmas Eve, many shops will be closed the whole day, and by the afternoon everything closes down.)
December 26

Festivals

Whatever time of the year you visit Budapest, there's almost certain to be something happening. Of the events listed in this chapter, the biggest are the **Spring Festival** in late March/early April, and the **Autumn Festival** from late September to late October – both of which feature music, ballet and drama, including star acts from abroad. Many theatres, concert halls and dance houses close down during the long, hot months of July and August, though open-air performances are staged in their place. The city's population returns from the countryside for the fireworks on August 20, and life returns to normal as school starts the following week. The new arts season holds fire until the last week of September, when there is a rash of music festivals and political anniversaries. The opening performance at the State Opera House is traditionally *Bánk Bán*, by Ferenc Erkel.

January and February

Farsang January 6 to Ash Wednesday. Farsang (carnival) is the Hungarian way of saying farewell to winter, as well as fattening everyone up before fasting begins in Lent (the word "carnival" being derived from the Italian for "the farewell to meat"). Revellers usually take to the streets in fancy dress during one weekend in January; they process across the Lánchíd and down to Vörösmarty tér, where prizes are given for the best-dressed. Unfortunately the inclement weather at this time of year often dampens the event's spirit.
Bears and Spring February 2. Tradition has it that if the bears in Budapest Zoo come out of their cave on this date and catch sight of their shadows, they will return to their lairs to sleep, and the winter will be a long one. If the sun doesn't shine, it means that spring is just around the corner.

Hungarian Film Festival (Magyar Filmszemle) Two weeks of the latest films from the Hungarian studios. See p.177 for more information.

March and April

Declaration of Independence of 1848 March 15. A public holiday in honour of the 1848 Revolution, which began with Petofi's declaration of the *National Song* from the steps of the National Museum. Budapest decks itself out with Hungarian tricolours (red, white and green), and there are speeches and gatherings outside the museum and by Petofi's statue on Marcius 15 tér. The more patriotic citizens wear little cockades in the national colours pinned to their lapels.
Budapest Spring Festival Late March/early April; ⓦ www.festivalcity.hu/btf. Budapest Tavaszi Fesztivál, as this is known in Hungarian, is the city's major arts festival. It comprises classical-music concerts in venues across the city, as well as some jazz and folk; exhibitions, including the World Press Photos show; dance, including the folk dance festival; theatre and cinema, with a series of Hungarian films with English subtitles often showing in one cinema in town.
Easter (Húsvét) Late March/early April. Easter has strong folk traditions in Hungary. Easter Saturday is marked by processions in churches, while on Easter Monday locsolkodás (splashing) takes place, when men and boys visit their female friends to spray them with cologne. Kids get a painted egg or money in return for splashing, while the men receive *pálinka* (schnapps). This is a tamer version of an older village tradition where a bucket of water was used instead of the perfume bottle. Regular events in the weeks preceding Easter are arts and craft fairs in the Museum of Ethnography, with traditional folk skills like egg painting on display; and free performances of the Bach Passions in the big, yellow Lutheran church on Deák tér.

May, June and July

Labour Day May 1. These days citizens are no longer obliged to parade past the Lenin statue that used to stand behind the Mucsarnok. Instead the major trade unions put on a big do in the park, with shows, games, talks, and of course food and drink in large quantities.
Book Week (Könyvhét) Early June. Vörösmarty tér and Szent István tér in front of the Basilica are lined with stalls, as Hungarian writers gather from neighbouring countries and further afield. Authors sign books for the punters – politicians have now joined the book circus, competing to see who can attract

the largest number of people wanting their books autographed – and there is singing and dancing on the temporary stages in the two squares. It is inspiring to see how popular such an event is. It has been going since 1929 and is as popular as ever.

World Music Festival (WOMUFE) Early June. A two- to three-day event at the Budai Parkszínpad in the park by Kosztolányi Dezso tér, hosting a collection of world music stars.

Worldwide Music Day Nearest weekend to June 21. Musical events around town mark this day, thought up by the French to celebrate music around the world.

Bridge Festival (Hídünnep) End of June; ⓦ www.festivalcity.hu/hidunnep. A new event that commemorates the building of the Lánchíd in the 1840s. The bridge itself is closed to traffic for the festival, and there is a river cavalcade, fireworks, folk dancing on the stage at Clark Ádám tér and general festivities.

Budapesti Bucsú Last weekend of June; ⓦ www. festivalcity.hu/bucsu. *Bucsú* means "farewell" in Hungarian, and the first Budapesti Bucsú was held in 1991 to celebrate the departure of Soviet troops from the country. Now it's an annual city-wide celebration of music, with events in the Tabán and in Hosök tere, where there is a large outdoor classical music performance.

Gay Pride Budapest Late June or early July. The largest event in the gay calendar is a four-day festival culminating in a march down Andrássy út and across the Danube.

August

Hungarian Grand Prix Usually second weekend of Aug. The Hungarian Grand Prix takes place at the Hungaroring circuit at Mogyoród on the northeastern edge of the city.

Sziget Festival Mid-August; ⓦ www.sziget.hu. One of the biggest rock and pop festivals in Europe takes place on Óbudai sziget, an island north of the centre. Rock, pop, world music, dance, theatre, films and children's events.

Budapest Beach (Budapest Plàzs) Most of August; ⓦ www.budapestplazs.hu. A kilometre and a half of the Pest riverside opposite Margit sziget, from Margit Bridge northwards, is closed to traffic and turned, like its Paris forebear, into a beach with live music and other entertainment.

St Stephen's Day August 20. A public holiday in honour of Hungary's national saint and founder, with day-long rites at his Basilica, a craft fair and folk dancing at different venues in the Várhegy, and a spectacular fireworks display at 9pm. Over a million people line the Danube to watch the fireworks fired off between the Erzsébet and Margit bridges, and

the traffic jam that follows is equally mind-blowing. Restaurants are also packed that night, so book well ahead if you want to eat out.

Budapest Parade August 25; ⓦ www .budapestparade.hu. A mini version of London's Notting Hill Carnival, when a procession of floats set up by radio stations and clubs parade through the city, ending up on Dózsa György út by the Városliget for a rave into the early hours.

Jewish Summer Festival End of August; ⓦ www .jewishfestival.hu. Attracts an international range of artists presenting classical, jazz and klezmer music and exhibitions.

September and October

Budapest Wine Festival Early September. The centrepiece of the Budapest Bor Fesztivál is Vörösmarty tér, where you can walk around the wine stalls tasting and buying wines. It has been a rather elitist event for many years, but that is now changing as more events are being opened up to appeal to the public.

European Heritage Days Late September. A Council of Europe initiative which takes place all over the Continent, with public buildings opened up for a weekend. Tours (in Hungarian) take you round the Art Nouveau Geological Institute on Stefánia út, the former Post Office Savings Bank in Hold utca, and the Interior Ministry on Roosevelt tér.

Budapest Music Weeks (Zenei hetek) Late September to early November. City-wide music events starting around the anniversary of Bartók's death on September 25.

Budapest Autumn Festival Late September to mid October; ⓦ www.festivalcity.hu/bof. Budapest Oszi Fesztivál is smaller than its spring counterpart, but stronger on contemporary music. There are also exhibitions and operatic and theatre performances.

Music of Our Time Early October. Two weeks of contemporary music played by Hungarian and foreign artists.

Titanic Film Festival Early October. An annual show of independent films shown over ten days in October, usually at the Toldi Cinema.

Arad martyrs anniversary October 6. Commemoration of the shooting of the thirteen Hungarian generals in 1849 in Arad in present-day Romania, when the 1848 revolution was crushed by the Austrians with Russian help. Wreaths are laid at the Eternal Flame (see p.60).

Commemoration of the 1956 Uprising October 23. A national holiday to commemorate the 1956 Uprising and the declaration of the Republic in 1990. Ceremonies take place in Kossuth tér, by the Nagy Imre statue nearby, and at Nagy's grave in the New Public Cemetery.

November and December

All Souls' Day (Mindenszentek napja)
November 1. Cemeteries stay open late around this day and candles are lit in memory of departed souls, making for an incredible sight as darkness falls.
Mikulás December 5–6. St Nicholas's Day. On December 5, children clean their shoes and put them in the window for "Mikulás", the Santa Claus figure, to fill with sweets. Naughty children are warned that if they behave badly, all they will get is virgács, a gold-painted bunch of twigs from Mikulás's little helpers. Nowadays most children get sweets, twigs and presents.
Christmas (Karácsony) December 24–25. The main celebration is on December 24, when the city becomes eerily silent by late afternoon. Children are taken out while their parents decorate the Christmas tree (until then the trees are stored outside, and on housing estates you can often see them dangling from windows). When the children return home, they wait outside until the bell rings, which tells them that "little Jesus" (Jézuska) has come. Inside, they sing carols by the tree, open presents, and start the big Christmas meal, traditionally spicy fish soup, among other things. In the preceding weeks there are Christmas fairs in several locations in town, the best being in the Museum of Ethnography, where traditional crafts are demonstrated.
New Year's Eve (Szilveszter) December 31. Revellers gather on the Nagykörút, engaging in trumpet battles at the junction with Rákóczi út. In the Opera House there is an all-night ball; tickets, which are expensive, can be bought from the usual ticket agencies on p.172.

Crime and personal safety

Hungary is one of the safest European countries to travel in and you should have little reason to worry about your personal security. However, whilst violent crime is extremely rare, the incidence of theft is growing, with Budapest in particular a prime target for pickpockets, car thieves and other scams. Unfortunately, the incidence of racist attacks is also increasing, with Asians, Arabs and, most commonly, the Hungarian Roma bearing the brunt of physical assaults.

As for offences you might commit, should you be caught in possession of **illegal drugs**, the police have the power to detain you for up to 48 hours and administer a mandatory drugs test. Note also that **drinking and driving** is totally prohibited and anyone caught doing so is liable for prosecution. As police occasionally ask to inspect **passports and visas**, you should keep your passport with you. Should you be arrested or need legal advice, ask to contact your embassy or consulate (see Budapest "Listings" for contact details).

Scams

Parts of Budapest area, notably Váci utca in the Belváros, are notorious for "**consume girls**", who target solo male foreigners. A couple of attractive young women (they're not difficult to spot) will approach you, get talking and, without wasting any time, "invite you" for a drink in a bar of their choice. A few drinks later you'll find yourself presented with a bill somewhat bigger than you bargained for and be strong-armed into paying up. The bars, and the waiters who work in them, are an integral part of the scam which makes any escape or complaint futile, although if you ever do find yourself caught up in such a situation then report it to the police.

Even if you disregard pick-ups and avoid places offering the "companionship of lovely ladies", there's a risk of **gross overcharging** at restaurants or bars which don't list their prices. The most notorious case was in 1997, when four Danes had to pay 1,300,000Ft for a meal. "As far as I'm concerned," said the owner of the restaurant involved, "we can charge tourists anything we like". While the worst offenders are out of business, it's still wise to be cautious and check prices before ordering. If you get stung, try insisting that you'll only pay in the presence of the police. Tourinform has a conference line with the police (☎1/438-8080), on which they'll translate from English or German.

There have been cases of **bogus ticket inspectors** working the transport system and demanding money from passengers. Genuine inspectors wear red armbands and work in twos or threes.

The police

The Hungarian **police** (*rendőrség*) always had a milder reputation than their counterparts in other Eastern Bloc states, and are generally keen to present a favourable image, though in recent years there are signs that they have become increasingly intrusive, particularly where ethnic minorities are concerned. The most visible police presence is in Budapest, particularly during the summer, when **tourist police** patrol the streets and metro stations, there mainly to act as a deterrent against thieves, but also to assist in any problems tourists may encounter.

Most Hungarian police have at least a smattering of German but rarely any other foreign language. To contact the **police**, call ☎107 or Policeinform (☎1/438-8080; 24hr; English spoken).

Religion

The majority of the Hungarian population is Roman Catholic, with the remainder comprising Reformed Protestants (Calvinists), Evangelical Protestants (Lutherans) and other, smaller groups such as Serb and Greek Orthodox. As in many other former Communist countries, there has been a steady rise in religious interest, with the church playing a more visible role in everyday life, although, Christmas and Easter aside, it's rare to see churches full.

Hungary has a very rich **Jewish heritage**, and is today the focus of huge donations aiming to build up communities and restore buildings that were devastated or obliterated in the Holocaust. Budapest still retains a sizeable and increasingly active Jewish community, which is far more visible that it was before 1989.

The Hungarian terms for the main religious denominations are: *Katolikus* (Catholic), *Református* (Calvinist), *Evangélikus* (Lutheran), *Görög* (Greek Orthodox), *Görög-Kato-* *likus* (Uniate), *Szerb* (Serb Orthodox) and *Zsidó* (Jewish).

Getting into **churches** may be problematic: the really important ones charge a small fee to see their crypts and treasures, and may prohibit sightseeing during services (*mise* or *istentisztelet*, or *Gottesdienst* in German). Visitors are expected to wear "decorous" dress – that is, no shorts or sleeveless tops. In Budapest, several churches offer religious services in English (see p.196).

Travellers with disabilities

Hungary has been painfully slow to acknowledge the needs of the disabled traveller, and while progress is being made, don't expect much in the way of special facilities. Not surprisingly, Budapest is the place where facilities are most advanced, with a number of hotels (albeit the more expensive ones) accommodating specially designed rooms, and an increasing number of museums providing ramps for wheelchairs. Aside from the Airport Minibus and a handful of BKV bus routes (see the "Passengers with disabilities" section on ⓦ www.bkv.hu for a list), public transport is largely inaccessible to wheelchair users.

The **Hungarian Disabled Association** (MEOSZ), San Marco utca 76, 1032 Budapest (☎ 1/388-5529, ⓦ www.meosz.hu), is doing a terrific job of trying to raise the profile of disabled persons' needs in Hungary. As well as advising on all aspects of coping with disabilities while in Hungary, they provide information on tourist facilities in the country specifically equipped for the physically disabled, including hotels, museums, restaurants and transportation (Budapest facilities are listed on their website). MEOSZ also operates its own special transport service in Budapest whereby, for a fixed payment, a bus equipped with lift or ramp can take you to your chosen destination.

Contacts for travellers with disabilities

UK and Ireland

Holiday Care ☎ 0845 124 9971 or ⓦ www .holidaycare.org.uk. Information on financial help for holidays available.

Irish Wheelchair Association ☎ 01/818 6400, ⓦ www.iwa.ie. Useful information provided about travelling abroad with a wheelchair.

Tripscope ☎ 0845 758 5641, ⓦ www.tripscope .org.uk. Free advice on UK and international transport for those with a mobility problem.

US

Directions Unlimited ☎ 1-800/533-5343 or 914/241-1700. Travel agency specializing in bookings for people with disabilities.

Wheels Up! ☎ 1-888/389-4335, ⓦ www .wheelsup.com. Discounted airfares and tours for disabled travellers.

Australia and New Zealand

ACROD (Australian Council for Rehabilitation of the Disabled) Australia ☎ 02/6282 4333 (also TTY), ⓦ www.acrod.org.au. Provides lists of travel agencies and tour operators for people with disabilities.

Disabled Persons Assembly NZ ☎ 04/801 9100 (also TTY), ⓦ www.dpa.org.nz. Resource centre with lists of travel agencies and tour operators for people with disabilities.

Work and study

Teaching English has traditionally been the main opportunity for work in Hungary, and now, more than ever, language teaching is big business. This is reflected in both the growing number of native speakers working in Budapest and in the number of schools which have opened up outside the capital in recent years. Being a native speaker of English is enough to secure employment at some state primary and secondary schools.

The most reputable **language school** in Hungary is International House, whose Budapest school is at II, Bimbó út 7 (☎1/212-4010, ⍟www.ih.hu); their minimum requirement is a CELTA or TESOL qualification, and preferably one year's experience. There are also teaching opportunities at the British Council, Benczúr utca 26 (☎1/478-4700, ⍟www.britishcouncil.hu), whose minimum requirements are a CELTA and two years' experience. Salaries work out at about 120,000–130,000Ft for a 22-hour week, while some schools, such as International House, will help arrange accommodation and offer some transport allowances, as well as one return flight. Although most language schools recruit year-round, the majority of teachers are in place by September. Another option is to give **private lessons**, the going rate for which is anywhere between 2500Ft and 3000Ft for a 45-minute lesson.

Although teaching in a **primary or secondary school** pays much less (around 70,000Ft per month), the deal usually includes subsidized or free accommodation. Expect to teach around twenty 45-minute periods a week, with a timetable that may also include exam preparation, marking, invigilation etc. Primary schools may take anyone who seems capable and enthusiastic, though you are likely to require at least a certificate in TEFL and/or a PGCE.

Study, work and exchange programmes

Several schools in Budapest cater for foreigners wishing to **learn Hungarian**, the best of which is the Hungarian Language School at VI, Rippl Rónai utca 4 (☎1/351-1191, ⍟www.hls.hu). The school runs a comprehensive range of short- and long-term courses, from beginners to advanced, as well as organizing cultural programmes and workshops.

Eager to publicize their cultural achievements and earn foreign exchange, the Hungarians also organize **summer courses** in everything from folk art to environmental studies. Full details are contained in a booklet published in the spring, which can be obtained by writing to TIT (Society for the Dissemination of Scientific Knowledge), H-1088 Budapest, VIII, Bródy Sándor utca 16. The deadline for most applications is May 1. Courses typically run for two or four weeks; a two-week course, including full-board accommodation, costs around £320/€450/US$580. There are also several organizations arranging summer **work camps** or **exchange programmes** in Hungary for people from a large number of countries.

Useful contacts

International

AFS Intercultural Programs ⍟www.afs.org. Exchange programmes for both students and grown-ups.
Earthwatch Institute ⍟www.earthwatch.org. A long-established charity offering the opportunity to work with eminent research scientists monitoring bird migration on the Ocsa wetland near Budapest (Aug/Sept, from around £700/US$1095).

UK and Ireland

British Council ⍟www.britishcouncil.org. The Council's Central Management of Direct Teaching (☎020/7389 4931) recruits TEFL teachers for posts worldwide.

Erasmus ⓦ europa.eu.int/comm/education/ programmes/socrates/erasmus/erasmus_en. Exchange programmes in Hungary are available from this EU-run scheme for students at participating universities in the UK and Ireland.

US

Council on International Educational Exchange (CIEE) ☏ 1-800/40-STUDY, ⓦ www .ciee.org. Summer, semester and academic-year programmes in Hungary and throughout Europe.

The City

The City

The Belváros

A buzz with pavement cafés, street artists, vendors, boutiques and night-clubs, the **BELVÁROS**, or Inner City, is the hub of Pest and, for tour-ists at least, the epicentre of what's happening. Commerce and pleasure have been its lifeblood as long as Pest has existed, first as a medieval market town and later as the kernel of a city whose *belle époque* rivalled Vienna's. Since their fates diverged, the Belváros has lagged far behind Vienna's Centrum in prosperity, but the gap is fast being narrowed, at least superficially. It's now increasingly like any Western city in its consumer culture, but you can still get a sense of the old atmosphere, especially in the quieter backstreets south of Kossuth utca.

The **Kiskörút** (Small Boulevard; comprising Károly körút, Múzeum körút and Vámház körút) that surrounds the Belváros follows the course of the medi-eval walls of Pest, showing how compact it was before the phenomenal expan-sion of the nineteenth century. However, little remains from further back than the eighteenth century, as the "liberation" of Pest by the Habsburgs in 1686 left the town in ruins. Some Baroque churches and the former Greek and Serbian quarters attest to its revival by settlers from other parts of the Habsburg empire, but most of the **architecture** dates from the era when Budapest asserted its right to be an imperial capital, between 1860 and 1918. Today, first-time visi-tors are struck by the statues, domes and mosaics on the Neoclassical and Art Nouveau piles, which are reflected in the mirrored banks and luxury hotels that symbolize the new order.

After a stroll along **Váci utca** from **Vörösmarty tér** and a look at the splendid view of Várhegy from the **embankment**, the best way to appreciate the Belváros is by simply wandering around. People-watching and window-shopping are the most enjoyable activities, and though prices are above average for Budapest, any visitor should be able to afford to sample the **cafés**. Shops are another matter – there are few bargains – and nightclubs are a trap for the unwary, but there's nothing to stop you from enjoying the **cultural life**, from jazz musicians and violinists on Vörösmarty tér to world-class conductors and soloists at the **Vigadó** concert hall, around the corner.

Vörösmarty tér

Vörösmarty tér, the leafy centre of the Belváros, is a good starting point for exploring the area. Crowds eddy around the portraitists, conjurers and saxo-phonists, and the craft stalls that are set up over summer, Christmas and the

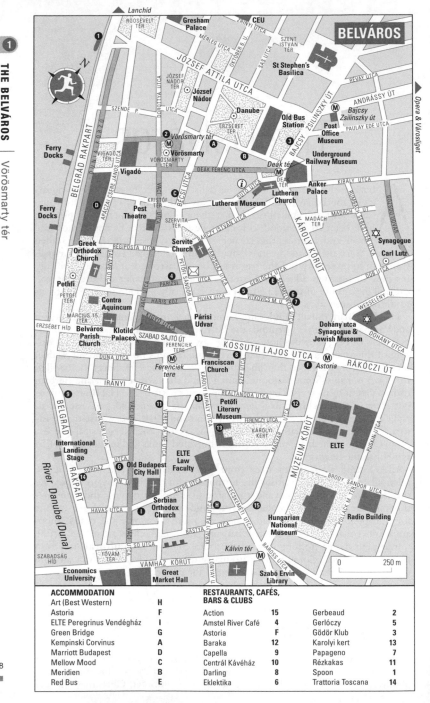

BELVÁROS

ACCOMMODATION

Art (Best Western)	H
Astoria	F
ELTE Peregrinus Vendégház	I
Green Bridge	G
Kempinski Corvinus	A
Marriott Budapest	D
Mellow Mood	C
Meridien	B
Red Bus	E

RESTAURANTS, CAFÉS, BARS & CLUBS

Action	15	Gerbeaud	2
Amstel River Café	4	Gerlóczy	5
Astoria	F	Gödör Klub	3
Baraka	12	Karolyi kert	13
Capella	9	Papageno	7
Centrál Kávéház	10	Rézkakas	11
Darling	8	Spoon	1
Eklektika	6	Trattoria Toscana	14

wine festival. While children play in the fountains, teenagers lounge around the **statue of Mihály Vörösmarty** (1800–50), a poet and translator whose hymn to Magyar identity, *Szózat* (Appeal), is publicly declaimed at moments of national crisis. Its opening line "Be faithful to your land forever, Oh Hungarians" is carved on the statue's pedestal. Made of Carrara marble, the statue has to be wrapped in plastic sheeting each winter to prevent it from cracking. The black spot above the inscription is reputedly a "lucky" coin donated by a beggar towards the cost of the monument.

On the north side of the square is the **Gerbeaud patisserie**, Budapest's most famous confectioners. Founded in 1858 by Henrik Kugler, it was bought in 1884 by the Swiss confectioner Emile Gerbeaud, who invented the *konyakos meggy* (cognac-cherry bonbon) – still a popular sweet with Hungarians. He sold top-class cakes at reasonable prices, making the *Gerbeaud* a popular rendezvous for the middle classes. His portrait hangs in one of the rooms, whose gilded ceilings and china recall the *belle époque*. The smaller *Kis-Gerbeaud* salon round on the right side of the building is no longer a haunt of octogenarian "Gerbeaud ladies" wearing furs and lace gloves; today it offers a cosier setting, fewer crowds and cheaper coffee and cakes than the main café.

From the terrace outside you can observe the entrance to the **Underground Railway** (Földalattivasút, the yellow line), whose vaguely Art Nouveau cast-iron fixtures and elegant tilework stamp it as decades older than the other metro lines. For its centenary in 1996, the line was equipped with the latest technology and its stations restored to their original decor. If you're curious to know more about its history, visit the Underground Railway Museum at Deák tér (see p.54). The Underground Railway's route along Andrássy út is covered in Chapter 3, with Hősök tere described in Chapter 4.

The east side of the square holds the oldfangled Luxus department store, which boasts a fine Art Nouveau staircase. At the southern end of the square, the Art Nouveau **Bank Palace** was built between 1913 and 1915, in the heyday of Hungarian self-confidence, by Ignác Alpár, who also designed the prewar Stock Exchange on Szabadság tér (see p.58). It now houses the **Budapest Stock Exchange**, which was reborn in 1990, 42 years after the Communists suppressed its predecessor. Count Mihály Károlyi, the radical liberal who became Prime Minister in 1918, had an office in the building across the street and used to address crowds from its balcony.

Váci utca

Váci utca has been famous for its shops and **korzó** (promenade) since the eighteenth century. During the 1980s, its vivid streetlife became a symbol of the "consumer socialism" that distinguished Hungary from other Eastern Bloc states. Since 1989 it has been a tourist haunt, with endless souvenir shops and rip-off bars where unsuspecting visitors would be tricked into paying huge bills. Today the northern half of the street, down to Ferenciek tere, has at least gained a touch of style from a number of outlets for big Western designer names. A few landmarks along the way might catch your eye, such as the scantily-clad **fisher-girl statue** on **Kristóf tér**, or the **Pest Theatre** (no. 9) on the site of the *Inn of the Seven Electors*, where the 12-year-old Liszt performed in 1823.

Váci's looks improve south of Március 15 tér, but pedestrianization of this stretch has brought a flood of cheap tat and tourist boutiques, as hordes of visitors walk from the coach park on Március 15 tér down to the Great Market Hall. You'll find a fair mix of architectural styles here, from the prewar **Officers' Casino** on the corner of Március 15 tér (now a bank's headquarters), or the nineteenth-century hulk of the **Old Budapest City Hall** at nos. 62–64, where the city council still meets, down to the more humble older buildings. Look out for the sculptural **plaque** on the wall of no. 47, commemorating the fact that the Swedish King Carl XII stayed here during his lightning fourteen-day horse-ride from Turkey to Sweden, in 1714.

Just beyond the Old Budapest City Hall, an eastward turn into Szerb utca will bring you to the **Serbian Orthodox Church**, built by the Serbian artisans and merchants who settled here after the Turks were driven out. Secluded in a high-walled garden, it's only open for High Mass on Sunday (10.30–11.45am), when the singing of the liturgy, the clouds of incense and flickering candles create an atmosphere that's quite unearthly. A block or so south of the church, part of the **medieval wall** of Pest can be seen running along the back of the car park on the corner of Bástya utca and Veres Pálné utca.

Szervita tér to Kálvin tér

If the hustle on Váci utca deters you, head towards **Szervita tér** – named after the eighteenth-century **Servite Church**, whose facade bears a relief of an angel cradling a dying horseman, in memory of the Seventh Kaiser Wilhelm Hussars killed in World War I. Across the way are two remarkable buildings from the golden age of Hungarian architecture. No. 3 has a gable aglow with a superb **Secessionist mosaic** of *Patrona Hungariae* (Our Lady) flanked by shepherds and angels, one of the finest works of Miksa Róth. The **Rózsavölgyi Building**, next door, was built a few years later between 1910 and 1913 by the "father" of Hungarian Modernism, **Béla Lajta**, whose earlier association with the National Romantic school is evident from the majolica decorations on its upper storeys, typical of the style. On the ground floor is the Rózsavölgyi music shop, one of the oldest and best in the city.

Behind the church, the Brutalist-style T-pont phone, fax and email centre is equally striking, but a rather less attractive presence on **Petőfi Sándor utca**, the street running parallel to Váci utca between Vörösmarty and **Ferenciek tere**. The square itself has been swallowed up by the expansion of the huge road leading down from the Érzsébet bridge. The six or so lanes squeeze down between a pair of imposing *fin-de-siècle* office buildings, named the **Klotild Palaces** after the Habsburg princess who commissioned them – they are sometimes mistakenly called the Klotild and Matilde palaces, though no one is certain which is which.

The most notable building on the Ferenciek tere is the **Párisi Udvar**, a flamboyantly eclectic shopping arcade, completed in 1915. Its fifty naked statues above the third floor were deemed incompatible with its intended role as a savings bank, symbolized by images of bees throughout the building. The neglected arcade, its dome designed by Miksa Róth (see p.74), is as dark as an Andalusian mosque and twice as ornate, and cries out for restoration.

The eastern side of Ferenciek tere seamlessly becomes **Kossuth Lajos utca**, which passes the **Franciscan church** that gave the square its name. The relief on the church's wall recalls the great flood of 1838, in which over four hundred citizens were killed; it depicts the heroic efforts of Baron Miklós Wesselényi, who personally rescued scores of people in his boat. The junction of Kossuth Lajos utca with the Kiskörút is named after the **Astoria Hotel** on the corner, a prewar haunt of spies and journalists that was commandeered as an HQ by the Nazis in 1944 and the Soviets after the 1956 Uprising. Today, its Neoclassical coffee lounge is redolent of Stalinist chic gone to seed.

Károlyi Mihály utca

Walking southwards from the Franciscan Church past the coloured dome of the university library, you come to another thoroughfare, the first part of which is named after Count Mihály Károlyi, the liberal politician who briefly led the government after World War I. Immediately to the right, on the corner, is the restored *Centrál Kávéház*, one of the grand old coffee houses where, during the early part of the last century, writers and intellectuals would sit day and night gathering inspiration.

Károlyi's birthplace at no. 16 houses the **Petőfi Literary Museum** (Petőfi Irodalmi Múzeum; Tues–Sun 10am–6pm; @www.pim.hu; permanent displays free), showcasing the personal effects of Sándor Petőfi, the nineteenth-century poet (see p.52), and other Hungarian writers. The mansion's garden, the **Károlyi-kert**, accessible from the streets running up the sides of the museum, is a delightful haven within the Belváros, but it didn't prove so for Lajos Batthyány, the head of the independent Hungarian government, following the 1848 revolution who was arrested here in 1849. It was also here, in the rose garden, that the "Butcher of Vienna", General Haynau, completed his exercises before signing the death warrants of the Hungarian leaders.

Along the embankment

The **Belgrád rakpart** (Belgrade Embankment) bore the brunt of the fighting in 1944–45, when the Nazis and the Red Army exchanged salvos across the Danube. As with the Várhegy in Buda, postwar clearances exposed historic sites and provided an opportunity to integrate them into the environment – but the magnificent **view** of Buda Palace and Gellért-hegy is hardly matched by the row of modern hotels on the Pest side. While such historic architecture as remains can be seen in a fifteen-minute stroll between the Erzsébet híd and the Lánchíd, **tram #2** enables you to see a longer stretch of the waterfront between Szabadság híd and Kossuth tér in the north, periodically interrupted by a tunnel that's the first to be flooded if the Danube overflows its embankments, as sometimes happens in the summer.

The bold white pylons and cables of the **Erzsébet híd** (Elizabeth Bridge) are as cherished a feature of the panorama as the stone Lánchíd to the north or the wrought-iron Szabadság híd to the south. Of all the Danube bridges blown up by the Germans as they retreated to Buda in January 1945, the Erzsébet híd was the only one not rebuilt in its original form. In fact it was not replaced until 1964 – and even then had to be closed down immediately due to faulty engineering.

In the shadow of the approach ramp, the grimy facade of the **Belváros Parish Church** (Belvárosi Plébánia Templom; Mon–Sat 7am–7pm, Sun 8am–7pm; free) masks its origins as the oldest church in Pest. Founded in 1046 as the burial place of St Gellért (see p.110), it was rebuilt as a Gothic hall church in the fifteenth century (his remains had been long shipped off to Venice), turned into a mosque by the Turks and then reconstructed as a church in the eighteenth century. This history is reflected in the church's interior, and after Latin Mass at 10am on Sunday you can see the Gothic sedilia and Turkish *mihrab* (prayer niche) behind the high altar, which are otherwise out of bounds. The vaulted nave and side chapels are Baroque.

Március 15 tér and Petőfi tér

On the square beside the Belváros Parish church, a sunken enclosure exposes the remains of **Contra-Aquincum**, a Roman fort that was an outpost of the settlement at Óbuda at the end of the third century. More pertinently to Hungarian history, the name of the square, **Március 15 tér**, refers to March 15, 1848, when the anti-Habsburg Revolution began, while the adjacent **Petőfi tér** is named after Sándor Petőfi, whose poem *National Song* – the anthem of 1848 – and romantic death in battle the following year made him a patriotic icon (see box below). Erected in 1882, the square's **Petőfi statue** has long been a focus for demonstrations as well as patriotic displays – especially on March 15, when the statue is bedecked with flags and flowers. Behind it looms the **Greek Orthodox Church**, built by the Greek community in the 1790s and currently the object of a tug-of-war between the Patriarchate of Moscow that gained control of it after 1945, and the Orthodox Church in Greece that previously owned it. Services (Sat 6pm & Sun 10am) are in Hungarian, accompanied by singing in the Orthodox fashion.

Just north of Petőfi tér, the gigantic **Marriott Hotel** is situated between the embankment and the street running parallel, Apáczai Csere János utca. Inaugurated as the *Duna Intercontinental* in 1969, it was the first hotel in the Eastern Bloc managed in partnership with a Western firm and the model for others on the *rakpart*. On the Danube side of the *Marriott*, the concrete esplanade is a sterile attempt at recreating the prewar **Duna-korzó**, the most informal of Budapest's promenades, where it was socially acceptable for strangers to approach celebrities and stroll beside them. The outdoor cafés here, which boast wonderful views, charge premium rates.

Sándor Petőfi

Born on New Year's Eve, 1822, of a Slovak mother and a southern Slav butcher-innkeeper father, **Sándor Petőfi** was to become obsessed with acting and by poetry, which he started to write at the age of 15. As a strolling player, soldier and labourer, he absorbed the language of working people and composed his lyrical poetry in the vernacular, to the outrage of critics. Moving to Budapest in 1844, he fell in with the young radical intellectuals who met at the *Pilvax Café* (its modern embodiment on Pilvax utca, off Váci utca, fails to capture the rebellious spirit), and embarked on his career as a revolutionary hero. He declaimed his *National Song* from the steps of the National Museum on the first day of the 1848 Revolution, and fought in the War of Independence with General Bem in Transylvania, where he disappeared during the battle of Segesvár in 1849. Though he was most likely trampled beyond recognition by the Cossacks' horses (as predicted in one of his poems), Petőfi was long rumoured to have survived as a prisoner. In 1990, a Hungarian entrepreneur sponsored an expedition to Siberia to uncover the putative grave, but it turned out to be that of a woman.

△ The Pest streets are full of charming architectural details

The Vigadó

Vigadó tér is an elegant square full of stalls and buskers, named after the **Vigadó** concert hall, whose name translates as "having a ball" or "making merry". Inaugurated in 1865, this splendidly Romantic pile by Frigyes Feszl has hosted performances by Liszt, Mahler, Wagner, von Karajan and other renowned artists. Badly damaged in World War II, it didn't reopen until 1980, such was the care taken to recreate its sumptuous decor. At the time of writing, the hall was once again closed for refurbishment.

Don't overlook the statue of the impish **Little Princess**, which has been sitting on the railings by the tram line since 1990. After dusk, you'll hardly notice that she isn't a person, if you notice her at all. By day, she looks like a cross-dressing boy in a Tinkerbell hat. Prince Charles was so taken by her that he invited her creator, László Marton, to hold an exhibition of his work in the UK.

Deák tér and Erzsébet tér

Three metro lines and several important roads meet at **Deák tér** and **Erzsébet tér** – two squares that merge into one another (making local addresses extremely confusing) to form a jumping-off point for the Belváros and Lipótváros. You'll recognize the area by two landmarks that stand astride Deák tér: the enormous mustard-coloured **Anker Palace** on the Kiskörút, and the **Lutheran Church** by the metro pavilion on the edge of the Belváros, which hosts some excellent concerts, including Bach's *St John Passion* over the fortnight before Easter. Next door, the **Lutheran Museum** (Evangélikus Múzeum; Tues–Sun 10am–6pm; 300Ft) displays a facsimile of Martin Luther's last will and testament, and a copy of the first book printed in Hungarian, a New Testament from 1541.

Erzsébet tér, once the site of a cemetery outside the medieval city walls, has gone through many names since then, notably Sztálin tér from 1946 until 1953, when it became Engels tér, before getting its older name back. The statue in the middle of the park is of Old Father Danube with his three bored tributaries, the Dráva, Száva and Tisza, designed in 1880 by Miklós Ybl. The long low functionalist building behind the trees used to house the main bus station until it moved out recently to Népliget. Much to the ire of some locals, the building is protected by a conservation order and so cannot be swept away. The space to the east has also been the cause of controversy: Gábor Demszky's plan to turn the former car park into the National Theatre in the 1990s was thwarted by the incoming Fidesz government, which halted work and set about commissioning its own theatre further down the Danube (see p.90). For several years this huge pit was christened the National Hole, until finally it was filled in and tidied up. Today it houses the *Gödör Klub*, comprising a bar, concert venue and exhibition space; from above, you can look down through a glass-bottomed pool at the art viewers below.

Underground Railway Museum

Accessible via the upper sub-level of Deák tér metro, the **Underground Railway Museum** (Földalattivasút Múzeum; Tues–Sun 10am–6pm; 160Ft or one BKV ticket) extols the history of Budapest's original metro. The exhibits include two elegant wooden carriages (one used up until 1973) and period fixtures and posters, which enhance the museum's nostalgic appeal.

The metro's genesis was a treatise by Mór Balazs, proposing a steam-driven tram network starting with a route along Andrássy út, an underground line being suggested as a fallback in case the overground option was rejected. Completed in under two years, it was inaugurated in 1896 – in time for the Millennial Exhibition – by Emperor Franz Josef, who agreed to allow it to bear his name, which it kept until 1918. The metro was the first on the European continent and the second in the world (after London's Metropolitan line), and originally ran from Vörösmarty tér as far as the Millennial Exhibition grounds at Hősök tere.

2

Lipótváros and Újlipótváros

L IPÓTVÁROS (Leopold Town), lying to the north of the Belváros, started to develop in the late eighteenth century, first as a financial centre and later as the seat of government and bureaucracy. Several institutions of national significance are found here, including **Parliament**, **St Stephen's Basilica**, the **National Bank** and the Television headquarters. Though part of the V District, as is the Belváros, Lipótváros has quite a different ambience, with sombre streets of Neoclassical buildings interrupted by squares flanked by monumental Art Nouveau or neo-Renaissance piles. It's busy with office workers by day, but used to be dead in the evenings and at weekends until good restaurants brought some life to the area. Another source of vitality is the Central European University (CEU), funded by the Hungarian-born billionaire financier George Soros.

It makes sense to start a Lipótváros visit either with Roosevelt tér, just inland of the Lánchíd, or St Stephen's Basilica, two minutes' walk from Erzsébet tér. Most of the streets between them lead towards the set-piece expanse of **Szabadság tér**, whence you can head on towards Parliament – though the Kossuth tér metro station or tram #2 from the Belgrád rakpart will provide quicker access.

Across the Nagykörút lies **ÚJLIPÓTVÁROS** (New Leopold Town; the XIII district), stretching from the bustling Pozsonyi út through quieter residential streets to another focus of activity, the market in the **Lehel Csarnok**. The way to get here is either by tram #4 or #6 along the Nagykörút or on the blue metro from Deák tér.

Roosevelt tér

At the Pest end of the Lánchíd, **Roosevelt tér** is blitzed by traffic, making it difficult to stand back and admire **Gresham Palace** – a splendid example of Art Nouveau – on the eastern side of the square. Commissioned by a British insurance company in 1904, the building is named after the financier Sir Thomas Gresham, the originator of Gresham's law, that bad money drives out good; Gresham described how the circulation of coins of equal face value but

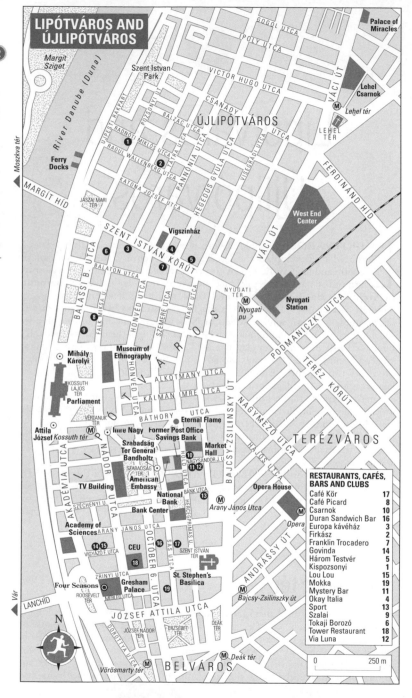

LIPÓTVÁROS AND ÚJLIPÓTVÁROS

Margit Sziget

Szent István Park

GOGOL UTCA

IPOLY UTCA

Palace of Miracles

VICTOR HUGO UTCA

VÁCI ÚT

Lehel Csarnok

CSANÁDY UTCA

Lehel tér

ÚJLIPÓTVÁROS

LEHEL TÉR

Moszkva tér

River Danube (Duna)

ÚJPESTI RAKPART

POZSONYI U.

BALZAC UTCA

RADNÓTI MIKLÓS UTCA ❶

RAOUL WALLENBERG UTCA ❷

LATRA UTCA

PANNÓNIA UTCA

HEGEDŰS GYULA UTCA

VISEGRÁDI UTCA

FERDINAND HÍD

Ferry Docks

KATONA JÓZSEF UTCA

JÁSZAI MARI TÉR

West End Center

MARGIT HÍD

SZENT ISTVÁN KÖRÚT

Vigszinház

❻ ❸ ❹ ❺ ❼

BALATON UTCA

VÁCI ÚT

BALASSI B. UTCA

FALK MIKSA U.

HONVÉD UTCA

SZEMERE UTCA

NAGY UTCA

NYUGATI TÉR

Nyugati Station

❽ ❾

Nyugati pu

PODMANICZKY UTCA

Mihály Károlyi

Museum of Ethnography

ALKOTMÁNY UTCA

TERÉZ KÖRÚT

KOSSUTH LAJOS TÉR

Parliament

KÁLMÁN IMRE UTCA

BÁTHORY UTCA

TERÉZVÁROS

VÉRTANUK TÉR

Eternal Flame

Attila József

Kossuth tér

Imre Nagy Former Post Office Savings Bank

NAGYMEZŐ UTCA

HAJÓS UTCA

Szabadság Ter General Bandholtz

Market Hall

NÁDOR UTCA

SZABADSÁG TÉR

American Embassy

❿

NAGYSÁNDOR J. U.

⓫⓬

Opera House

RESTAURANTS, CAFÉS, BARS AND CLUBS

TV Building

National Bank

BANK UTCA

⓭

AKADÉMIA UTCA

SZÉCHENYI U.

Bank Center

HERCEGPRIMÁS U.

Arany János Utca

Opera

Café Kör	17
Café Picard	8
Csarnok	10
Duran Sandwich Bar	16
Europa kávéház	3
Firkász	2
Franklin Trocadero	7
Govinda	14
Három Testvér	5
Kispozsonyi	1
Lou Lou	15
Mokka	19
Mystery Bar	11
Okay Italia	4
Sport	13
Szalai	9
Tokaji Borozó	6
Tower Restaurant	18
Via Luna	12

Academy of Sciences

ARANY JÁNOS UTCA

⓮⓯

VIGYÁZÓ F. UTCA

CEU ⓰ ⓱

SAS UTCA

SZENT ISTVÁN TÉR

OKTÓBER 6. UTCA

⓲

ZRINYI UTCA

Four Seasons

Gresham Palace

St. Stephen's Basilica

ROOSEVELT TÉR

MÉRLEG UTCA

⓳

Bajcsy-Zsilinszky út

Vár

LÁNCHÍD

JÓZSEF ATTILA UTCA

DOROTTYA UTCA

JÓZSEF NÁDOR TÉR

ERZSÉBET TÉR

DEÁK TÉR

ANDRÁSSY ÚT

BAJCSY-ZSILINSZKY ÚT

N

Vörösmarty tér

Deák tér

BELVÁROS

0   250 m

of different metals led to the coins of the more expensive metal being hoarded, and thus disappearing from use.

The building was in a very poor state when it was handed over to the Four Seasons chain to turn it into a hotel, and many feared that big money would drive out the architectural good. These concerns have been allayed by the loving restoration job: original materials and even the original workshops were painstakingly sought out for the work, so that today you can once again see Sir Thomas's bust high up on the facade, the interior glass-roofed arcade and the stained-glass windows by Miksa Róth on the staircases in all their glory. The management understands that it has one of the city's finest buildings in its hands, and so has made a point of drawing people in to show them round, rather than shutting its fine wrought-iron peacock gates. Ask at the reception desk in the foyer if you can look round inside.

Statues of Count Széchenyi (see p.106) and Ferenc Deák, another major nineteenth-century politician, stand at opposite ends of the square. The statue of the former isn't far from the **Hungarian Academy of Sciences** (Magyar Tudományos Akadémia), founded after Széchenyi pledged a year's income from his estates towards its establishment in 1825 – as depicted on a relief on the wall facing Akadémia utca.

While the Academy and the Lánchíd are tangible reminders of Széchenyi's enterprise, there is no reminder of Deák's achievement in forging an Ausgleich (Compromise) with the Habsburgs. This was symbolized by the crowning of Emperor Franz Josef as King of Hungary in 1867, when soil from every corner of the nation was piled into a Coronation Hill, on the site of the present square. Here the emperor flourished the sword of St Stephen and promised to defend Hungary against all its enemies – a pledge that proved almost as ephemeral as the hill itself. Eighty years later, the square was renamed Roosevelt tér in honour of the late US president – a rare example of Cold War courtesy that was never revoked.

St Stephen's Basilica and Bajcsy-Zsilinszky út

St Stephen's Basilica (Szent István-Bazilika; Mon–Fri 9am–5pm, Sat 9am–1pm, Sun 1–4pm) took so long to build that Budapesters used to joke, when borrowing money, "I'll pay you back when the basilica is finished". Work began in 1851 under the supervision of József Hild, continued after his death under Miklós Ybl, and was finally completed by Joseph Krauser in 1905. At the inaugural ceremony Franz Josef was seen to glance anxiously at the dome, whose collapse during a storm in 1868 had set progress back. At 96m, it is exactly the same height as the dome of the Parliament building – both allude to the putative date of the Magyars' arrival in Hungary (896 AD). After recent restoration work that seemed to take as long as the original construction, the Basilica looks fabulous today. It is best visited when the interior is open for sightseeing, as its beauty lies in the carvings, frescoes and chapels, the variegated marble, gilded stucco and bronze mouldings, and the splendid **organ** above the doorway.

In the second chapel to the right is a painting of King Stephen offering the Crown of Hungary to the Virgin (see p.96), while a statue of him haloed as a saint (but with a sword at his side) forms the centrepiece of the altar. In a chapel to the left at the back is the gnarled **mummified hand of St Stephen**, Hungary's holiest relic. The Szent Jobb (literally, "holy right") is paraded with great pomp through the surrounding streets on August 20, the anniversary of his death, but at other times you can see it in the chapel by inserting 100Ft to illuminate the casket.

Although the **treasury** (250Ft) is paltry compared to that at Esztergom's Basilica, you shouldn't miss the so-called **Panorama Tower** (daily April–Oct 10am–6pm; 500Ft). You can only go to the base of the cupola 65m up (the stairs up to the top are closed indefinitely), but that nonetheless offers a grand **view** over Pest; save the 302 or so steps for the return and go up by lift. (Note that when you come out of the first lift, you change to a second lift over to your right.)

While Stephen is revered as the founder and patron saint of Hungary, the pantheon of national heroes includes a niche for Endre Bajcsy-Zsilinszky (1866–1944), after whom the avenue that runs past the Basilica is named. Originally a right-winger, he ended up an outspoken critic of Fascism, was arrested in Parliament (a statue on Deák tér captures the moment) and shot as the Russians approached. **Bajcsy–Zsilinszky út** runs northwards to **Nyugati tér**, dominated by **Nyugati Station**, an elegant, iron-beamed terminal built in 1874–77 by the Eiffel Company of Paris. The avenue is also the demarcation line between the Lipótváros and Terézváros districts. Beside the station, the **Westend City Center** is one of Budapest's largest malls, boasting four hundred outlets and an artificial waterfall three storeys high. Its newest attraction is the **Budapest Eye** (Budapest Kilátó; weather permitting: May–Oct Mon–Thurs & Sun 11am–10pm, Fri & Sat 11am–midnight; Nov–April daily noon–8pm; 3300Ft; ⊚www.budapestkilato.hu), a hot-air balloon that takes visitors up 150m for excellent views over the city. The whole thing takes about twenty minutes, though you only spend five minutes at the top height. In summer, you may need to book tickets in advance (call ☎1/238 7623).

Szabadság tér and around

For over a century Lipótváros was dominated by a gigantic barracks where scores of Hungarians were imprisoned or executed, until this symbol of Habsburg tyranny was demolished in 1897 and the site redeveloped as **Szabadság tér** (Liberty Square). Invested with significance from the outset, it became a kind of record of the vicissitudes of modern Hungarian history, where each regime added or removed monuments, according to their political complexion. For an excellent vantage point from which to admire the square's buildings, head to the café pavilion in the centre of the square.

The Stock Exchange and National Bank

In the early years of the last century, Hungary's burgeoning prosperity was expressed by two monumental temples to capitalism on opposite sides of the square. To the west stood the **Stock Exchange**, one of the grandest buildings in Budapest. Designed by Ignác Alpár, it has blended motifs from Greek and Assyrian architecture and is crowned with twin towers resembling Khmer temples. After the Communists closed down the Stock Exchange in 1948, it became the headquarters of Hungarian Television.

Alpár also designed the **National Bank** (Nemzeti Bank), which still functions as such and is notable for the reliefs on its exterior, representing such diverse aspects of wealth creation as Magyars ploughing and herding, ancient Egyptians harvesting wheat, and Vikings loading their longships with loot. The building, entered at Szabadság tér 8, contains a small **Museum of Banknotes** (Thurs 9am–2pm; free) featuring curiosities like the "Kossuth" banknotes that were issued in America during the politician's exile after the failed War of Independence, and notes denominated in billions of forints from the period of hyper-inflation in 1946. The mirrored-glass and granite **Bank Center** at the southern end of the square is a triumphant affirmation that Hungary has rejoined the capitalist system.

Szabadság tér's monuments

The square has seen quite a high turnover in its **statuary** as the winds of politics have changed. Dominating the northern end of the square is the **Soviet Army Memorial** set up after World War II to commemorate the liberation of Budapest from the Nazis, with reliefs of Red Army troops and tanks advancing on Ferenciek tere and Parliament. This replaced a collection of statues erected after World War I by the Hungarian government mourning the 1920 Treaty of Trianon, which gave away two-thirds of Hungary's territory and a third of its Magyar population to the "Successor States" of Romania, Czechoslovakia and Yugoslavia. The most notable of these was the Monument to Hungarian Grief – featuring a flag at half-mast and a quotation from Lord Rothermere (the proprietor of the British *Daily Mail*, whose campaign against Trianon was so appreciated that he was offered the Hungarian crown) – and four statues called North, South, East and West, whose inauguration in 1921 was attended by 50,000 people. When the Communist regime got the boot in 1990, there were calls to remove the Soviet memorial and restore the old nationalist ones, though wiser counsels prevailed; the Soviet Army Memorial survived on the grounds that it contains the remains of Soviet soldiers.

The way in which the statues have been placed has a certain irony. The Soviet memorial stands near the former headquarters of the Fascist Arrow Cross, and directly in front of the US Embassy, which for fifteen years gave shelter to Cardinal Mindszenty, the Primate of Hungary's Catholic Church, in the aftermath of the 1956 Uprising. Later, however, the US became embarrassed by his presence, as did the Vatican, who finally persuaded him to leave for Austria in 1971 (see box on p.142). Nearby is the statue of **General Harry Bandholtz** of the US Army, who intervened with a dogwhip to stop Romanian troops from looting the Hungarian National Museum in 1919. The statue was erected in the 1930s, removed after World War II, and reinstated by the Communists prior to the first President Bush's visit in 1989.

The former Post Office Savings Bank

Behind the US Embassy, the **former Post Office Savings Bank** on Hold utca is a classic example of Hungarian Art Nouveau, its tiled facade patterned like a quilt, with swarms of bees (symbolizing savings) ascending to the polychromatic roof, which is the wildest part of the building. Its architect, Ödön Lechner, once asked why birds shouldn't enjoy his buildings too, and amazing roofs are a feature of his other masterpieces in Budapest, the Applied Arts Museum and the Geological Institute. You can see the foyer during bank hours, but the rest of the interior is open to the public on only one day a year – European Heritage Day, in September (ask Tourinform for details). Diagonally across the street is a wrought-iron **market hall**, one of five opened on a single day in 1896, which continue to serve the centre of Budapest to this day.

The Batthyány and Nagy Monuments

At the junction of Hold utca and Báthory utca, a lantern on a plinth flickers with an **Eternal Flame** commemorating Count Lajos Batthyány, the Prime Minister of the short-lived republic declared after the 1848 War of Independence, whom the Habsburgs executed on this spot on October 6, 1849. As a staunch patriot – but not a revolutionary – Batthyány is a hero for conservative nationalists, and his monument is the destination of annual marches on October 6.

The refrains and paradoxes of Hungarian history are echoed on Vértanuk tér (Martyrs' Square), between Szabadság tér and Kossuth tér, where a **statue of Imre Nagy** – the reform Communist who became Prime Minister during the 1956 Uprising and was shot in secret two years afterwards – stands on a footbridge, gazing towards Parliament. With his raincoat, trilby and umbrella hooked over his arm, Nagy cuts an all-too-human, flawed figure – and is scorned by those who pay homage to Batthyány.

Kossuth tér

The apotheosis of the government district and Hungary's romantic self-image comes at **Kossuth tér**, with its colossal Parliament building and memorials to national heroes and epic moments in Hungarian history. The square is named after **Lajos Kossuth**, the leader of the 1848 Revolution against the Habsburgs (see box opposite), who was originally represented by a sculptural tableau showing him and his ministers downcast by their defeat in 1849. However, the Communists replaced it with a more "heroic" one of Kossuth rousing the nation to arms, by Kisfaludy-Strobl, also responsible for the Liberation Monument on Gellért-hegy. The other main statue is of **Prince Ferenc Rákóczi II**, an earlier hero of the struggle for Hungarian independence, whose plinth is inscribed with the words "The wounds of the noble Hungarian nation burst open!" This is a reference to the anti-Habsburg war of 1703–11, but also perfectly describes the evening of October 23, 1956, when crowds filled the square, chanting anti-Stalinist slogans at Parliament – the prelude to the Uprising that night. An **eternal flame** burns in memory of those who died on Kossuth tér on October 25, when ÁVO snipers opened fire on a peaceful crowd that was fraternizing with Soviet tank-crews.

On either side of Parliament near the river stand two statues of note. To the south, nearer to the Kossuth tér metro station, sits the brooding figure of **Attila József**, one of Hungary's finest poets. Too radical for the Communist Party, which rejected him in the 1930s for trying to reconcile Marx and Freud, he committed suicide in 1937 after being rejected by his lover, too. His powerful, turbulent verse has never lost its popularity, and he earns his place here for his poem *By the Danube*. To the north of Parliament stands the forlorn figure of **Károly Mihályi**, the liberal count who led the short-lived government after the collapse of the Habsburg Empire at the end of World War I. He was swept

Lajos Kossuth

Lajos Kossuth was the incarnation of post-Napoleonic bourgeois nationalism. Born into landless gentry in 1802, he began his career as a lawyer, representing absentee magnates in Parliament. His Parliamentary reports, which advocated greater liberalism than the Habsburgs would tolerate, became widely influential during the Reform era, and he was jailed for sedition. While in prison, Kossuth taught himself English by reading Shakespeare. Released in 1840, he became editor of the radical *Pesti Hírlap*, was elected to Parliament and took the helm during the 1848 Revolution.

After Serbs, Croats and Romanians rebelled against Magyar rule and the Habsburgs invaded Hungary, the Hungarians proclaimed a republic with Kossuth as de facto dictator. After the Hungarians surrendered in August 1849, Kossuth escaped to Turkey and later toured Britain and America, espousing liberty and trying to win support for the Hungarian cause. So eloquent were his denunciations of Habsburg tyranny that London brewery workers attacked General Haynau, the "Butcher of Vienna", when he visited the city. One man who did his best to undermine Kossuth's efforts was Karl Marx, who loathed Kossuth as a bourgeois radical and wrote hostile articles in the New York *Herald Tribune* and the London *Times*.

As a friend of the Italian patriot Mazzini, Kossuth spent his last years in Turin, where he died in 1894. His remains now lie in the Kerepesi Cemetery (see p.87).

aside by the Republic of Councils and forced into exile, returning briefly after World War II, when he soon became disillusioned with the Soviet-backed regime. He died in 1955 in France.

Parliament

The Hungarian **Parliament** building (Országház; @www.parliament.hu) makes the Houses of Parliament in London look humble, its architect Imre Steindl having larded Pugin's Gothic Revival style with Renaissance and Baroque flourishes. Sprawling for 268m along the embankment, its symmetrical wings bristle with finials and 88 statues of Hungarian rulers, surmounted by a dome 96m high (alluding to the date of the Magyar conquest; see p.199). Though most people are impressed by the building, the popular poet and writer Gyula Illyés (1902–83) once famously dismissed it as "no more than a Turkish bath crossed with a Gothic chapel" – albeit one that cost 38,000,000 gold forints. One weakness in the design was the white limestone of the exterior, which has been battered by the elements and pollution; since 1925 it has required almost constant cleaning and replacement.

For centuries, Hungarian assemblies convened wherever they could, and it wasn't until 1843 that it was resolved to build a permanent "House of the Motherland" in Pest-Buda (as the city was then called). By the time work began in 1885, the concept of Parliament had changed insofar as the middle classes were now represented as well, though over ninety percent of the population still lacked the right to vote. Gains were made in 1918, but they were soon curtailed under the Horthy regime, just as the attainment of universal adult suffrage in 1945 was rendered meaningless after 1948 by a Communist dictatorship. The introduction of multiparty democracy in 1990 was symbolized by the removal of the red star from Parliament's dome and the replacement of Communist emblems by the traditional coat of arms featuring the double cross of King Stephen – whose Coronation Regalia is now on show in the building's Cupola Hall.

The interior – and the Coronation Regalia

How much you see on the **tours** of the interior (daily at 10am, noon, 2pm & 6pm in English; free for EU citizens, passport needed for proof, 2070Ft for others; no flash photography) depends on Parliament's activities, but you can be sure of seeing the main staircase, the Cupola Hall and the Lords Chamber, if nothing else. Statues, carvings, gilding and mosaics are ten a penny, lit by lamps worthy of the Winter Palace – but there are also cosy touches such as the individually numbered brass ashtrays where peers left their cigars smouldering in the lounge while they popped back into the chamber to hear someone speak; a good speaker was said to be "worth a Havana". **Tickets** are bought from Gate X, though getting them can involve a palaver – you'll see a huddle of people to the right of the central span of the building, and guards will usually let you through to get tickets ten minutes before tours start.

Guards holding drawn sabres flank the **Coronation Regalia**, whose centrepiece, **St Stephen's Crown**, has symbolized Hungarian statehood for over a thousand years. It consists of two crowns joined together: the cruciform crown that was sent as a gift by Pope Sylvester II to Stephen for his coronation in 1000, and a circlet given by the Byzantine monarch to King Géza I. The distinctive bent cross was caused by the crown being squashed as it was smuggled out of a palace in a baby's cradle. At other times it has been hidden in a hay-cart or buried in Transylvania, abducted to Germany by Hungarian Fascists and thence taken to the US, where it reposed in Fort Knox until its return home in 1978, together with Stephen's crystal-headed sceptre, a fourteenth-century gold-plated orb and a sixteenth-century sword made in Vienna, used by his successors. Under the Dual Monarchy, Habsburg emperors ruled Hungary in the name of St Stephen, and travelled to Budapest for a special coronation ceremony, traditionally held in the Mátyás Church on Várhegy.

On a humbler note, there's a **scale model** of Parliament made of 100,000 matchsticks, built by a patriotic family over three years.

Museum of Ethnography

Across the road from Kossuth's statue stands a neo-Renaissance building housing the **Museum of Ethnography** (Néprajzi Múzeum; Tues–Sun: March–Oct 10am–6pm; Nov–Feb 10am–5pm; free, visiting exhibitions 500Ft; @www .neprajz.hu). Little visited by tourists, it's actually one of the finest museums in Budapest, originally built as the Palace of the Supreme Court; petitioners would have been overawed by its lofty, gilded main hall, whose ceiling bears a fresco of the goddess Justitia surrounded by allegories of Justice, Peace, Revenge and Sin.

The museum's permanent exhibition on **Hungarian folk culture** occupies thirteen rooms on the first floor (off the left-hand staircase) and is fully captioned in English, with an excellent catalogue available. Habsburg-ruled Hungary comprised a dozen ethnic groups, represented by exhibits arranged under headings such as "Institutions" and "Peasant Work"; the only groups not represented are the Jews and the gypsies. Though the beautiful costumes and objects on display are no longer part of everyday life in Hungary, you can still see them in parts of Romania, such as Maramures and the Kalotaszeg, which belonged to Hungary before 1920.

Temporary exhibitions (on the second floor) cover anything from Bedouin life to Hindu rituals, while over Easter and Christmas there are **concerts** of Hungarian folk music and dancing, and **craft fairs**.

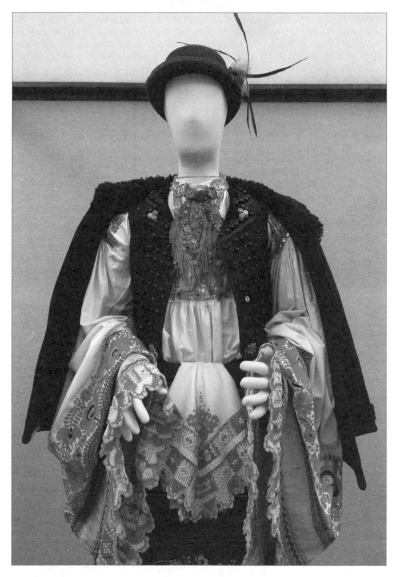

△ The Museum of Ethnography has a large collection of folk costumes

Újlipótváros

Szent István körút, the section of the Nagykörút running from Nyugati Station to the Danube, marks the end of Lipótváros – but there are a few sights
further out in Újlipótváros (District XIII) that are worth a mention. The bank
of the Danube north of the Margit híd is the site of the summertime **Budapest**

Beach (Budapest Plázs; ⓦwww.budapestplazs.hu), which takes its cue from the Paris original. For the month of August the 1500-metre stretch of the Újpesti rakpart is closed to traffic and covered in sand and palm trees, recreating a seaside feel, and there are stages, live music, children's programmes and numerous food stalls and restaurants to keep beach-goers happy.

Running up from the *körút* parallel to the beach is Pozsonyi út, a bustling tree-lined street that leads up to **Szent István Park**, the prewar social hub of the wealthy Jewish neighbourhood, and which still boasts the finest flowerbeds in the city. It's an apt site for a **monument to Raoul Wallenberg**, who gave up a playboy life in neutral Sweden to help the Jews of Budapest in 1944 (see p.71). The monument was constructed in the 1950s but "exiled" to Debrecen in eastern Hungary before being stashed away for decades, only taking its rightful place in Budapest in 1999.

Heading eastwards for 500m along Csanádi utca brings you to Lehel tér. Here you can't miss the **Romanesque church** on a traffic island to your left, a 1930s reconstruction of the ruined church at Zsámbék, west of Budapest. Beyond lies the **Lehel tér market hall** (Lehel Csarnok), which may look like a stylistic mish-mash but has an excellent range of food stalls inside.

Visitors with kids or an interest in science should enjoy the **Palace of Miracles** (Csodák palotája; Jan to mid-April Tues–Fri 9am–5pm, Sat & Sun 10am–6pm; mid-April to Dec Mon–Fri 10am–5pm, Sat & Sun 10am–6pm; 650Ft; ⓦwww.csodapalota.hu) at Váci út 19 (not to be confused with Váci utca in the Belváros), a couple of blocks further on. This interactive playhouse was the brainchild of two Hungarian physicists and aims to explain scientific principles to 6- to 12-year-olds, using devices such as optical illusions, a bed of nails, a simulated low-gravity "moonwalk" and a "miracle bicycle" on a tightrope.

Terézváros and Erzsébetváros

ERÉZVÁROS (Theresa Town, the VI District) is home to the **State Opera House**, the **Academy of Music** and the Hungarian equivalent of Broadway, making it one of the most vibrant parts of the city. Its main thoroughfare, **Andrássy út**, marking the border between it and Lipótváros, is Budapest's longest, grandest avenue, running in a perfect straight line for two and a half kilometres up to Hősök tere and the Városliget, covered in chapter 4. With its coffee houses and grey stone edifices laden with dryads, not to mention the Opera House, the avenue retains something of the style that made it so fashionable in the 1890s, when "Bertie" the Prince of Wales drove its length in a landau, offering flowers to women as he passed.

To the south of Király utca, the mainly residential **ERZSÉBETVÁROS** (Elizabeth Town, the VII District) is composed of nineteenth-century buildings whose bullet-scarred facades, adorned with fancy wrought-ironwork, conceal a warren of dwellings and leafy courtyards. It is also traditionally the **Jewish quarter** of the city, which was transformed into a ghetto during the Nazi occupation and almost wiped out in 1944–45, but has miraculously retained its cultural identity. Its current resurgence owes much to increased contacts with international Jewry, and a revival of interest in their religion and roots among the eighty-thousand-strong Jewish community of Budapest, which had previously tended towards assimilation, reluctant to proclaim itself in a country where anti-Semitic prejudices linger. There is no better part of Pest to wander around, soaking up the atmosphere.

The stretch of Andrássy út up to the Oktogon – where it meets the Nagykörút (Great Boulevard) – is within walking distance of Deak tér, and the whole length of the boulevard is served by the metro. Trams and buses circle the Nagykörút 24-hourly, and several trolleybus lines run through the two districts out to the Városliget.

Terézváros

Laid out in the late nineteenth century, **Terézváros** was heavily influenced by Haussmann's redevelopment of Paris, and at that time it was one of the smart-

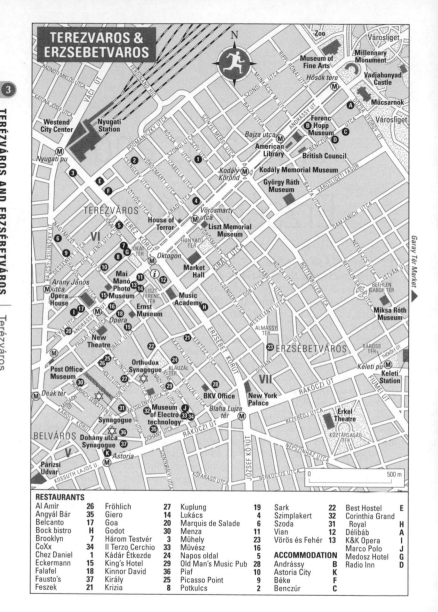

TERÉZVÁROS & ERZSÉBETVÁROS

RESTAURANTS								ACCOMMODATION	
Al Amir	26	Fröhlich	27	Kuplung	19	Sark	22	Best Hostel	E
Angyál Bár	35	Giero	14	Lukács	4	Szimplakert	32	Corinthia Grand	
Belcanto	17	Goa	20	Marquis de Salade	6	Szoda	31	Royal	H
Bock bistro	H	Godot	30	Menza	11	Vian	12	Délibáb	A
Brooklyn	7	Három Testvér	3	Mühely	23	Vörös és Fehér	13	K&K Opera	I
CoXx	34	Il Terzo Cerchio	33	Müvész	16			Marco Polo	J
Chez Daniel	1	Kádár Étkezde	24	Napos oldal	5	ACCOMMODATION		Medosz Hotel	G
Eckermann	15	King's Hotel	29	Old Man's Music Pub	28	Andrássy	B	Radio Inn	D
Falafel	18	Kinnor David	36	Piaf	10	Astoria City	K		
Fausto's	37	Király		Picasso Point	9	Béke	F		
Feszek	21	Krizia	8	Potkulcs	2	Benczúr	C		

est districts in the city. In recent decades the area became pretty run-down, but the appeal of the old apartment blocks lining its streets is gradually bringing in the middle classes; meanwhile the villas near the park have recovered their value and café society flourishes around Liszt Ferenc tér.

Andrássy út was inaugurated in 1884 as the Sugár (Radial) út, but was soon renamed after the statesman Count Gyula Andrássy, and it was this name which stayed in popular use throughout the years when this was officially Stalin Avenue (1949–56) or the Avenue of the People's Republic (1957–89). The first point of interest as you head out along the boulevard is at no. 3, where the **Post Office Museum** (Posta Múzeum; Tues–Sun 10am–6pm; 100Ft) occupies a fabulous old apartment complete with parquet floors, marble fireplaces, Venetian mirrors and frescoes by Károly Lotz; its owners fled to the US in 1938. Besides offering a window into how wealthy Budapestis lived before World War II, it also features a wealth of postal exhibits including a compressed-air mail tube, vintage delivery vehicles and a display on the inventor and telephone pioneer Tivadar Puskás, a colleague of Thomas Edison.

The State Opera House and New Theatre

The **State Opera House** (Állami Operaház; ⓦwww.opera.hu) was founded by Ferenc Erkel, the composer of Hungary's national anthem, and occupies a magnificent neo-Renaissance pile built in 1875–84 by Miklós Ybl. It can boast of being directed by Mahler (who was driven out by the anti-Semitism he experienced in the city), hosting performances conducted by Otto Klemperer and Antal Doráti, and sheltering two hundred local residents (including Kodály) in its cellars during the siege of Budapest. The 1260-seat auditorium was the first in Europe to feature an iron fire curtain (installed after a fire at the Vienna Opera House), underfloor heating and air-conditioning. Its chandelier weighs three tonnes, and 2.7 kilos of gold were used to gild the fixtures. To the left of the stage is the box used by Emperor Franz Josef's wife, Sissi (see p.114), who loved Hungarian opera as much as he detested it. The upstairs reception rooms and downstairs foyer are equally lavish, festooned with portraits and busts of Hungarian divas and composers. Tickets for English-language **tours** of the interior (daily 3 & 4pm; 2200Ft) are available from the shop to the right of the main entrance; see p.174 for details of tickets for performances.

In a similar vein, on Paulay Ede utca, off the opposite side of Andrássy, stands the **New Theatre** (Új Színház), whose blue and gold Art Nouveau facade and foyer (by Béla Lajta) look superb. Continuing north along Andrássy, you'll pass the stylish new **Goethe Institut** at no. 24 (with regular art exhibitions, and a good place to stop for coffee) followed by a pharmacy that retains its original fixtures from 1889. Across the road at no. 29 is the *Művész* coffee house – where the magnificent interior is more enticing than the cakes or service.

Nagymező utca

One block beyond the Opera, Andrássy út is crossed by **Nagymező utca** – nicknamed "**Broadway**" because of the clubs and theatres on either side of the street, whose pavement features bronze impressions of the hand- or footprints of Hungarian entertainers. During the interwar years, the best known club was the *Arizona*, run by Sándor Rozsnyai and his wife Miss Arizona (which inspired Pal Sándor's 1988 film of the same name, starring Hanna Schygulla and Marcello Mastroianni); the Rozsnyais were murdered by the Arrow Cross in 1944. Their club was at Nagymező utca 20, in the former home of the Habsburg court photographer who lends his name to the **Mai Manó Photography Museum** (Mon–Fri 2–7pm, Sat, Sun & holidays 11am–7pm; 200Ft, students 100Ft; ⓦwww.fotomuzeum.hu), occupying two floors of the building and worth a visit for its fine exhibitions and photographic bookshop.

Across Andrássy út at Nagymező utca 8, the **Ernst Múzeum** holds excellent temporary fine arts exhibitions on the first floor (Tues–Sun 11am–7pm; 500Ft;

@www.ernstmuzeum.hu) – but it's worth visiting for the building alone, which has Art Nouveau features by József Rippl-Rónai and Ödön Lechner. Dating from 1911, the museum takes its name from Lajos Ernst, a Hungarian art collector. Pop into the Tivoli theatre in the same building, if it's open, to see its Art Deco lobby.

Further along Andrássy út, the **Divatcsarnok** (Fashion Hall) is worth a brief detour. Also built in 1911, this seven-floor department store has rather gone to seed, but still retains its modernist inner hall. At the back on the first floor is the contrastingly sumptuous Lotz Room, a ballroom decorated with frescoes by Károly Lotz. The roof terrace, which once served as an ice-rink with views over the city, is sadly closed.

The Oktogon and around

Further up Andrássy, two elongated squares lined with pavement **cafés** provide a vibrant interlude. On the left (north of Andrássy ut) is **Jókai tér**, with a large statue of the novelist Mór Jókai, while across the road on **Liszt Ferenc tér**, the composer hammers an imaginary keyboard with his vast hands, blind to the strolling crowds and the **Music Academy** that bears his name, at the far end at no. 8. If you're enticed in by the sounds of practising musicians and singers, you'll come upon a magnificent Art Nouveau entrance hall, designed by Aladár Körösfői Kriesch. The two gilded auditoriums are highly atmospheric concert halls, well matched to the quality of the music that you can hear there.

Continuing up Andrássy út, you cross the Nagykörút at the **Oktogon**, an eight-sided square flanked by eclectic buildings. With 24-hour fast-food chains ensconced in two of them, and buses and taxis running along the Nagykörút through to the small hours, the Oktogon never sleeps. During the Horthy period it rejoiced in the name of Mussolini tér, while under the Communists it was called November 7 tér after the date of the Bolshevik revolution.

The House of Terror

You can't miss the **House of Terror** (Terror Háza; Tues–Fri 10am–6pm, Sat & Sun 10am–7.30pm; 1200Ft; not recommended for small children; @www.terrorhaza.hu) looming out of an otherwise ordinary corner house at Andrássy út 60, with its ominous black frame. In the mid-twentieth century this was the most terrifying address in Budapest, the headquarters of the secret police. Jews and other victims of the Arrow Cross were tortured here during World War II, and the ÁVO (see box below) later used the building for the same purpose. When it was captured by insurgents in 1956, no trace was found of the giant meat-grinder rumoured to have been used to dispose of

---

The ÁVO

The **Communist secret police** began as the party's private security section during the Horthy era, when its chief, **Gábor Péter**, betrayed Trotskyites to the police to take the heat off their Stalinist comrades. After World War II it became the Államvédelmi Osztály or **ÁVO** (State Security Department), its growing power implicit in a change of name in 1948 – to the State Security Authority or **ÁVH** (though the old acronym stuck). Ex-Nazi torturers were easily persuaded to apply their skills on its behalf, and its network of spies permeated society. So hated was the ÁVO that any members caught during the Uprising were summarily killed, and their mouths stuffed with banknotes (secret policemen earned more than anyone else).

corpses. Today the House of Terror is a cross between a museum and a memorial, featuring a series of powerful images and artefacts – such as the Soviet tank that fills the courtyard – linked together by constant loud music; the moment you step in through the spooky automatic door you are bombarded with funereal sounds. English-language audio-guides (1000Ft) save you having to read the English-language sheets in each room, though the latter pack more information.

The House was set up by the right-of-centre Fidesz government, and has been accused of bias in its emphasis on the Stalinist terror – for example, the video in the ticket hall repeatedly plays the image of a man weeping at the many deaths at the hands of the Communists, and saying "this was their socialism". However, balance is impossible here in such a sensitive area, and the public treatment of the Stalinist years is at least a much-needed, if simplified, beginning.

The displays begin on the second floor (you take the lift there, then work downwards) with a couple of rooms glossing over how Hungary came to join the Axis powers, dealing briskly with the death of more than 400,000 Jews, Gypsies and others in the Holocaust. Subsequently there are rooms covering the Soviet "liberation", the deportations of unwanted elements (class enemies, as well as Germans and Slavs), rigged elections, collectivization, and the crushing of the 1956 Uprising. The most harrowing part is the lift that leads down to the basement: when the doors shut a video starts of an executioner quietly explaining his job. When the doors open at the bottom, you emerge into a re-creation of the old torture section, the cells where the prisoners were softened up before being taken for interrogation. Here, the music mercifully stops as the exhibits are allowed to speak for themselves.

The House of Terror attracts a large number of groups, and can get crowded. On the ground floor is a **café** for much needed refreshment, or you can escape up the road to the *Lukács* (see p.164).

The Liszt Memorial Museum

A little further on the opposite side, the Old Music Academy at no. 67 harbours the **Liszt Memorial Museum** (Liszt Ferenc Emlékmúzeum; Mon–Fri 10am–6pm, Sat 9am–5pm; closed Aug; 380Ft; ⊛www.lisztmuseum.hu), entered from around the corner at Vörösmarty utca 35, where the composer – who was the first president of the Academy – lived from 1881 until his death in 1886. His glass piano and travelling keyboard are the highlights of an extensive collection of memorabilia and scores. Concerts are performed here by young pianists every Saturday at 11am (250Ft; Budapest Card covers entry to the museum but concert tickets must be bought separately).

Just down to the right (south) from the museum along Vörösmarty utca lies **Hunyadi tér**, which has a fine old market hall that has not been modernized yet, and some fruit and vegetable stalls in the square itself.

Kodály körönd to Hősök tere

Kodály körönd, named after the composer Zoltán Kodály, is one of Budapest's most elegant squares, flanked by four neo-Renaissance mansions. At no. 1 on the northeast corner, the flat where he lived until his death in 1967 is a **Kodály Memorial Museum** (Wed 10am–4pm, Thurs–Sat 10am–6pm, Sun 10am–2pm; 200Ft; ⊛www.kodaly-inst.hu), preserving his library, salon, dining room and folk-art collection – press the buzzer for apartment 11 to get in. During World War II the *körönd* was named Hitler tér, prompting the émigré

Bartók to vow that he would not be buried in Hungary so long as anywhere in the country was named after Hitler or Mussolini.

Two fine collections of Asian art lurk just beyond the *körönd*. The **György Ráth Museum** (Tues–Sun 10am–6pm; free) displays artefacts from the vast collection amassed by the optician and art collector Ferenc Hopp (1833–1919), drawn from all the great Eastern civilizations. The museum is in an Art Nouveau villa at Városligeti fasor 12, on an avenue parallel to Andrássy. The statue in the garden of a Buddhist monk actually depicts Sándor Kőrösi-Csoma, a Hungarian who achieved fame by compiling the first English–Tibetan dictionary, though his real goal was a vain search for the ancestors of the Hungarian people. Nearby, the **Ferenc Hopp Museum** (same hours; 400Ft) at Andrássy út 103 presents temporary displays of works from the same collection.

From here, the final stretch of Andrássy út up to Hősök tere is lined with spacious villas set back from the avenue, mostly housing embassies.

The Erzsébetváros

The official boundary between the Terézváros and **Erzsébetváros** runs down the middle of **Király utca**, which used to be a main thoroughfare before Andrássy út was built. In the 1870s the street contained 14 of the 58 licensed brothels in Budapest, and as late as 1934 Patrick Leigh Fermor was told that "any man could be a cavalier for five pengöes" here. After decades of shabby respectability under Communism the street is undergoing a revival: the recent semi-pedestrianization has given it a further boost, and it boasts an excellent café, bars and a rash of interior design and furniture boutiques. Though not the most logical place to start exploring the Jewish quarter, the route here from the direction of Andrássy út makes a wonderful approach, as you zigzag down through the backstreets. However, if you approach the area from the **Kiskörút**, as most people do, then the Dohány utca Synagogue is the obvious first objective.

Walking tours, with commentary in English, of the Jewish quarter (daily except Sat; 5000Ft; book in advance with Chosen Tours on ℡01/355 2202) reveal local colour and historical details you might otherwise miss; you can sign up at the main synagogue.

The Dohány utca Synagogue

The splendid **Dohány utca Synagogue** (Dohány utcai Zsinagóga; Mon–Thurs 10am–5pm, closing at 3pm Oct–March, Fri 10am–2pm, Sun 10am–2pm; 1000Ft for synagogue and museum), which also contains the **Jewish Museum**, is one of the landmarks of Pest. Located only five minutes' walk from Deák tér, just off Károly körút, it's Europe's largest synagogue and the second biggest in the world after the Temple Emmanuel in New York; it can hold three thousand worshippers, members of the **Neolog** community, a Hungarian denomination combining elements of Reform and Orthodox Judaism.

The building, designed by a Viennese Gentile, Ludwig Förster, epitomizes the so-called Byzantine-Moorish style that was popular in the 1850s, and attests to the patriotism of Hungarian Jewry – the colours of its brickwork (yellow, red and blue) being those of Budapest's coat of arms. In the 1990s the synagogue was restored at a cost of over $40 million; the work was funded by the Hungarian government and the Hungarian-Jewish diaspora, notably the Emmanuel Foundation, fronted by the Hollywood actor Tony Curtis, born of 1920s emigrants.

You have time to admire the gilded onion-domed towers while waiting to pass through a security check, and can opt for a guided **tour** (1900Ft), though this doesn't add much to the experience. The marvellous **interior** is by Frigyes Feszl, the architect of the Vigadó concert hall; arabesques and Stars of David decorate the ceiling, the balconies for female worshippers are surmounted by gilded arches, and the floor is inset with eight-pointed stars. The layout reflects the synagogue's Neolog identity, with the *bemah*, or Ark of the Torah, at one end, in the Reform fashion, but with men and women seated apart, according to Orthodox tradition. On Jewish festivals, the place is filled to the rafters with Jews from all over Hungary, whose chattering disturbs their more devout co-religionists. At other times, the hall is used for concerts of classical or klezmer music, as advertised outside.

Next, visitors cross a courtyard full of simple headstones, marking the **mass grave** of 2281 Jews who died here during the icy winter of 1944. You can also see part of the brick wall that surrounded the ghetto, with a plaque commemorating its liberation by the Red Army on January 18, 1945. Behind the courtyard looms the cuboid, domed **Heroes' Temple**, erected in 1929–31 in honour of the 10,000 Jewish soldiers who died fighting for Hungary during World War I. These days it serves as a synagogue for everyday use and is not open to tourists.

The Jewish Museum

Heading upstairs to the **Jewish Museum** (Zsidó Múzeum), to the left of the main synagogue entrance, note a relief of Tivadar (Theodor) Herzl, the founder of modern Zionism, who was born and taught on this site. In the foyer is a gravestone inscribed with a menorah (seven-branched candlestick) from the third century AD – proof that there were Jews living in Hungary six hundred years before the Magyars arrived. The first three rooms are devoted to Jewish festivals, with beautifully crafted objects such as Sabbath lamps and bowls for the Seder festival, some from medieval times. The final room covers the Holocaust in Hungary, with chilling photos and examples of anti-Semitic propaganda. Oddly, the museum says nothing about the huge contribution that Jews have made to Hungarian society, in every field from medicine to poetry.

Upon leaving, turn the corner on to Wesselényi utca and enter the **Raoul Wallenberg Memorial Garden**, named after the Swedish consul who saved 20,000 Jews during World War II. Armed with diplomatic status and money for bribing officials, Wallenberg and his assistants plucked thousands from the cattle trucks and lodged them in "safe houses", manoeuvring to buy time until the Russians arrived. He was last seen alive the day before the Red Army liberated the ghetto; arrested by the Soviets on suspicion of espionage, he died in the Gulag. The park's centrepiece is a **Holocaust Memorial** by Imre Varga, shaped like a weeping willow, each leaf engraved with the names of a family killed by the Nazis. On the plinth are testimonials from their relatives living in Israel, America and Russia. Behind it, glass panels by the artist Klára Szilárd commemorate the sixtieth anniversary of the Goldmark Hall, named after Károly Goldmark, the composer of the opera *The Queen of Sheba*.

Behind the synagogue

Fanning out behind the synagogue is what was once the Jewish **ghetto**, created by the Nazis in April 1944. Initially, the Hungarian government

△ The Heroes' Temple, with the Holocaust Memorial in the foreground

feared that concentrating all the Jews within one area would expose the rest of Budapest to Allied bombing raids, but by November such considerations were forgotten, and all Jews living outside the ghetto were compelled to move there. As their menfolk had already been conscripted into labour battalions intended to kill them from overwork, the 70,000 inhabitants of the ghetto were largely women, children and old folk, crammed into 162 blocks of flats, with over 50,000 of them (in buildings meant for 15,000) around Klauzál tér alone.

Directly across the road from the Wallenberg Memorial Garden, **Rumbach Sebestyén utca** leads northwards to the **synagogue** of the so-called "Status Quo" or middling-conservative Jews. For many years after the war it lay in ruins, and even though it has now been restored, it isn't open to the public – you have to peek through the gates to glimpse the magnificence of its interior. Negotiations stumble on about the building – rumour had it that Yoko Ono was buying it – but there was local outrage when it was rented as a backdrop for a film about tigers in a circus a few years back. With a Moorish-style facade in yellow and red brick, inset with blue crosses, it's outwardly akin to the Dohány utca synagogue, but its interior conforms to conservative prescriptions, with a detached gallery for women, and the Ark of the Torah in the centre of the hall. As a plaque outside notes, the building served as a detention barracks in August 1941, from where up to 1800 Slovak and Polish refugees were deported to the Nazi death camps.

En route to the Status Quo synagogue, as you cross Dob utca, you'll see a **monument to Carl Lutz**, the Swiss consul who began issuing Schutzpasses to Jews, attesting that they were Swiss or Swedish citizens – a ruse subsequently used by Wallenberg. Lutz was a more ambiguous figure, who ceased issuing passes and tried to prevent others from doing so after being threatened by the Gestapo. After the war he was criticized for abusing Swiss law and, feeling slighted, proposed himself for the Nobel Peace Prize. His monument – a gilded angel swooping down to help a prostrate victim – is locally known as "the figure jumping out of a window".

Just beyond Lutz's memorial, a grey stone portal at no. 16 leads into the **Gozsdu udvar**, a 200-metre-long passageway built in 1904 and running through to Király utca 11. Connecting seven courtyards, it was a hive of life and activity before the Holocaust; after many years of dereliction, it is now being redeveloped as a sanitized luxury plaza containing flats and shops.

The kosher *Fröhlich* patisserie at Dob utca 22 is one of several Jewish businesses around **Kazinczy utca**, the centre of the 3000-strong Orthodox community, where Yiddish can still be heard. There's a butcher's in the yard of Dob utca 35, with wigmakers at nos. 31 and 46, while down to the right at Kazinczy utca 28 is a kosher baker and the non-kosher Jewish *Carmel* restaurant at no. 31. Almost next door to the last stands the **Orthodox Synagogue**, an Art Nouveau edifice that melds into the curve of the street, its pediment bearing a Hebrew inscription asserting: "This place is none other than the house of God and the gate to heaven." Its interior is open for religious purposes only. The gate to the right leads into an L-shaped courtyard containing a Jewish school and the *Hanna* Orthodox kosher restaurant – also accessible via an arcade on Dob utca.

For something quite different, visit the **Museum of Electrotechnology** (Magyar Elektrotechnikai Múzeum; ☎1/342 5750 or ✉info@emuzeum.hu to book visits; free) in a former electricity substation at Kazinczy utca 21. Its curators demonstrate the world's first dynamo (invented in 1859 by Áynos Jedlik, a Benedictine monk) and other devices in rooms devoted to such topics as the history of light bulbs and the Hungarian section of the Iron Curtain, along the border with Austria. Though the current was too weak to kill and the minefields were removed in 1965, patrols kept it inviolate until 1989, when the Hungarians ceased shooting escapees, thereby spelling the end of the Iron Curtain as a whole.

Walking on down Kazinczy utca and left along Dohány utca, you come to a relic of Budapest's past glory – the rotting Art Nouveau facade of the **Hungária Baths** at no. 44, by the corner of Nyár utca. The baths were once one of the most popular in the city, with room for a thousand bathers, but were never salvaged after subsidence caused their closure in 1955, and talk of restoration looks increasingly forlorn.

Across the Nagykörút

Pressing on along Dohány utca, you come to another piece of old Budapest that for many years lay rotting while negotiators fiddled. Like the Gresham Palace on Roosevelt tér (see p.55), the **New York Palace** on the corner of the Nagykörút is a Budapest landmark that is being converted into a luxury hotel. It too is associated with an insurance company, in this case the New York, which commissioned the building in 1895 and included in the plans a magnificent coffee house, which became one of the great literary cafés in interwar Budapest. Under Communism the building was home to one of the big state-run publishers, and the Beaux Arts façade – with a small Statue of Liberty high up on the corner – survived being rammed by a tank in 1956. When the new hotel opens, it'll be worth checking if the coffee house has been restored to its former function and glory.

Further along Dohány utca the district changes, becoming more working class and tinged with Arab and Chinese influences as you near the "**Garment District**" around **Garay tér**. The bustling **market hall** is a lunch spot for workers from the sweatshops in a neighbourhood where wholesalers do business in a dozen languages and travel agents offer trips to Mecca.

One of the rewards here is a small museum dedicated to the man behind so much of the city's stained-glass windows. The **Miksa Róth Museum** (Róth Miksa Múzeum; Tues–Sun 2–6pm; 500Ft) at Nefelejcs utca 26 uses Róth's own furniture to recreate his rooms – this was once his house – and also shows the breadth of his work, both in stained glass and in mosaics. Róth (1865–1944) was a leading figure in the Hungarian Art Nouveau movement and his work can be seen in the Parliament, the Gresham Palace, the Music Academy and the Jewish Museum.

The Városliget and the stadium district

Both **Hősök tere** (Heroes' Square) and the **VÁROSLIGET** (City Park), at the end of Andrassy út, were created in the late nineteenth century for the nationwide celebrations of the millennium of the Magyar conquest of Hungary, but as neither was ready on time the anniversary was rescheduled for the following year. Historians revised the date of the conquest accordingly and have stuck to 896 ever since. The millennial celebrations were unashamedly nationalistic but full of contradictions, as the Dual Monarchy tried to flatter Hungarians without alienating other ethnic groups that resented Magyar chauvinism, so each was represented at the exhibition. Today, the chief attractions are the **Museum of Fine Arts** and the romantic **Vajdahunyad Castle**, followed by a wallow in the **Széchenyi Baths**. Budapest's **zoo**, **circus** and amusement park are also located in the vicinity, together with two of the city's classiest restaurants, and a handful of other museums. Nearby is the collection of indoor and outdoor **stadiums** that host sporting competitions, concerts and other events. Next door to the stadiums is another of the city's fine Art Nouveau specimens, the **Geology Institute**.

The best ways to reach the Városliget from the centre are on the yellow metro line or bus #4, but trolleybus #74 from the Dohány utca Synagogue and #72 from Arany János utca metro station are also useful. To reach the stadium district, catch trolleybus #75 from Hősök tere or the red metro from the centre of town to Stadionok station.

Hősök tere and the Museum of Fine Arts

The enormous ceremonial plaza of **Hősök tere** is flanked by two galleries resembling Greek temples. At its centre is the **Millenary Monument** – Budapest's answer to London's Nelson's Column – consisting of a 36-metre-high column topped by the figure of the Archangel Gabriel who, according to legend, appeared to Stephen in a dream and offered him the crown of Hungary. Around the base are figures of Prince Árpád and his chieftains, who led the seven Magyar tribes into the Carpathian Basin. They look like a wild bunch; one of their number, Huba, even has stag's antlers strapped to his horse's head.

As a backdrop to this, a semicircular colonnade displays statues of Hungary's most illustrious leaders, from King Stephen to Kossuth.

During the brief Republic of Councils in 1919, when the country was governed by revolutionary Soviets, the square was decked out in red banners and the column enclosed in a red obelisk bearing a relief of Marx. More recently, in June 1989, it was the setting for the ceremonial reburial of Imre Nagy and other murdered leaders of the 1956 Uprising (plus an empty coffin representing the "unknown insurgent") – an event which symbolized the dawning of a new era in Hungary. Today it's more likely to be filled with coach parties of tourists, and with rollerbladers and skateboarders, for whom the smooth surface is ideal. The square was originally laid out as a garden, but was paved over for the Eucharistic Congress of 1932.

On the south side of the square is the **Műcsarnok** (Exhibition Hall; Tues–Sun 10am–6pm; 150Ft) also called the Palace of Art (not to be confused with the Palace of Arts, covered on p.90), a Grecian pile with gilded columns and a mosaic of St Stephen as patron of the arts. Its magnificent facade and foyer are in contrast to the four austere rooms used for **temporary exhibitions** (two or three at a time), which are often first-rate. Since the palace was inaugurated in 1896, its steps have been a stage for the state funeral of the painter Mihály Munkácsy, the reburial of Nagy, and other public ceremonies.

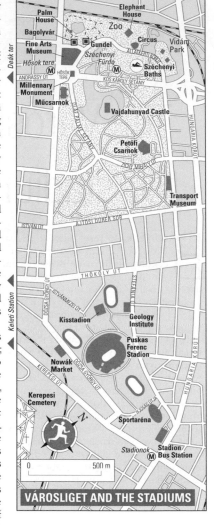

VÁROSLIGET AND THE STADIUMS

Dózsa György út, the wide avenue running off alongside the Városliget, serves as the setting for occasional **fairs** and **concerts**. In Communist times it was here that Party leaders reviewed parades from a grandstand, beneath a 25-metre-high statue of Stalin that was torn down during the Uprising, dragged to the Nagykörút and hammered into bits for souvenirs. A statue of Lenin was erected in its place, which remained until it was taken away "for structual repairs" in 1989 and finally ended up in the Statue Park (see p.128).

△ The Millenary Monument on Hősök tere

Museum of Fine Arts

To the north of the square, the **Museum of Fine Arts** (Szépművészeti Múzeum; Tues–Sun 10am–5.30pm; free, temporary exhibitions 800Ft; @www .szepmuveszeti.hu) is the pan-European equivalent of the Hungarian National Gallery, housed in an imposing Neoclassical building completed in 1906. The majority of exhibits are labelled in English, but if you want more information you should go on an English-language **tour** (Tues–Sat at 11am from the lobby) or invest in a catalogue. On the lower ground floor there's an excellent **shop** for art books, posters and contemporary ceramics, and a decent **café**.

The museum is undergoing changes, with the appointment of a new director who wants to sweep away its dusty image. Besides rehanging the pictures, he is moving the excellent **bookshop** to new premises to the left of the entrance on the ground floor, after which some of the sections described below will also move. All the sections are laid out in the traditional chronological manner, although the new layout for the twentieth century may be executed according to themes – the director is adopting the more modern approach to its modern art.

One of the best art secrets in town is the museum's **library**, which art historians will find to be a treasure trove of information, in various languages. It's housed nearby at VI, Szondi utca 77 (Mon–Fri 9am–5pm).

Lower ground floor

To the right of the stairs is a small but choice **Egyptian Collection**, chiefly from the Late Period and Greco-Roman eras of Egyptian civilization. The highlights of the first room are a huge painted coffin and a child-sized one from Gamhud in Middle Egypt; *shabiti* figures, intended to perform menial tasks in the afterlife; and a mummified crocodile, cat and ibis from the Late Period, when animal cults reached their apogee. In the second room, look out for the sculpted heads of a nameless pharaoh and a bewigged youth from the New Kingdom, the painted coffin of a priestess of Amun bearing an uncanny resemblance to Julia Roberts, a tautly poised bronze of the cat goddess Bastet and three more fine coffins.

On the left-hand side of the foyer, the **Twentieth-Century Art Collection** features relatively few artists that you're likely to have heard of, but is nonetheless stimulating. In the museum's Majovszky Hall, a scumbled Expressionist portrait by **Oskar Kokoschka** faces **Maurice Utrillo**'s *Street Scene*. There's a wonderfully simple Fauvist landscape by János Máttis, and two realist portraits in violet and green impasto by Gino Severini. **Marc Chagall**'s *Village in Blue* is a typically lyrical composition of floating figures, while **Roberto Guttuso**'s *Seizure of the Land in Sicily* speaks of the urgency of the land reform cause in terms of Cubism and Social Realism. Sex pervades the **Symbolist and Decadent** works' section, notably Franz von Stuck's *The Kiss of the Sphinx*, John Quincey Adams's vampish *Lilli* and Hans Makart's *Nessus Raptures Deianeira*.

Ground floor

To the right of the lobby are several rooms devoted to **ancient Mediterranean cultures** from Etruria to Athens, mainly represented by jugs and vases. Highlights include a pair of bronze shin-guards decorated with rams' heads, terracotta tiles portraying bestial deities, a man's torso and head from the pediment of a Campanian temple, lifelike busts of Roman worthies, and an Attic marble sarcophagus carved with hunting scenes.

Across the hall are the **bookshop** and rooms specially designed for temporary exhibitions. There are also two halls displaying large allegorical or religious works on loan from other European museums, notably Artemesia Gentileschi's *Salome with the Head of St John the Baptist*. The **Prints and Drawings Room**, at the far end on the right, beyond the less appealing Baroque collection, regularly has temporary displays drawn from the museum's extensive holdings, including works by Raphael, Leonardo, Rembrandt, Rubens, Dürer, Picasso and Chagall.

First floor

The museum's forte is its hoard of **Old Masters**, based on the collection of Count Miklós Esterházy, which he sold to the state in 1871. As a notice explains, this section has been rehung in what is allegedly the once-again fashionable style of stacking one painting above another, which, though it may facilitate comparisons, doesn't allow visitors to appreciate the pictures well above eye-level. Furthermore the room numbering is baffling – not least because Roman numerals refer to the main rooms, while Arabic numerals are used for the smaller outer rooms – but the quality of the art transcends all these failings.

The **Spanish Collection** of seventy works is perhaps the best in the world outside Spain. Recently rehung in rooms to the right on the first floor, it starts off with vivid altarpieces by unknown Catalonians, including a *Bishop-Saint Enthroned*, whose obvious bewilderment belies his magnificent attire. In room II are several **Murillos**, of which *Ecce Homo* and *The Holy Family with the Infant St John and Christ* are superlative, while through in room VI you'll find the moving *Martyrdom of St Andrew* by **Ribera**. Room V next door is dominated by seven **El Grecos**, most notably *Christ Stripped of His Garments*, *The Agony in the Garden*, *The Apostle St Andrew* and *The Penitent Magdalene*, though Eugenio Cajes's *Adoration of the Magi* is equally awe-inspiring. Then at the far end in room 1 are five **Goyas**, ranging from war scenes (*2nd of May*) to portraits of the rich (*Señora Ceán Bermudez*) and humble (*The Knife-Grinder*), plus **Velázquez**'s *Peasant's Repast*.

From here, the simplest thing is to move on to room VIII, but starting from this room means you see the **Dutch and German Collection** in reverse chronological order (you can avoid this by going back through the Spanish collection, then turning right and right again into room XI). In room VIII, the serenity of **Van Dyck**'s *St John the Evangelist* contrasts with the melodrama of **Rubens**' *Mucius Scaevola before Porsenna* and **Jordeans**' *The Satyr and the Peasant*, while room IX is largely given over to **Brueghels**, from Pieter the Elder's *Sermon of St John the Baptist* to Pieter the Younger's *Blind Hurdy-Gurdy Player* and Jan's *The Garden of Eden with the Fall of Man*. Through in one of the small rooms with windows is a small Bosch, *The Bacchus Singers*; note the man on the left making himself vomit.

If you take the lift from here to the second floor to a collection of seventeenth-century Dutch paintings, you'll be rewarded with couple of **Frans Hals** portraits, but better lies ahead in the **German collection** back on the first floor. Pausing in room X to catch **Angelika Kauffmann**'s depiction of *The Wife of Count Esterházy as Venus*, which shows a strumpet with her jewellery box, you come to the dramatic paintings of **Cranach** the Elder in room XI. The suppressed violence of his *Crucifixions* seem like presentiments of the Thirty Years War a century ahead, while in his *Salome with the Head of St John the Baptist*, Salome displays St John's head on a platter with the nonchalance of a hostess bringing out the roast. At the far end of the room, every emotion from awe to jealousy appears on the faces in **Holbein**'s *Dormition of the Virgin*. The small room 14 to the right has a dazzling array of works by **Altdorfer**, while elsewhere in the same room, **Dürer**'s *Young Man* has an enigmatic smile.

To the left at the top of the stairs, the **Nineteenth-Century Art** collection opens with a fanfare of Barbizons and Impressionists. However, the drama of **Courbet**'s wild landscapes and life-sized *Wrestlers*, the delight of **Monet**'s *Plum Trees in Blossom* and **Corot**'s *Remembrance of Coubrou* aren't sustained by weaker pictures like **Cézanne**'s *The Cupboard*, **Toulouse-Lautrec**'s *Three Ladies in the Refectory* or **Manet**'s *Lady with a Fan*, though *Eternal Springtime* and *The Kiss* by Rodin both deserve an honourable mention. There's also a small assortment of **English art** – a dullish portrait apiece by Hogarth, Reynolds and Gainsborough, and a melodramatic *Theatre Scene* by Zoffany.

The **Italian Collection**, being reorganized at the time of writing, is also impressive. Look out for **Raphael**'s small but exquisite *Esterházy Madonna* – a Virgin and Child with the infant St John – and a picture of a youth with a Mona Lisa-esque mystique. The latter's psychological depth is matched by portraits by **Giorgione** (whose own self-portrait exudes sensitivity) and **Titian** (of a Venetian Doge, stern and watchful in his cloth of gold). **Tintoretto**'s self-portrait is less focused, while **Bellini**'s pig-eyed *Queen of Cyprus* verges on caricature. Tintoretto steals the show next door with *Hercules Expelling the Faun from Omphade's Bed* and a *Supper at Emmaus*. **Veronese** is represented by his *Allegory of Venice* and *Crucifixion*; you'll also find **Boccacio**'s *Adoration of the Infant Christ*, with the cheerfully gory *Judith with the Head of Holoferenes* and the cruel *Mocking of Job* nearby. Acknowledging that art transcends nationality, this collection also features well-travelled artists such as **Canaletto**, who died in Warsaw after painting *The Palace of Kaunitz in Vienna*; and **Tiepolo**, whose *St James the Great Conquering the Moors* once served as an icon for the Habsburgs.

The Városliget

The **Városliget** (City Park) starts just behind Hősök tere, where the fairy-tale towers of **Vajdahunyad Castle** rear above an island girdled by an artificial lake that's used for boating in the summer and, during winter, is transformed into the most splendid outdoor ice-rink in Europe. Like the park, the castle was created for the Millenary Anniversary celebrations of 1896, and proved so popular that the temporary structures were replaced by permanent ones. The castle is a catalogue in stone of architectural styles from the kingdom of Hungary, incorporating parts of two Transylvanian castles and a replica of the chapel at Ják, as well as a Renaissance courtyard that makes a romantic setting for evening **concerts** from July to mid-August.

In the main wing of the castle, the **Agriculture Museum** (Mezőgazdasági Múzeum; March to mid-Nov Tues–Fri & Sun 10am–5pm, Sat 10am–6pm; mid-Nov to Feb Tues–Fri & Sun 10am–4pm, Sat 10am–5pm; 300Ft; ⊛www .mezogazdasagimuzeum.hu) traces the history of hunting and farming in Hungary. Its most interesting sections relate to the early Magyars and such typically Hungarian breeds of livestock as longhorned grey cattle (favoured for their draught power rather than their milk) and woolly pigs. Upstairs, the hunting section is notable for a prehistoric dugout boat carved from a single piece of oak, which was found at Lake Balaton southwest of the capital, and antique crossbows and rifles exquisitely inlaid with leaping hares and other prey.

Even if you decide to skip the museum, don't miss the hooded **statue of Anonymous** outside. This nameless chronicler to King Béla is the prime source of information about early medieval Hungary, though the existence of several monarchs of that name during the twelfth and thirteenth centuries makes it hard to date him (or his chronicles) with any accuracy.

The Petőfi Csarnok and Transport Museum

Leaving Vajdahunyad island by the causeway at the rear, you're ten minutes' walk away from the **Petőfi Csarnok** (Petőfi Hall; ℡01/363-3730 or ⊛www .petoficsarnok.hu for information), a shabby 1970s "Metropolitan Youth Centre" that regularly hosts concerts (outdoors in summer), films and parties, and a fine **flea market** at weekends. Trolleybuses #70, #72 and #74 from the centre of town all go near the hall. At the back of the building is a stairway leading to the **Aviation and Space Flight Exhibition** (Repüléstörténeti és Űrhajózási kiállítás; April–Nov Tues–Fri 10am–5pm, Sat & Sun 10am–6pm; free), which, among other items, contains the space capsule used by Hungary's first astronaut, Bertalan Farkas, and his Soviet colleague on the Soyuz-35 mission of 1980; and an L-2 monoplane sporting an Italian Fascist symbol, which broke world speed records in the Budapest–Rome races of 1927 and 1930. Alas, there seems to be nothing about Count László Almássy, Hungary's foremost aviator of that time, now better known abroad as the hero of the book and film *The English Patient*.

Not far away is the **Transport Museum** (Közlekedési Múzeum; Tues–Fri 10am–5pm, Sat & Sun 10am–6pm; free) on the edge of the park, of which the aviation exhibition above is an outgrowth. Captions in English explain that the Hungarian transport network of the 1890s was among the most sophisticated in Europe; despite the country starting from a low technological base, railways, canals, trams and a metro had all been created within fifty years. Displays include vintage locomotives and scale models of steamboats, and a wonderful collection

Bathing
matters

"The hot baths are the most remarkable things of Buda: the water springs up in several places in great abundance in the narrow scrap of land that lies between the Danube and the hill on which the fortress stands. The Turks could not fail of applying it to their favourite pastime; some of the baths, and the greatest, are Turkish remains."

Robert Townson, *Travels in Hungary in the Year 1793*

Some two hundred years after these words were published, they remain as true as ever – Budapest's **baths** *are* remarkable. Housed in some of the city's finest buildings, they are impressive sights in their own right; with their medicinal properties, the thermal waters are reputed to cure myriad ailments – and of course there's the swimming itself. The smaller Rudas and Király baths are first and foremost steam baths, with saunas and small pools fed by thermal springs. In the larger baths, such as the Gellért or Széchenyi, you can go back and forth between a brisk dip in the swimming pool and a leisurely soak in the steam section. Finally – and this contributes to the appeal of the baths – they are an important social hub, where people come to sit and chat as they follow the rituals. As you admire the light filtering through the dome in the Rudas, watch the chess players ponder their next move in the outdoor pool of the Széchenyi or peer through the mists in the steam rooms at the Gellért, there's a real sense of being part of a tradition that has lasted centuries.

Bath house history

With more than a hundred springs offering a seemingly endless supply of hot water at temperatures of up to 76°C, Budapest is deservedly known as a spa city. Even though the water's sulphurous healthy content means that it doesn't always smell very pleasant, its therapeutic qualities have long been exploited. The earliest remains of baths here date back to the Bronze Age, and a succession of invaders have since capitalized on the benefits of the local waters. The **Romans**, who appreciated a good bath, set up camp along the banks of the Danube – you can see the ruins of their bath houses in Óbuda. After their arrival from the east, the **Hungarian tribes** also recognized the value of the thermal springs, as testified by the remnants of a hospital bath house from 1178 found near the Lukács.

During their occupation, the **Ottomans** played a vital role in the development of Budapest's baths – the precept, under Islamic law, for washing five times a day before prayers is thought to have engendered a popular bathing culture here. The oldest baths that survive today are the Turkish baths on the Buda side of the river: built in the late sixteenth century, the Király and the Rudas baths have preserved their original layout, with a central bathing pool surrounded by smaller pools that lie below the old Turkish cupolas.

The next **golden age of bathing** occurred in the late nineteenth and early twentieth centuries, as a fashion for spas swept across Europe. Budapest's baths were dressed up in a new magnificence, and splendid buildings such as the neo-Baroque Széchenyi baths in the Városliget and the Art Nouveau Gellért baths were erected. During the **Communist era**, the baths were as popular as ever – a place to meet and gossip in the murky mists – but they suffered prolonged neglect. In recent years, however, major investments have seen the buildings restored and their facilities upgraded by way of new features such as whirlpools – Budapest's baths are now far more salubrious places to visit. And it's not just people who have benefited from the thermal waters. The success of the hippopotamus breeding programme at Budapest Zoo is thought to be partly due to the zoo's constant supply of hot water from the Széchenyi baths across the road – the hippos clearly benefit from wallowing in lovely hot water. The thermal springs also saved them during the bitter winter siege of the city in 1944–45, when most of the zoo's other animals died in the freezing temperatures.

The changing rooms

Once inside the **changing room** (*öltöző*), an attendant will direct you to a cabin or locker. In most single-sex steam baths, swimsuits are still rare – though you can wear one if you want, and the authorities do sometimes make them compulsory. In the steam baths, the attendant will give you a *kötény* – a small loincloth for men or an apron for women – which offers a vestige of cover.

Gellért Baths

Once you've changed, you need to find the attendant again; they will lock your locker or cabin door and give you a tag (or another key with which to double lock your door for security). You tie the tag or key to your swimming costume or the strings of your *kötény*, making a note of your cabin number and taking with you any supplementary tickets (if you're booked in for a massage, bring a couple of hundred forints for tipping the masseur). In all baths bring flip-flops if you have them, as well as your own soap and shampoo; in the steam baths, you don't need a towel as a sheet is provided to dry yourself with.

The tickets

Palatinus Strand

A standard **ticket** purchased from the ticket office (*pénztár*) gets you into the pools as well as the sauna and steam rooms; supplementary tickets will buy you a massage (*masszázs*), a soak in a private tub (*kádfürdő*) or a mud bath (*iszapfürdő*) – a list by the office will detail the available services. In terms of changing facilities, you'll often have the choice between changing in a communal room and using a locker (*szekrény*), or a slightly more expensive cubicle (*kabin*) – the latter gives you more privacy and, in the mixed-sex baths, this allows couples to change together.

Recently, attempts have been made to control the numbers of visitors to the baths: the Király and Rudas impose strict limits on the length of your stay, while several of the big baths offer a small refund if you stay less than four hours – the shorter the stay, the higher the refund. As you go into the baths, you're given a counter to feed into the turnstile at the entrance – there is usually a member of staff standing around to show you what to do as it can be confusing. When you leave, put your counter into the turnstile at the exit; this feeds out a chit, which you take to the *pénztár* for your refund.

Király Baths

Széchenyi Baths

The steam baths

The best way to enjoy the **steam baths** is to go from room to room, moving on when the heat gets too much. A popular sequence is: sauna (dry steam – often divided into three rooms, the furthest being the hottest), cool pool, steam room, cold plunge (if you can bear it), hot plunge (this makes your skin tingle wonderfully, but don't stay in for long), followed by a wallow in the larger, warmer pools that are usually at the centre of the baths. Most people then repeat the whole thing again, but the sequence you choose is entirely up to you – the main thing is not to stay in any one section if you feel uncomfortable.

When you're completely finished, take a sheet from the pile to dry yourself. Relax in the rest room if you feel exhausted – certainly don't plan on anything too strenuous afterwards – and then find the attendant to unlock your cabin or locker. It's usual to tip the attendant a couple of hundred forints.

The swimming pools

In many **pools**, bathing caps (*uszósapka*) are compulsory: in the Széchenyi, they're only required in the middle of the three outdoor pools (the one reserved for swimming proper); go in without a cap and you'll be whistled at by the attendant and told to get out. Like swimsuits and towels, caps can be rented at the *pénztár* – though at the Gellért you can pick up an unattractive blue plastic one inside for free.

Another tip in the swimming pools: some, such as the main inside pool of the Gellért, have an anti-clockwise swimming policy: you may be whistled at if you don't follow the arrows.

Gellért Steam Baths

of Hungarian Railways posters from 1900 to 1980. The model train set on the floor above the foyer attracts a crowd when it's switched on – for fifteen minutes every hour, on the hour. Collectors can buy Hungarian model trains in the museum shop. Outside the building are remnants of two of the Danube bridges that were wrecked in 1945: the cast-iron Erzsébet híd (replaced by a new bridge) and a few links of the original chains from the Lánchíd, which is now supported by cables.

The Széchenyi Baths

On the far side of the park's main axis, Kós Károly sétány, the **Széchenyi Baths** (Széchenyi Gyógyfürdő; see p.183 for details) could be mistaken for a palace, so grand is its facade. Outside is a statue of the geologist Zsigmondy Vilmos, who discovered the thermal spring that feeds its outdoor pool and Turkish baths. This is perhaps the best venue for mixed-sex bathing, and in one of the large outdoor pools you can enjoy the surreal spectacle of people playing **chess** while immersed up to their chests in steaming water – so hot that you shouldn't stay in for more than twenty minutes. The best players sit at tables around the pool's edge (the former world champion **Bobby Fischer** was among them, when he was freer to travel). Bring your own set if you wish to participate.

The Circus, Vidám Park and the Zoo

Beyond the baths, on the far side of Állatkerti körút, the **Municipal Circus** (Fővárosi Nagycirkusz) traces its origins back to 1783, when the Hetz Theatre played to spectators on what is now Deák tér (all year except September Wed, Fri & Sun 3pm & 7pm, Thurs 3pm, Sat 10am, 3pm & 7pm; 1200–1900Ft; ⓦwww.maciva.hu). To the right is **Vidám Park**, an old-fashioned fairground known as the "English Park" before the war (daily 11am–6pm, open till 8pm July–Aug; 300Ft, free for children under 120cm in height). The funfair was the setting for Ferenc Molnár's play *Liliom*, which inspired the musical *Carousel*. The gilded merry-go-round to the left of the entrance and the wooden switchback at the back of the fairground both predate World War II.

Further down towards Hősök tere you'll find the delightful Elephant Gates of Budapest's **Zoo** (Állatkert; daily: March, April, Sept & Oct 9am–5pm; May–Aug 9am–6pm; Nov–Feb 9am–4pm; 1300Ft; ⓦwww.zoobudapest.com) which opened its doors in 1866. Its Art Nouveau pavilions by Károly Kós (dating from 1911) seemed the last word in zoological architecture, but it slowly stagnated until the 1990s, when a new director aided by private sponsors began long-overdue improvements to give the animals better habitats and make the zoo more visitor-friendly. Don't miss the exotic **Elephant House**, resembling a Central Asian mosque, the **Palm House** with its magnificent **aquarium** below (300Ft), or the **Bonsai garden**. Look out for other events in the zoo – such as concerts and children's events. The children's corner is signposted "Állatóvoda", to the left from the main entrance past the Palm House.

The stadium district

The **stadium district**, north of Kerepesi út, is chiefly notable for the **Puskás Ferenc Stadium**, where league championship and international **football** matches, **concerts** by foreign rock stars and events such as the national dog show are held. Originally known as Népstadion (People's Stadium; it was renamed recently after the great Hungarian footballer of the 1950s), it was built in the early 1950s by fifty thousand Budapesters who "volunteered" their labour, unpaid, on Soviet-style "free Saturdays". To the west of the stadium is the smaller Kisstadion, while to the east Stalinist statues of healthy proletarian youth line the court that leads to the indoor **Papp László Sportaréna** (or Aréna), a silver mushroom-shaped affair which also hosts concerts and sporting events – Papp was the first boxer to win three Olympic gold medals (1948, 1952 and 1956). The Stadion **bus station** completes this concrete ensemble.

Catching trolleybus #75 along Stefánia út, past the Aréna, you can admire the **Geological Institute** at no. 14, one of the major edifices in Budapest designed by Ödön Lechner. The exterior is as striking as the Post Office Savings Bank (see p.59) and the Applied Arts Museum (see p.89), with a gingerbread facade, scrolled gables and steeply pitched Transylvanian roofs patterned in bright-blue tiles, crowned by figures holding globes on their backs. By visiting its small geological **museum** (Thurs, Sat & Sun 10am–4pm; closed Dec 20 to Jan 6; 250Ft), you can also see something of the interior.

Walking in the other direction past the tall *Hotel Stadion* and down Dózsa György út brings you to a weekend **flea market**, the Nowák piac, at nos. 1–3. There are plenty of uninteresting video and CD stalls squeezed in between the road and the railway tracks, but among the dross there are some interesting stalls selling knick-knacks.

Józsefváros and Ferencváros

Separated from Erzsébetváros by Rákóczi út, which runs out to Keleti Station, **JÓZSEFVÁROS** (the VIII District) is an amalgam of high and low life. Although it boasts several prestigious institutions around the Kiskörút, including the **Hungarian National Museum**, Eötvös Loránd University and the **Erkel Theatre**, its hinterland beyond the Nagykörút was nicknamed "Chicago" during the 1920s and 1930s, and is still associated with prostitution and criminal activities. While the area between the Kiskörút and Nagykörút is nothing to worry about, caution is warranted elsewhere, especially after dark.

Bordering Józsefváros to the south is **FERENCVÁROS** (Franz Town, the IX District), the most solidly working-class of the inner-city districts, whose tenements are swelteringly hot in the summer. The area is chiefly of interest for the wonderful **market hall** on Vámház körút, the **Applied Arts Museum** and the **Palace of Arts** complex – but **football** fans will want to see Fradi in action at the FTC Stadium, and children will enjoy the **Natural History Museum**.

Transport options for the two districts include the red and blue metro lines, trams #4 and #6 along the Nagykörút and tram #2, which runs down the Pest bank of the Danube.

Józsefváros

Part of the Kiskörút, **Múzeum körút** separates the Belváros and Józsefváros. Aside from being curved rather than straight, it resembles Andrássy út in miniature, lined with trees, shops and grandiose buildings. Immediately beyond the East–West Business Centre by the Astoria junction stands the old faculty of the **Eötvös Loránd Science University** (known by its Hungarian initials as ELTE). It's named after the physicist Loránd Eötvös, whose pupils included many of the scientists who later developed the US atomic bombs at Los Alamos, including Edward Teller, "Father of the Hydrogen Bomb".

Across the street, on Ferenczy utca, you can see a small crenellated section of the **medieval wall of Pest**. Originally 2km long and 8m high, the walls gradually disappeared as the city was built up on either side, but fragments

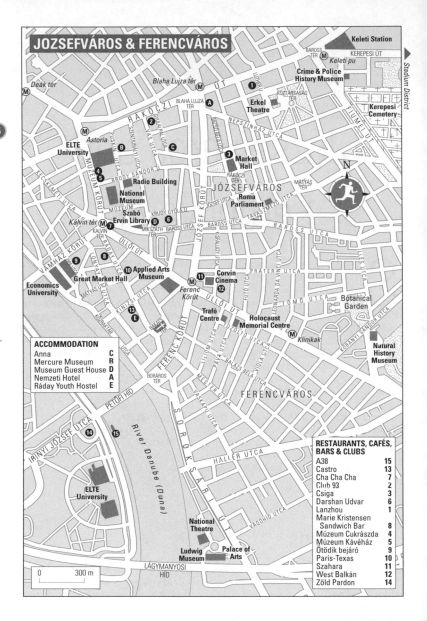

JOZSEFVÁROS & FERENCVÁROS

Keleti Station

Keleti pu

Crime & Police History Museum

Kerepesi Cemetery

Deák tér

Blaha Lujza tér

Erkel Theatre

Astoria

ELTE University

Market Hall

JÓZSEFVÁROS

Radio Building

National Museum

Roma Parliament

Szabó Ervin Library

Kálvin tér

Corvin Cinema

Economics University

Great Market Hall

Applied Arts Museum

Ferenc Körút

Botanical Garden

Trafó Centre

Holocaust Memorial Centre

Klinikak

Natural History Museum

FERENCVÁROS

River Danube (Duna)

ELTE University

PETŐFI HÍD

National Theatre

Ludwig Museum

Palace of Arts

LÁGYMÁNYOSI HÍD

0   300 m

ACCOMMODATION
Anna	C
Mercure Museum	B
Museum Guest House	D
Nemzeti Hotel	A
Ráday Youth Hostel	E

RESTAURANTS, CAFÉS, BARS & CLUBS
A38	15
Castro	13
Cha Cha Cha	7
Club 93	2
Csiga	3
Darshan Udvar	6
Lanzhou	1
Marie Kristensen Sandwich Bar	8
Múzeum Cukrászda	4
Múzeum Kávéház	5
Ötödik bejáró	9
Paris-Texas	10
Szahara	11
West Balkán	12
Zöld Pardon	14

remain here and there – a larger freestanding chunk lurks in the courtyard of no. 21.

Staying on the outer edge of Múzeum körút, you'll find the **Múzeum Kávéház** at no. 12, which was one of the earliest coffee houses in Pest. Its original frescoes and Zsolnay ceramic reliefs dating from 1885 still grace what has long since become a restaurant (see p.161). Dining here is a must, but it's essential to reserve. From here, you can wander down **Bródy Sándor utca**, which runs along the garden of the Hungarian National Museum. At no. 4, the **Italian Institute** housed the lower chamber of the Hungarian Parliament from 1867 until its present building was completed, while at nos. 5–7 is the **Radio Building**. It was here that ÁVO guards fired upon students demanding access to the airwaves, an act which turned the hitherto peaceful protests of October 23, 1956 into an uprising against the secret police and other manifestations of Stalinism.

Hungarian National Museum

Like the National Library on Várhegy, the **Hungarian National Museum** (Magyar Nemzeti Múzeum; Tues–Sun 10am–6pm; free; ⊛www.hnm.hu) was the brainchild of Count Ferenc Széchenyi (father of István), who donated thousands of prints and manuscripts to form the basis of its collection. Housed in a Grecian-style edifice by Mihály Pollack, it was only the fourth such museum in the world when it opened in 1847, and soon afterwards became the stage for a famous event in the **1848 Revolution**, when Sándor Petőfi (see p.52) first declaimed the *National Song* from its steps, with its rousing refrain – "Choose! Now is the time! Shall we be slaves or shall we be free?" ("Some noisy mob had their hurly-burly outside so I left for home," complained the museum's director.) Ever since, March 15 has been commemorated here with flags and speeches.

By way of amends for losing the Coronation Regalia in 2000 (now on display in Parliament – see p.62), the National Museum has undergone a major refit. This has resulted in two new subterranean levels, devoted to **medieval and Roman sculptures** – the latter starring a third-century mosaic floor from a villa at Balácpuszta in western Hungary. To the left from the ground-floor foyer is a darkened room displaying King Stephen's Byzantine silk **coronation robe**, which is far too fragile to be exhibited in the Parliament building, while to the right is a series of rooms covering the history of the **pre-Hungarian peoples** in the Carpathian basin. There have been extensive finds from excavations of prehistoric, Roman and later cultures, and the new display – with the Bronze Age tombs set in the floor, among other things – is excellent.

Hungarian history exhibition

The main exhibition on the upper floor traces Hungarian history from the Árpád dynasty to the end of Communism, presenting objects from each era with brief descriptions in English. Room 1 – to the left at the top of the stairs – contains Béla III's crown, sceptre and sword, and room 2, the Anjou Fountain from the royal palace at Visegrád (see p.137). Don't miss the ivory saddles inlaid with hunting scenes in room 3, the suit of armour of the child-king Sigismund III in room 5, or the huge Renaissance pew in room 6. Turkish weaponry and the gold-embroidered tunic of Prince Gábor Bethlen of Transylvania in room 7 speak of the 150 years when Hungary was divided and its destiny decided by intriguers and warlords, including the Forgáchs and Nádasdys depicted in the oldest **portraits** in Hungary (almost naive in style), hung in room 8 – except for the infamous "Blood Countess", whose picture is kept in storage. The Countess, widow of national hero Ferenc Nádasdy, was charged with torturing six hundred women to death and reputedly bathing in their blood to preserve her beauty; she was walled up in her castle and the atrocity hushed up.

From here, proceed back to the top of the stairs; on the other side the Reform era and the *belle époque* are covered in rooms 11–18, followed by World War II and the Communist era in room 20. The last features newsreel footage and such items as a radio set dedicated to Stalin's 70th birthday, a fragment of the Stalin statue and the crest of Party headquarters torn down by crowds in 1956, and kitsch tributes to János Kádár, who reimposed Communist rule with a vengeance, but later liberalized it to the point that his successors felt able to abandon it entirely. Not to be missed are the **propaganda** films from the Horthy, Fascist and Stalinist eras, whose resemblance to each other makes the point.

Kálvin tér

Múzeum körút ends at **Kálvin tér**, a busy intersection with roads going to the airport and the east, and westwards across the river. In 1956 street fighting was especially fierce here as insurgents battled tanks rumbling in from the Soviet base on Csepel island. It seems almost miraculous that the ornate reading rooms of the **Szabó Ervin Library** (Mon–Fri 10am–8pm, Sat 10am–4pm; closed July, reduced hours in August; free), on the corner of Baross utca, survived unscathed. The library, built in 1887 by the Wenckheim family – who enjoyed a near-monopoly on Hungary's onion production – has come through a thorough modernization in sparkling form. Entering via the main entrance on Reviczky utca, you can ask at the information desk about visiting the reading rooms up on the fourth level. They may ask you to register (which you will also have to do if you want to use the Internet stations upstairs) but will probably just wave you through.

The very name of the "**Fountain of Hungarian Truth**" (Magyar Igazság kútja) in front of the library sets alarm bells ringing, with its nationalist connotations of seeking justice after the wrongs that history imposed upon the country. This is one of the few surviving public monuments marking the Trianon treaty, and was set up in 1928 in honour of Lord Rothermere (see p.59), whose profile features on the fountain. Below the figure of Justice comforting poor Hungary, the inscription speaks of the gratitude of the Hungarian people to the peer. On June 4, the anniversary of the treaty's signing, right-wing and Fascist groups gather to pay their respects.

To the Nagykörút and Keleti Station

To stretch your legs, take a stroll through the atmospheric quarter behind the library, with its crumbling churches and parochial schools, wine cellars and workshops. Eventually you'll emerge on the **József körút**, one of the sleazier arcs of the Nagykörút. Following a law in 1999 to restrict **prostitution**, a crackdown on the adjacent **Rákóczi tér** merely drove the trade into brothels more easily controlled by the Mafia – hence the lesbian shows on the *körút*. As for Rákóczi tér itself, by day the shabby square is simply a place for locals to shop in the market hall and a centre for Chinese wholesalers, though the *Csiga* bar on the corner just across from the market hall is a decent hangout.

While theatre-goers bestow bourgeois respectability upon **Köztársaság tér** – the home of Budapest's "second" opera house, the **Erkel Theatre** (named after the composer of the national anthem, Ferenc Erkel) – the grittier side of life prevails at **Keleti Station** on Baross tér. As the station is Budapest's "gateway to the east", it's not surprising that Chinese takeaways and Arab shops are a feature of the area – as are incessant ID checks by the **police**, who patrol here in threes ("One can read, one can write, and the third one keeps an eye on the two intellectuals", as the old joke has it).

The Crime and Police History Museum

Handily for the police, their precinct HQ is only two blocks from the station, at Mosonyi utca 5. Tourists who'd never go there otherwise can visit the bizarre **Crime and Police History Museum** (Bűnügyi és Rendőrség-Történeti Múzeum; Tues–Sun 10am–5pm; free) at no. 7, guarded by a dummy sentry. Since the museum is captioned in Hungarian only, you can easily miss the ideological cast of the display of uniforms and memorabilia going back to Habsburg times, which harbours a tribute to the Communist border guards and militia, and CIA leaflets inciting the Uprising. Be thankful you're not an exhibit in the other hall, where many displays depict murders and mutilations in horrific detail, unlike the staged – and very Sixties – crime scene with a sign listing key points for trainee investigators. Stuff on forgery and art theft in the 1980s begs the question why there's nothing about crime in Hungary nowadays. The show ends with a fraternal display of police uniforms from fellow forces in the EU.

Kerepesi Cemetery

Five minutes' walk from the museum, along Fiumei út, you'll find **Kerepesi Cemetery** (Kerepesi temető; daily: April & Aug 7am–7pm, May–July 7am–8pm, Sept 7am–6pm, Oct 7am–5.30pm, Nov–March 7.30am–5pm; free), the Père Lachaise of Budapest, where the famous, great and not-so-good are buried. Vintage hearses and mourning regalia in the **Funerary Museum** (Mon–Thurs 10am–3pm, Fri 10am–1pm; free) near the main gates illuminate the Hungarian way of death and set the stage for the necropolis. In Communist times, Party

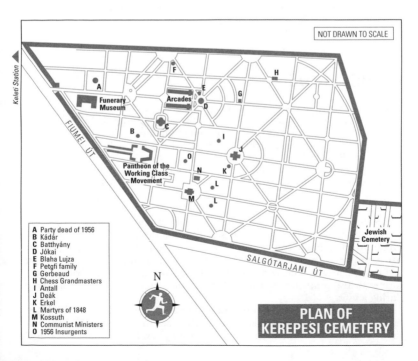

A Party dead of 1956
B Kádár
C Batthyány
D Jókai
E Blaha Lujza
F Petőfi family
G Gerbeaud
H Chess Grandmasters
I Antall
J Deák
K Erkel
L Martyrs of 1848
M Kossuth
N Communist Ministers
O 1956 Insurgents

NOT DRAWN TO SCALE

Keleti Station

Funerary Museum

Arcades

Pantheon of the Working Class Movement

Jewish Cemetery

FIUMEI ÚT

SALGÓTARJANI ÚT

N

PLAN OF KEREPESI CEMETERY

members killed during the Uprising were buried in a prominent position near the entrance and government ministers in honourable proximity to Kossuth, while leaders and martyrs who "Lived for Communism and the People" were enshrined in a starkly ugly **Pantheon of the Working Class Movement**, which was so shoddily built that it's falling apart; some have been removed by their relatives since the demise of Communism. Party leader János Kádár – who ruled Hungary from 1956 to 1988 – rates a separate grave, heaped with wreaths from admirers; his reputation has risen in recent years, and there's even talk of a monument.

Further in lie the florid **nineteenth-century mausoleums** of Kossuth, Batthyány, Deák and Petőfi (whose family tomb is here, though his own body was never found). Don't miss the Art Nouveau funerary arcades between Batthyány's and the novelist Jókai's mausoleums, nor the nearby tomb of the diva Lujza Blaha, the "Nation's Nightingale", whose effigy is surrounded by statues of serenading figures. Other notables include the composer Erkel, the confectioner Gerbeaud and three chess grandmasters whose tombs are engraved with the chess moves that won them their titles. A more recent addition is József Antall, the first post-Communist prime minister of Hungary, honoured by an allegorical monument with horses struggling to burst free of a sheet.

Next to Kerepesi lies an overgrown **Jewish cemetery** (Mon–Fri & Sun 8am–2pm), with some beautiful Art Nouveau tombs of artists, politicians and industrialists, several designed by the brilliant architect Béla Lajta. That of Manfred Weiss, founder of the big Csepel ironworks that once dominated the industrial island south of the city centre, is still maintained by Csepel's council, in gratitude and by way of apology for the fact that Weiss had to sign his factory over to the government in return for being allowed to leave Hungary with his family in 1944. The cemetery gates are on Salgótarján utca, about ten minutes' walk from the main entrance to Kerepesi.

Ferencváros

Ferencváros was developed to house workers in the latter half of the nineteenth century, and remains the most working-class of Budapest's inner suburbs. During the 1930s and 1940s, its population confounded Marxist orthodoxy by voting for the extreme right, who returned the favour by supporting the local football team **FTC** – popularly known as "**Fradi**" – which became the unofficial team of the opposition under Communism and is nowadays known for its hardcore hooligan supporters. The club's green and white colours can be seen throughout the district; for more on Fradi and the football scene in general, see p.179.

Initially, Ferencváros takes its tone from two institutions on Vámház körút, the section of the Kiskörút that separates it from the Belváros. The wrought-iron **Great Market Hall** (Nagycsarnok; Mon 6am–5pm, Tues–Fri 6am–6pm, Sat 6am–2pm) is as famous for its ambience as for its produce, with tanks of live fish downstairs and stalls festooned with strings of paprika at the back, where former British prime minister Mrs Thatcher once endeared herself by haggling during a visit.

Nearer the Danube, the **Economics University** (named after Karl Marx during Communist times) makes a fine sight from Buda at night, reflected in the river, and adds to the liveliness of the area by day. The building was originally Budapest's main Customs House (Vámház) – hence the name of the *körút*. A freestanding section of the **medieval walls** of Pest can be found in Vámház körút in the courtyard of no. 16, if the door is open.

Running down from Kalvin tér, **Ráday utca** is a semi-pedestrianized street lined with bars and cafés spilling out on to the street, giving it a very lively feel. Half a kilometre down the street, Bakáts tér hosts concerts during the **Ferencváros festival** at the end of June.

Along Üllői út

Down Üllői út at nos. 33–37, the **Applied Arts Museum** (Iparművészeti Múzeum; Tues–Sun 10am–6pm; 600Ft; free; ⓦwww.imm.hu) is worth a visit purely to see the building by Ödön Lechner, who strove to create a uniquely Hungarian form of architecture emphasizing the Magyars' Ugric roots, but was also influenced by Art Nouveau. Inaugurated by Emperor Franz Josef during the 1896 Millennial celebrations, it has an enormous dome tiled in green and yellow and a portico with ceramic Turkic motifs on an egg-yolk-coloured background, from the Zsolnay porcelain factory in Pécs. By contrast, the all-white interior is reminiscent of Mogul architecture: at one time it was thought that the Magyars came from India. The museum has a large collection but no permanent displays; instead they mount frequent small exhibitions of their own material as well as regular major shows drawn from other collections.

One block beyond the Applied Arts Museum, the underpass at the junction of the Nagykörút will bring you out on Üllői út beside two buildings associated with the 1956 Uprising. On the right (south) side stands the former **Kilián Barracks**, whose Hungarian garrison was the first to join the insurgents. As the Uprising spread, it became the headquarters of Colonel Pál Maleter and teams of teenage guerillas (some as young as 12) who sallied forth from the alleys surrounding the **Corvin Cinema**, on the other side of Üllői út, to lob Molotov cocktails at Soviet tanks. Since the fall of Communism they have been honoured by a statue of a young insurgent outside the cinema. Its auditoriums are named after illustrious Hungarian actors or directors such as Alexander Korda – one of many Magyars who made it in Hollywood (see p. 176).

A couple of streets further down are two very different buildings. On Liliom utca, an old transformer plant has been turned into the **Trafó**, an outstanding contemporary arts centre (see p.173), while on the parallel Páva utca you'll find the newly established **Budapest Holocaust Memorial Centre** (Holocaust Emlékközpont; Tues–Sun 10am–6pm; free; ⓦwww.hdke.hu). The core of the centre is a beautiful 1920s synagogue designed by Leopold Baumhorn (responsible for some of Hungary's finest synagogues). A new wing was added to the old building to house the first government-funded documentation centre in the region, which has been set up to collect information about the Holocaust in Hungary, promote educational activities in schools and hold exhibitions. The centre doesn't just cover the Jewish exterminations, but also that of the Roma and others, hence the importance of its location outside the main Jewish quarter. By the time you read this a permanent exhibition should be open, which ought to give this fine setting greater ballast.

The Natural History Museum

A kilometre further down Üllői út just past the Klinikák metro stop, a left turn up Korányi Sándor utca brings you to the newly refurbished **Hungarian Natural History Museum** (Magyar Természettudományi Múzeum; daily

except Tues 10am–6pm; free, 1800Ft for temporary displays; @www.nhmus
.hu). Though slightly out on a limb, it is worth the hike, especially if you
have children: the presentation is captivating, with lots of colour, wide open
spaces, explanations in English and, for the weary, benches made from huge
tree trunks.

From the large entrance hall, dominated by a huge whale skeleton, you walk
through to a fantastic **underwater room**, which has colourful fish in sea- and
freshwater aquariums – the mock seabed under the glass floor makes you feel
as if you are walking on water. The first floor has lots of interesting displays
of animals around the world, recreating their habitats, for instance in a jungle
scene. On the top floor is a Noah's Ark focusing on animals under threat, and
showcasing what Hungary is doing for the environment. The shop downstairs
by the entrance sells an excellent range of animal-related bits, from fridge mag-
nets to games and books.

Across the road is a small **Botanical Garden** (Fűvészkert; daily 9am–5pm,
greenhouses closed noon–1pm and from 4pm; 800Ft). Delightfully jungle-like,
it derives part of its appeal from its rather run-down state.

The National Theatre and Palace of Arts

Further south on the banks of the Danube is a major new **cultural complex**
in a strange location 3km from Deák tér, though perhaps when the intervening
area is built up these new blocks will look less forlorn. The best way to get here
is by taking tram #2 to the penultimate stop, Vágóhíd utca.

The first sight that greets you across the wasteland is the **National Theatre**
(Nemzeti Színház), a tortured creation looking like a Ceausescu folly stranded
by the decline of Communism. The theatre's exterior and surroundings are
strewn with random architectural references and assorted statuary; the Classical facade lying under water at the front is a replica of the frontage of the old
National Theatre torn down in 1964.

Next door is the **Palace of Arts** (Művészetek Palotája; @www.mupa.hu), a
vast palace indeed, that is the new home of the Ludwig Museum, the excellent
Philharmonic Orchestra and the National Dance Theatre. By day it looks like
a dull office block, but comes alive in the evening with some impressive light-
ing. No expense has been spared to make this a top arts venue, and this is most

---

The sorry saga of Budapest's National Theatre

Until the construction of the metro in the 1960s, the National Theatre had been
housed in a grand building on **Blaha Lujza tér** – its demolition was seen by many as
an evil plot by the Communist regime to undermine the nation's cultural identity. For
many years the theatre was temporarily housed in a hideous building in the backstreets of Pest, while the debate continued as to where the great national institution
should stand. In 1997 the centre-left city authorities finally started the construction
of a huge development on **Erzsébet tér**, which incorporated very costly foundations so that the underground car park would not disturb the performances. Hardly
had the foundations been laid, however, when in 1998 the new centre-right national
government halted construction and started a new debate about where to put the
theatre. In the end it chose the current site on the Pest riverbank, but controversy
has continued: the government minister in charge awarded the job of designing the
building to the architect who designed his holiday house; the site of the new theatre
is a long way from the centre, with poor transport links; and the end result has been
widely mocked – to say nothing of the standard of the performances.

apparent in the concert hall, a state-of-the-art construction where the acoustics are excellent – so good, say wicked tongues, that some orchestras dislike it as you can hear the mistakes.

To the right of the main entrance, the **Ludwig Museum** or Museum of Contemporary Art (Kortárs Művészti Múzeum; Tues–Sun 10am–6pm; free, though temporary shows cost 1000Ft; ⓦwww.ludwigmuseum.hu) was established in 1996 to build upon an earlier bequest by the late German industrialist Peter Ludwig. The collection includes US pop art such as Warhol's *Single Elvis* and Lichtenstein's *Vicky*, as well as Picasso's *Musketeer with a Sword* and a *Sealed Letter* by Beuys, but most of the recent acquisitions are works by lesser-known Europeans, in such styles as Hyper-Realism and Neo-Primitivism.

6

Várhegy and central Buda

V ÁRHEGY (Castle Hill), often referred to simply as the **Vár**, is Buda's
most prominent feature. A 1500-metre-long plateau encrusted with
bastions, mansions and a huge palace, it dominates both the Víziváros
below and Pest, over the river, making this stretch of the river one of
the grandest, loveliest urban waterfronts in Europe. The hill is studded with
interesting museums, from the big **National Gallery** and the **Budapest History Museum** in the **Royal Palace** to the small **Golden Eagle Pharmacy**
and the **Telephone Museum**, but it's also enjoyable just walking the streets
and admiring such florid creations as the **Mátyás Church** and the **Fishermen's Bastion**.

Between the castle and the river, the **Víziváros** is something of a quiet residential backwater in the heart of Buda, with a distinctive atmosphere but few
specific sights other than the Lánchíd and the Sikló funicular at the southern
end, the **Church of St Anne** on **Batthyány tér** in the middle, and the **Király
Baths** further up.

The area to the **north of Várhegy** has a variety of attractions in the backstreets off Margit körút: a lively **market** and the **Millenaris Park**, a major
concert venue, exhibition centre and children's playground all in one. Further
down, on the edge of the affluent Rózsadomb district, is one of Budapest's
Turkish remnants, **Gül Baba's tomb**.

The simplest and most novel approach to Várhegy is to ride up to the palace
by the aforementioned **Sikló**, a renovated nineteenth-century **funicular** that
runs from Clark Ádám tér by the Lánchíd. From Pest, the most direct approach
is to get bus #16 from Erzsébet tér across the Lánchíd to the lower terminal of
the Sikló, or to the end of the line on Dísz tér, near Buda Palace. From Moszkva tér (on the red metro line) you can either take the small **Várbusz** (Castle
Bus; every 15min; usual BKV tickets apply) that leaves from the raised side of
Moszkva tér and terminates by the palace, or walk uphill to the Vienna Gate
at the northern end of the Castle District. Walking from Batthyány tér via the
steep flights of steps (*lépcső*) off Fő utca involves more effort, but the dramatic
stairway up to the Fishermen's Bastion is worth the sweat. The red metro line
and bus #16 will also get you to the Víziváros, while the southern Rózsadomb
is skirted by trams #4 and #6 between Pest and Moszkva tér.

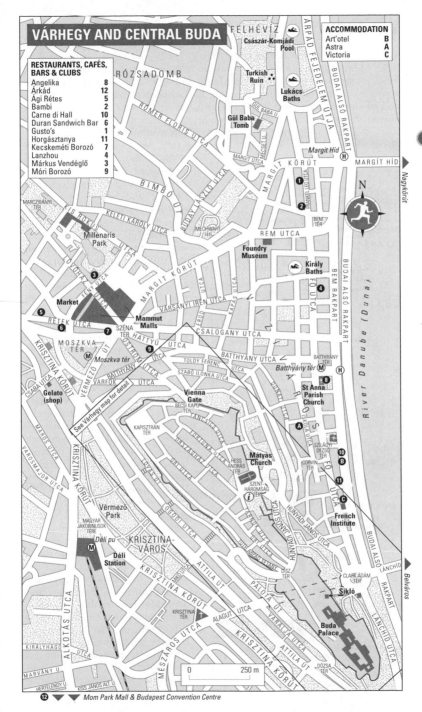

VÁRHEGY AND CENTRAL BUDA

ACCOMMODATION
Art'otel	B
Astra	A
Victoria	C

RESTAURANTS, CAFÉS, BARS & CLUBS
Angelika	8
Árkád	12
Ági Rétes	5
Bambi	2
Carne di Hall	10
Duran Sandwich Bar	6
Gusto's	1
Horgásztanya	11
Kecskeméti Borozó	7
Lanzhou	4
Márkus Vendéglő	3
Móri Borozó	9

FELHÉVÍZ

Császár-Komjádi Pool

RÓZSADOMB

Turkish Ruin

Lukács Baths

Gül Baba Tomb

Gül Baba Tomb

RÓMER FLÓRIS UTCA

MARGIT UTCA

Margit Híd

MARGIT KÖRÚT

MARGÍT HÍD

BIMBÓ UT

BUDAI LÁSZLÓ UTCA

MARCZIBÁNYI TÉR

KELETI KÁROLY UTCA

MECHWART TÉR

BEM TÉR

Millenáris Park

REM UTCA

Foundry Museum

Király Baths

MARGIT KÖRÚT

VÁRSÁNYI IRÉN UTCA

FŐ UTCA

Market

RÉTEK UTCA

SZÉNA TÉR

Mammut Malls

CSALOGÁNY UTCA

BUDAI ALSÓ RAKPART

MOSZKVA TÉR

Moszkva tér

HATTYÚ UTCA

BATTHYÁNY UTCA

BATTHYÁNY TÉR

TOLDY FERENC UTCA

SZABÓ ILONKA UTCA

Batthyány tér

River Danube (Duna)

KRISZTINA KÖRÚT

VÉRMEZŐ UTCA

VÁRFOK UTCA

Gelato (shop)

Vienna Gate

BÉCSI KAPU TÉR

LÁNCHÍD UTCA

St Anna Parish Church

VÁROSMAJOR UTCA

KAPISZTRÁN TÉR

FORTUNA UTCA

HESS ANDRÁS TÉR

Mátyás Church

Vérmező Park

MAGYAR JAKOBINUSOK TERE

Déli pu

KRISZTINA-VÁROS

SZENT-HÁROMSÁG TÉR

CORVIN TÉR

French Institute

Déli Station

KRISZTINA KÖRÚT

ATTILA ÚT

HUNYADI JÁNOS UTCA

DÍSZ TÉR

CLARK ÁDÁM TÉR

Siklo

KRISZTINA KÖRÚT

Buda Palace

ALKOTÁS UTCA

MÉSZÁROS UTCA

ALAGÚT UTCA

VÁRALJA UTCA

ATTILA ÚT

LÁNCHÍD UTCA

KRISZTINA TÉR

KRISZTINA KÖRÚT

DÓZSA TÉR

KIRÁLYHÁGÓ U

MÁRVÁNY U

HERTELENDY U

KISS JÁNOS ALT. U.

0	250 m

Mom Park Mall & Budapest Convention Centre

Várhegy

Várhegy's striking location and its strategic utility have long gone hand in hand: Hungarian kings built their palaces here because it was easy to defend, a fact appreciated by the Turks, Habsburgs and other occupiers. **Buda Palace** serves as a reminder of this past, rising like a house of cards at the southern end of the hill, as proud yet insubstantial as those who ruled there while Hungary's fate was determined by mightier forces.

The hill's buildings have been almost wholly reconstructed from the rubble of 1945, when the Wehrmacht and the Red Army battled over the hill while Buda's inhabitants cowered underground. This was the eighty-sixth time that Várhegy had been ravaged and rebuilt over seven centuries, rivalling the devastation caused by the recapture of Buda from the Turks in 1686. It was this repeated destruction that caused the melange of styles characterizing the hill. While the palace is a faithful postwar reconstruction of the Habsburg behemoth that bestrode the ruins of earlier palaces, the Neo-Gothic **Mátyás Church** and **Fishermen's Bastion** are romantic nineteenth-century evocations of medieval glories, interweaving past and present national fixations.

The streets of the **Várhegy** (Castle District), the residential area to the north of the palace, still follow their medieval courses, with Gothic arches and stone carvings half-concealed in the courtyards and passages of eighteenth-century Baroque houses, whose facades are embellished with fancy ironwork grilles. For many centuries, residence here was a privilege granted to religious or ethnic groups, each occupying a specific street. This pattern persisted through the 145-year-long Turkish occupation, when Armenians, Circassians and Sephardic Jews established themselves under the relatively tolerant Ottomans. The liberation of Buda by a multinational Christian army under Habsburg command was followed by a pogrom and ordinances restricting the right of

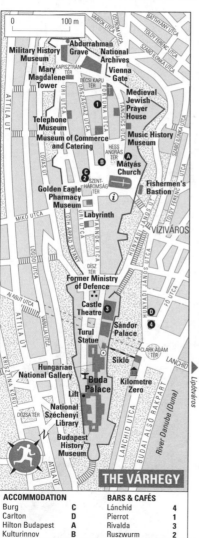

THE VÁRHEGY

ACCOMMODATION		BARS & CAFÉS	
Burg	C	Lánchíd	4
Carlton	D	Pierrot	1
Hilton Budapest	A	Rivalda	3
Kulturinnov	B	Ruszwurm	2

residence to Catholics and Germans, which remained in force for nearly a century. Almost every building here displays a stone *műemlék* (listed) plaque giving details of its history (in Hungarian), and a surprising number are still homes rather than embassies or boutiques – there are even a couple of schools and corner shops. At dusk, when most of the tourists have left, pensioners walk their dogs and toddlers play in the long shadows of Hungarian history.

Szentháromság tér

The obvious starting point is **Szentháromság tér** (Holy Trinity Square), the historic heart of the district, named after an ornate **Trinity Column** erected in 1713 in thanksgiving for the abatement of a plague; a scene showing people dying from the Black Death appears on the plinth. To the southwest stands the former **Town Hall**, Buda having been a municipality until its unification with Pest and Óbuda in 1873; note the corner statue of Pallas Athene, bearing Buda's coat of arms on her shield.

Down the road at Szentháromság utca 7, the tiny **Ruszwurm patisserie** has been a pastry shop and café since 1827 and was a gingerbread shop in the Middle Ages. Its Empire-style decor looks much the same as it would have done under Vilmos Ruszwurm, who ran the patisserie for nearly four decades from 1884.

Mátyás Church

The square's most prominent feature is the Neo-Gothic **Mátyás Church** (Mátyás templom; Mon–Fri 9am–5pm, Sat 9am–2.30pm, Sun 1–5pm; 600Ft; audioguide 300Ft), with its wildly asymmetrical diamond-patterned roofs and toothy spires. Officially dedicated to Our Lady but popularly named after "Good King Mátyás", the building is a late nineteenth-century recreation by architect Frigyes Schulek, grafted onto those portions of the original thirteenth-century church that survived the siege of 1686. Ravaged yet again in World War II, the church was laboriously restored by a Communist regime keen to show its patriotic credentials, and the transition to democracy in 1989/90 saw the sanctity of this "ancient shrine of the Hungarian people" reaffirmed – which means that visitors are expected to be properly dressed and respectfully behaved.

As you enter the church through its twin-spired **Mary Portal**, the richness of the interior is overwhelming. Painted leaves and geometric motifs run up columns and under vaulting, while shafts of light fall through rose windows onto gilded altars and statues with stunning effect. Most of the **frescoes** were executed by Károly Lotz or Bertalan Székely, the foremost historical painters of the nineteenth century. The **coat of arms of King Mátyás** can be seen on the wall to your left, just inside; his family name, Corvinus, comes from the raven (*corvus* in Latin) that appeared on his heraldry and on every volume in his famed Corvin Library.

Around the corner, beneath the south tower, is the **Loreto Chapel**, containing a Baroque Madonna, while in the bay beneath the **Béla Tower** you can see two medieval capitals, one carved with monsters fighting a dragon, the other with two bearded figures reading a book. The tower is named after Béla IV, who founded the church, rather than his predecessor in the second chapel along, who shares a **double sarcophagus** with Anne of Chatillon. The tomb, originally located in the old capital, Székesfehérvár, 60km southwest of Budapest, was moved here after its discovery in 1848. Although Hungary's medieval kings were crowned at Székesfehérvár, it was customary to make a prior appearance in Buda – hence the sobriquet, the "Coronation Church".

The church also has a small collection of **ecclesiastical treasures** and relics, including the right foot of St János. The **crypt**, normally reserved for prayer, contains the red-marble tombstone of a nameless Árpád prince. Otherwise, climb a spiral staircase to the **Royal Oratory** overlooking the stained-glass windows and embossed vaulting of the nave; here votive figures and vestments presage a **replica of the Coronation Regalia**, whose attached exhibition is more informative about the provenance of St Stephen's Crown than that accompanying the originals, on display in Parliament (see p.62).

Mass is celebrated in the Mátyás Church daily at 7am, 8.30am and 6pm, and at 10am and noon on Sundays and public holidays. The 10am mass on Sunday is in Latin with a full choir. The church is also a superb venue for **concerts** during the festival seasons, and evening organ recitals throughout the year. Details appear in listings magazines and on the church's own website, ⓦwww .matyas-templom.hu. Tickets are available on the spot or from any booking agency (see p.172).

Fishermen's Bastion

After the Mátyás Church, the most impressive sight in Várhegy is the **Fishermen's Bastion** (Halászbástya) just beyond. An undulating white rampart of cloisters and stairways intersecting at seven tent-like turrets (symbolizing the Magyar tribes that conquered the Carpathian Basin), it looks as though it was dreamt up by the illusionist artist Escher, but was actually designed by Schulek as a foil to the Mátyás Church. Although fishermen from the Víziváros reputedly defended this part of the hill during the Middle Ages, the bastion is purely decorative. The **view** of Pest across the river, framed by the bastion, is only surpassed by the vistas from the terrace of Buda Palace, and the Citadella on Gellért-hegy. However, you might baulk at paying 330Ft to go up to the top level – tickets from the machine nearby (students and OAPs have to go to

---

King Stephen

If you commit just one figure from Hungarian history to memory, make it **King Stephen**, for it was he who welded the tribal Magyar fiefdoms into a state and won recognition from Christendom. Born Vajk, son of Grand Duke Géza, he emulated his father's policy of trying to convert the pagan Magyars and develop Hungary with the help of foreign preachers, craftsmen and merchants. By marrying Gizella of Bavaria in 996, he was able to use her father's knights to crush a pagan revolt after Géza's death, and subsequently received an apostolic cross and crown from Pope Sylvester II for his coronation on Christmas Day, 1000 AD, when he took the name Stephen (István in Hungarian).

Though noted for his enlightened views (such as the need for tolerance and the desirability of multiracial nations), he could act ruthlessly when necessary. After his only son Imre died in an accident and a pagan seemed likely to inherit, Stephen had the man blinded and poured molten lead into his ears. Naming his successor, he symbolically offered his crown to the Virgin Mary rather than the Holy Roman Emperor or the pope; ever since, she has been considered the Patroness of Hungary. Swiftly canonized after his death in 1038, **St Stephen** became a national talisman, his mummified right hand a holy relic, and his coronation regalia the symbol of statehood. Despite playing down his cult for decades, even the Communists eventually embraced it in a bid for some legitimacy, while nobody in post-Communist Hungary thinks it odd that the symbol of the republic should be the crown and cross of King Stephen.

the ticket office in the adjacent park to get their half-price tickets) – as the free view from the lower level is just as good.

Between the bastion and the church, an equestrian **statue of King Stephen** honours the founder of the Hungarian nation, whose conversion to Christianity and coronation with a crown sent by the pope presaged the Magyars' integration into European civilization (see box). The relief at the back of the plinth depicts Schulek offering a model of the Mátyás Church to Stephen. Like the church and the bastion, his statue is reflected in the copper-glass facade of the **Budapest Hilton**, incorporating chunks of a medieval Dominican church and monastery on the side facing the river, and an eighteenth-century Jesuit college on the other, which bears a copy of the **Mátyás Relief** from Bautzen in Germany that's regarded as the only true likeness of Hungary's Renaissance monarch.

Museum of Commerce and Catering

Be sure to visit the fascinating **Museum of Commerce and Catering** (Kereskedelmi és Vendéglátóipari Múzeum; Wed–Fri 10am–5pm, Sat & Sun 10am–6pm; free, or 500Ft for temporary exhibitions) at Fortuna utca 4, which captures something of the atmosphere of Budapest during its bustling golden age in the late nineteenth and early twentieth century. To the right of the courtyard, the commerce section contains antique shopfronts and interiors, complete with artefacts such as an early twentieth-century illuminated sign advertising beer, and a model dog that raps shop windows with its paws to attract passersby in. The display ends with images of nationalization after the Communist takeover in 1948, which would suppress commercial activity for forty years. The catering – or hospitality – part to the left pays homage to the restaurateur Károly Gundel, the confectioner Emil Gerbeaud, and Alfred Dobos, who became a celebrity when his *dobostorta*, a caramel-topped layered sponge cake, won a prize at the Vienna Exhibition. Among its displays you'll find furnishings from old coffee houses, antique culinary implements and a reconstructed bedroom from the *Gellért Hotel*.

Along Táncsics Mihály utca

In the fifteenth century, Táncsics Mihály utca was known as Zsidó utca (Jewish Street), when both Ashkenazi and Sephardic Jews lived here – the Ashkenazi community was established in 1251 in the reign of Béla IV. The Jewish community was completely wiped out when Buda was captured from the Ottomans in 1686. The Jews, who had fared well under Turkish rule, assisted in the defence of Buda, and those who had not fled or died in the siege were carted away as prisoners by the victorious Christian army. After several name changes, the street was renamed in 1948 after **Mihály Táncsics**, a radical Hungarian politician of the 1848 uprising who was imprisoned here. As it happens Táncsics, though not Jewish, joined a Jewish platoon of the National Guard in protest against anti-Semitism.

The **Music History Museum** (Zenetörténeti Múzeum; ✆www.zti.hu /museum.htm) at no. 7 occupies the Baroque Erdödy Palace where Beethoven was a guest in 1800, and where Bartók once had a workshop before he emigrated. The museum focuses on splendid instruments that represent three centuries of music, but was closed for major restoration work at the time of writing, and is not due to reopen until 2007. The collection ranges from a Holczman harp made for Marie Antoinette and a unique tongue-shaped violin in the classical section to hurdy-gurdies, zithers, cowhorns and bagpipes, as well as many Bartók scores and jottings. On your way out, have a look at no. 9 next door, which was once the Joseph Barracks where the Habsburgs jailed Hungarian radicals such as Táncsics.

Evidence of Buda's Jewish past can be found at no. 26, which contains a **Medieval Jewish Prayer House** (Középkori Zsidó Imaház; May–Oct Tues–Sun 10am–5pm; 400Ft). Around 1470, King Mátyás allowed the Jews to build a synagogue and appointed a Jewish council led by Jacobus Mendel; part of Mendel's house survives in the entrance to the prayer house. All that remains of its original decor are two Cabbalistic symbols painted on a wall, and though the museum does its best to flesh out the history of the community with maps and prints, all the real treasures are in the Jewish Museum in Pest (see p.71).

Kapisztrán tér

At the end of Táncsics Mihály utca lies **Bécsi kapu tér**, named after the **Vienna Gate** (Bécsi kapu) that was erected on the 250th anniversary of the recapture of Buda. Beside it, the forbidding-looking Neo-Romanesque **National Archives** (no admission) guard the way to **Kapisztrán tér**, a larger square centred on the **Mary Magdalene Tower** (Magdolna-torony), whose accompanying church was wrecked in World War II. In medieval times this was where Hungarian residents worshipped (Germans used the Mátyás Church), so its reconstruction is occasionally mooted by vote-hungry nationalist politicians. Today the tower boasts a peal of ornamental bells that jingles through a medley composed by the jazz pianist György Szabados, including Hungarian folk tunes, Chopin *Études* and the theme from *Bridge over the River Kwai*.

Beyond the tower is a statue of **Friar John Capistranus**, who exhorted the Hungarians to victory at the siege of Belgrade in 1456, a triumph which the pope hailed by ordering church bells to be rung at noon throughout Europe. The statue, showing Capistranus bestriding a dead Turk, is aptly sited outside the Military History Museum.

The Military History Museum

The **Military History Museum** (Hadtörténeti Múzeum; April–Sept 10am–6pm; Oct–March 10am–4pm; closed Mon; free), in a former barracks on the north side of the square, has gung-ho exhibitions on the history of hand weapons from ancient times till the advent of firearms, and the birth and campaigns of the Honvéd (national army) during the 1848–49 War of Independence. However, what sticks in the memory are the sections on the Hungarian Second Army that was decimated at Stalingrad (ask to see newsreel footage as there are no regular shows). In the courtyard are post-Communist memorials to the POWs who never returned from the Gulag.

The entrance to the museum is on **Tóth Árpád sétány**, a promenade lined with cannons and chestnut trees on the western side of the hill, looking across to the Buda Hills. At its northern end it turns east, past a giant **flagpole** striped in Hungarian colours, to the symbolic **grave of Abdurrahman**, the last Turkish Pasha of Buda, who died on the walls in 1686 – a "valiant foe", according to the inscription.

Országház utca and Úri utca

Back towards Szentháromság tér, there's more to be seen on **Országház utca**, which was the district's main thoroughfare in the Middle Ages and was known as the "street of baths" during Turkish times. Its present name, Parliament Street, recalls the sessions of the Diet held in the 1790s in a former Poor Clares' cloister at no. 28, where the Gestapo imprisoned 350 Hungarians and foreigners in 1945. No. 17, over the road, consists of two medieval houses joined together and has a relief of a croissant on its keystone, from the time when it was a bakery. A few doors down from the old parliament building, Renaissance sgraffiti survive on the underside of the bay window of no. 22 and a Gothic trefoil-arched cornice on the house next door, while the one beyond has been rebuilt in its original fifteenth-century form.

Úri utca (Gentleman Street) also boasts historic associations, for it was at the former Franciscan monastery at no. 51 that the five Hungarian Jacobins were held before being beheaded on the "Blood Meadow" below the hill in 1795. Next door is a wing of the Poor Clares' cloister that served as a postwar telephone exhange before being turned into a **Telephone Museum** (Telefónia Múzeum; Tues–Sun 10am–4pm; 200Ft). The museum's curator strives to explain the development of telephone exchanges since their introduction to Budapest in the early 1900s – activating a noisy rotary one that's stood here since the 1930s – and you're invited to dial up commentaries in English or songs in Hungarian, check out the webcam and Internet facilities, and admire the personal phones of Emperor Franz Josef, Admiral Horthy and the Communist leader János Kádár.

Further down the street, on either side, notice the statues of the four seasons in the first-floor niches at nos. 54–56, Gothic sedilia in the gateway of nos. 48–50, and three arched windows and two diamond-shaped ones from the fourteenth and fifteenth centuries at no. 31.

The Buda Castle Labyrinth

An unusual attraction is the **Buda Castle Labyrinth** (Budavári Labirintus; daily 9.30am–7.30pm; 1400Ft including optional 25min tour and a cup of warming tea; ⓦwww.labirintus.com), whose main entrance is at Úri utca 9. There's another entrance, which offers wheelchair access to sections of the cave, beyond the castle walls at Lovas út 4.

Under the castle are 10km of galleries formed by hot springs and cellars dug since medieval times; they were converted into an air-raid shelter for up to ten thousand people in the 1930s and were used as such in World War II. The labyrinth, which covers 1200m and is 16m below ground, remained in military hands till the 1980s. Since opening as a tourist attraction it has struggled to find interesting displays to enliven what is a fairly simple set of caves. At present the displays include copies of the cave paintings of Lascaux (Buda's caves also sheltered prehistoric hunters), and a "bravery labyrinth", where you have to make your way through a section of cave in total darkness. Masked figures and a giant head sunken into the floor enliven other dank chambers.

The Golden Eagle Pharmacy

Heading south from Szentháromság tér towards the palace, check out the **Golden Eagle Pharmacy Museum** (Arany Sas Patikamúzeum; Tues–Sun 10.30am–6.30pm; free) at Tárnok utca 18. The Golden Eagle was the first pharmacy in Buda, established after the expulsion of the Turks, and moved to its present site in the eighteenth century. Its original murals and furnishings lend authenticity to dubious nostrums, including the skull of a mummy used to make Mumia powder to treat epilepsy; there's also a reconstruction of an alchemist's laboratory, complete with dried bats and crocodiles, and other obscure exhibits such as the small, long-necked Roman glass vessel for collecting widows' tears. The museum has no handouts in English, but the staff can usually explain the more interesting bits. Notice the portrait of the Dominican nun pharmacist – it was common practice for nuns and monks in the Middle Ages to double up as apothecaries. The *Tárnok* coffee house, next door but one, occupies a medieval building with a Renaissance sgraffiti facade of red and yellow checks and roundels, and, like the street, is named after the royal treasurers who once lived there.

6 Dísz tér and the Turul statue

Both Tárnok utca and Úri utca end in **Dísz tér** (Parade Square), whose cobbled expanses are guarded by a mournful Honvéd memorial to the dead of 1848–49. To the south lies the scarred hulk of the old **Ministry of Defence**, to the east of which stands the **Castle Theatre** (Várszínház), which was a Carmelite church until the order was dissolved by Josef II; its conversion was supervised by Farkas Kempelen, inventor of a chess-playing automaton. It was here that the first-ever play in Hungarian was staged in 1790, and where Beethoven performed in 1808. The last building in the row is the **Sándor Palace** (Sándor Palota), formerly the prime minister's residence, where Premier Teleki shot himself in protest at Hungary joining the Nazi invasion of Yugoslavia. It is now the residence of the country's president, a figurehead who is elected by parliament – during the 1989 negotiations over the transition to democracy, the opposition was afraid the Communists would slip in a populist figure to hijack the process and insisted that it be Parliament, rather than the electorate at large, who should choose the president.

Next door to Sándor Palace, the upper terminal of the **Sikló** funicular (see p.105) is separated from the terrace of Buda Palace by stately railings and the ferocious-looking **Turul statue** – a giant bronze eagle clasping a sword in its talons, which is visible from across the river. In Magyar mythology the Turul sired the first dynasty of Hungarian kings by raping the grandmother of Prince Árpád, who led the tribes into the Carpathian Basin. The Turul also accompanied their raids on Europe, bearing the sword of Attila the Hun in its talons. During the nineteenth century it became a symbol of Hungarian identity in the face of Austrian culture, but wound up being co-opted by the Habsburgs, who cast Emperor Franz Josef as a latter-day Árpád for the next millennium. Today, the Turul has been adopted as an emblem by Hungary's skinheads.

From here, you can go through the wrought-iron gates and down some steps to the **terrace** of the palace, commanding a sweeping **view** of Pest. Beyond the souvenir stalls prances an equestrian **statue of Prince Eugene of Savoy**, who captured Buda from the Ottomans in 1686. The bronze statues nearby represent **Csongor and Tünde**, the lovers in the play of the same name by Mihály Vörösmarty (1800–50).

Buda Palace

As befits a former royal residence, the lineage of **Buda Palace** (Budavári palota) can be traced back to medieval times, the rise and fall of various palaces on the hill reflecting the changing fortunes of the Hungarian state. The first fortifications and dwellings, hastily erected by Béla IV after the Mongol invasion of 1241–42, were replaced by the grander palaces of the Angevin kings, who ruled in more prosperous and stable times. This process of rebuilding reached its zenith in the reign of Mátyás Corvinus (1458–90), whose palace was a Renaissance extravaganza to which artists and scholars from all over Europe were drawn by the blandishments of Queen Beatrice and the prospect of lavish hospitality. The rooms had hot and cold running water, and during celebrations the fountains and gargoyles flowed with wine. After the Turkish occupation and the long siege that ended it, only ruins were left – which the Habsburgs, Hungary's new rulers, levelled to build a palace of their own.

From modest beginnings under Empress Maria Theresa (when there were a mere 203 rooms, which she never saw completed), the palace expanded inexorably throughout the nineteenth century, though no monarch ever dwelt here, only the Habsburg palatine (viceroy). After the collapse of the empire following World War I, Admiral Horthy inhabited the building with all the pomp of monarchy until he was deposed by a German coup in October 1944. The palace was left unoccupied, and it wasn't long before the siege of Buda once again resulted in total devastation. Reconstruction work began in the 1950s in tandem with excavations of the medieval substrata beneath the rubble. The medieval section was incorporated into the new building, whose interior is far less elegant than the prewar version, being designed to accommodate cultural institutions.

The complex houses the **Hungarian National Gallery** (Wings A, B, C and D), the **Budapest History Museum** (E) and the **National Széchenyi Library** (F) – the first two of which are definitely worth seeing and could easily take an afternoon. There are separate entrances for each.

The Hungarian National Gallery

Most people's first port of call is the **Hungarian National Gallery** (Magyar Nemzeti Galéria; Tues–Sun 10am–6pm; free for permanent displays, 800Ft for visiting shows; ⓦwww.mng.hu), devoted to Hungarian art from the Middle Ages to the present. It contains much that's superb, but the vastness of the collection and the confusing layout can be fatiguing. Though all the paintings are labelled in English, other details are scanty, so it's worth investing in a guidebook or guided tour (3000Ft for up to five people; book a couple of days in advance on ☎06-20/439-7449). The main entrance is on the eastern side of Wing C, overlooking the river, behind the statue of Eugene of Savoy. Don't buy a special ticket (500Ft) to see the separate **Habsburg crypt**, containing the tombs of several Habsburgs who ruled as palatines of Hungary up until 1849, until you've checked that a tour is scheduled, as they require at least 25 people.

Through the shop to the left of the ticket office, a lovely **wooden ceiling** from a sixteenth-century church and marble reliefs of Beatrice and Mátyás are the highlights of a **Medieval and Renaissance Lapidarium**. Between the two, doors on the left lead to the fantastic collection of fifteenth-century **Gothic altarpieces** and panels at the rear of Wing D. Salvaged from churches great and small that escaped destruction by the Turks, some are artful and others rustic, but all are full of character and detail: notice the varied reactions expressed within the *Death of the Virgin* from Kassa (Kosice, a Slovakian centre of altar-painting) and the gloating spectators in the Jánosrét *Passion*. From the same church comes a *St Nicholas* altar as long as a limo and lurid as a comic strip, whose final scene shows cripples being cured by the saint's corpse. Also strange to modern eyes are *The Expulsion of St Adalbert*, who seems blithely oblivious to the burning of his church, and the woodcarving of *St Anthony the Hermit*, carrying a hill upon his back. The pointed finials on the high altar from Liptószentmária (Liptovská Mara in Slovakia) anticipate the winged altarpieces of the sixteenth century on the floor above. To get there without returning to the foyer, use the small staircase outside the doors to this section and turn left, left and left again at the top.

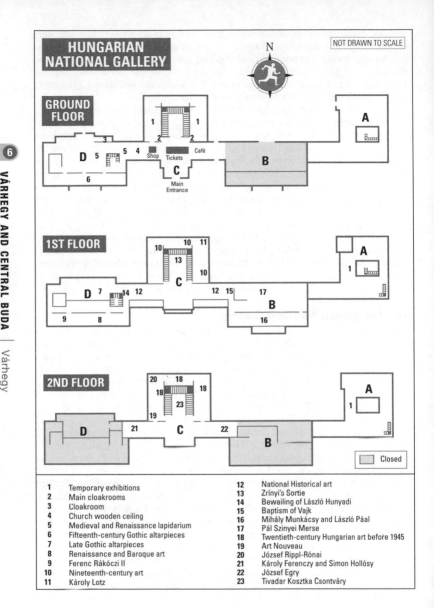

HUNGARIAN NATIONAL GALLERY

NOT DRAWN TO SCALE

N

GROUND FLOOR

1 1
2 2
3
D 5 5 4 Shop Tickets Café
C B
6 Main Entrance
A

1ST FLOOR

10 10 11
10 13 10
C
D 7 14 12 12 15 17 B
9 8 16
A
1

2ND FLOOR

20 18
18 18
19 23
D 21 C 22 B
A
1

Closed

1	Temporary exhibitions	12	National Historical art
2	Main cloakrooms	13	Zrínyi's Sortie
3	Cloakroom	14	Bewailing of László Hunyadi
4	Church wooden ceiling	15	Baptism of Vajk
5	Medieval and Renaissance lapidarium	16	Mihály Munkácsy and László Páal
6	Fifteenth-century Gothic altarpieces	17	Pál Szinyei Merse
7	Late Gothic altarpieces	18	Twentieth-century Hungarian art before 1945
8	Renaissance and Baroque art	19	Art Nouveau
9	Ferenc Rákóczi II	20	József Rippl-Rónai
10	Nineteenth-century art	21	Károly Ferenczy and Simon Hollósy
11	Károly Lotz	22	József Egry
		23	Tivadar Kosztka Csontváry

The first floor covers the widest range of art and is likely to engage you the longest. It picks up where the ground floor left off in the former Throne Room, where **late Gothic altarpieces** with soaring pinnacles and carved surrounds are displayed. Most of them come from churches now in Slovakia or Romania, such as the altarpiece of the Virgin from Csíkmenaság (now Armaseni in Romania) or the homely St Anne altarpiece from Kisszeben (Sabinov, Slovakia), which looks like a medieval playgroup. On an altar from Berki (Rokycany,

Slovakia), Mary Magdalene is raptured by angels as bishops are impaled, while another piece from Liptószentandrás (Liptovsky Ondrej, Slovakia) shows St Andrew clutching the poles for his crucifixion. Also look out for *The Visitation* by the anonymous "Master MS", in the anteroom, and the coffered ceiling from Gogánváralija (Gogan-Varolea, Romania), in the room behind the Kisszeben altarpiece.

Many of the works in the adjacent section on **Baroque art** once belonged to Count Miklós Esterházy (including his portrait), or were confiscated from private owners in the 1950s. The prolific Austrian **Anton Maulbertsch**, who executed scores of altars and murals reminiscent of Caravaggio, is represented here by smaller works such as *Christ Carrying His Cross*. On the back of one panel running across the room, don't miss **Ádám Mányoki**'s portrait of Ferenc Rákóczi II from 1712, a sober study of a national hero that foreshadowed a new artistic genre of **National Historical art** in the nineteenth century.

People coming up the stairs from the ticket office are confronted on the mid-floor landing by *Zrínyi's Sortie*, a vast canvas by **Peter Krafft** depicting the suicidal sally by the defenders of Szigetvár against a Turkish army fifty times their number. Not a drop of blood spatters the melee, as Count Zrínyi leads the charge across the bridge. Facing you as you come to the first floor is **Gyula Benczúr**'s *Reoccupying of Buda Castle*, whose portrayal of Eugene of Savoy and Karl of Lotharingia suggests a mere exchange of Turkish rulers for Habsburg ones, while *The Bewailing of László Hunyadi* by **Viktor Madarász**, down to the right, would have been read as an allusion to the execution of Hungarian patriots after the War of Independence. At the far end to the left, Benczúr's *The Baptism of Vajk* depicts the future St Stephen's conversion to Christianity. Nearby are two disparate battle scenes by **Bertalan Székely**: *Recovering the Corpse of Louis II* after the catastrophic Hungarian defeat at Mohács in 1526, and *The Women of Eger*, exalting their defiance of the Turks in 1552.

Wings B and C cover other trends in **nineteenth-century art**, namely genre painting, rural romanticism and Impressionism. Through the door to the right of *The Baptism of Vajk* is a section devoted to works by **Mihály Munkácsy** and **László Paál**, exhibited together since both painted landscapes – though Paál did little else, whereas Munkácsy was internationally renowned for pictures with a social message (*The Condemned Cell, Tramps of the Night*) and bravura historical works like *The Conquest* (in the Parliament building). Many canvases have suffered from his use of bitumen in mixing paint, which has caused them to darken and crack – a problem that hasn't affected **László Mednyánszky**'s moonlit *Fishing on the Tisza*. Another section displays works by **Pál Szinyei Merse**, the "father of Hungarian Impressionism", whose models and subjects were cheerfully bourgeois, for example *A Picnic in May*. The pick of the works in Wing C are *Thunderstorm on the Puszta* and *Horses at the Watering Place*, evoking the hazy skies and manly world of the Hungarian "Wild West" – the Great Plain southeast of Budapest. Both are by **Károly Lotz**, better known for his frescoes around the city, such as in the Mátyás Church, Opera House and Parliament.

Walking upstairs to the second floor, you come face to face with three huge canvases by the visionary artist **Tivadar Kosztka Csontváry**, whose obsession with the Holy Land and the "path of the sun" inspired scenes such as *Pilgrimage to the Cedars in Lebanon* and *Ruins of the Greek Theatre at Taormina*, with its magical twilight colours. When Picasso saw an exhibition of his works years later, he remarked: "And I thought I was the only great painter of our century."

In the display to the left of the main landing are works by **József Egry**, a painter in the first half of the twentieth century, whose simple lines bear the

6

influences of both plein air and constructivism. To the right are works by two plein-air painters from the same period, Károly Ferenczy – look out for *Morning Sunshine* and *Picnic in May* – and Simon Hollósy (*Peasant Courtyard* and *Rákóczi March*). Both were members of the **Nagybánya school**, the influential group of Hungarian artists based in Baia Mare in Romania.

Heading through the doors to the left of the stairs, you arrive at **twentieth-century art before 1945** in Wing C, which starts at the end of the nineteenth century: the strong Hungarian **Art Nouveau** movement, represented by János Vaszary (Golden Age), Lajos Gulácsi and Aladár Körösfői Kriesch (who is best known for his work in the Liszt Music Academy – see p.68). Further on are works by **József Rippl-Rónai**, a pupil of Munkácsy whose portraits went mostly unrecognized in his lifetime but are now regarded as Art Nouveau classics – such as *Woman in a White-dotted Dress*. The genre was more rewarding for contemporary applied artists such as Miksa Róth, Károly Kernstok and the architect Ödön Lechner. Csontváry is also represented here with a couple of smaller paintings, including the magically lit *Carriage Ride at Full Moon in Athens*. You then come to the twentieth century proper, with Constructivists such as **Béla Uitz**, the Cubist **János Kmetty**, the expressionist **Vilmos Ába-Novak**, and finally two works by **Imre Ámos**, who worked with Chagall, among others, before he died in a Nazi concentration camp in 1944. More of the work of Imre Amos and Károly Ferenczy can be seen in Szentendre (see p.133).

At the top of the stairs to the third floor, a sculpture called *Throne of Fire*, portraying the awful fate of the peasant rebel leader Dózsa, is the introduction to the museum's **twentieth century art after 1945** section. The display has works by some of the leading artists of the modern era, including Endre Bálint (1914–86) and Attila Szűcs (1967–).

The Mátyás Fountain, Lion Courtyard and the National Library

The square outside the museum is flanked on three sides by the palace and overlooks Buda to the west, though the **view** is marred by the MTI (Hungarian News Agency) building on Nap-hegy. By the far wall stands the flamboyant **Mátyás Fountain**, whose bronze figures recall the legend of Szép Ilonka. This beautiful peasant girl met the king while he was hunting incognito, fell in love with him, and died of a broken heart after discovering his identity and realizing the futility of her hopes. The man with a falcon is the king's Italian chronicler, who recorded the story for posterity (it is also enshrined in a poem by Vörösmarty).

A gateway guarded by lions leads into the **Lion Courtyard**, totally enclosed by further wings. To the right is the **National Széchenyi Library** (Országos Széchenyi Könyvtár), occupying the nineteenth-century Ybl block, whose full size is only apparent from the far side of the hill, where it looms over Dózsa tér like a mountain. The library was founded in 1802 on the initiative of Count Ferenc Széchenyi, the father of István (see p.106). A repository for publications in Hungarian and material relating to the country from around the world, by law it receives a copy of every book, newspaper and magazine that is published in Hungary. The central reading room is open to the public (Mon 1–9pm, Tues–Sat 9am–9pm; free) and there are temporary exhibitions on diverse subjects. During library hours, a passenger **lift** (100Ft) in the adjacent building by the Lion Gateway provides direct access to and from Dózsa tér, at the foot of Várhegy.

The Budapest History Museum

On the far side of the Lion Courtyard, the **Budapest History Museum** (Budapest Történeti Múzeum; March to mid-May and mid-Sept to Oct daily except Tues 10am–6pm; mid-May to mid-Sept daily 10am–6pm; Nov–Feb daily except Tues 10am–4pm; 900Ft, audioguide 800Ft) covers two millennia of history on three floors, and descends into original vaulted, flagstoned halls from the Renaissance and medieval palaces unearthed during excavations. It's worth starting with **prehistory**, on the top floor, to find out about the ancient Magyars. Here you can see the artefacts of their nomadic precursors who overran the Pannonian Plain after the Romans left, such as a gold bridle and stirrup fastenings in a zoomorphic style from Avar burial mounds. Owing to the ravages inflicted by the Mongols and the Turks, there's little to show from the time of the Conquest or Hungary's medieval civilization, so most of the second floor is occupied by **Budapest in Modern Times**, an exhibition giving insight into urban planning, fashions, trade and vices, from 1686 onwards. At either end of the section, two lifesize replicas of the lions on the Lánchíd bracket the period starting with the hopes of the Reform era in the 1840s and ending with the devastated city of 1945. Other items range from an 1880s barrel organ to one of the Swedish Red Cross notices affixed to Jewish safe houses by Wallenberg (see p.71).

The **remains of the medieval palace** are reached from the basement via an eighteenth-century cellar spanning two medieval yards on a lower level. A wing of the ground floor of King Sigismund's palace and the cellars beneath the Corvin Library form an intermediate stratum overlaying the cross-vaulted crypt of the **Royal Chapel** and a **Gothic Hall** displaying statues from later in the fourteenth century, which were found in 1974. In another chamber are portions of red marble fireplaces and a massive portal carved with cherubs and flowers from the palace of King Mátyás. Emerging into daylight, bear left and up the stairs to reach another imposing hall, with a view over the castle ramparts.

The Sikló and the Lánchíd

Between the Buda Palace and the Sándor Palace stands the upper station of the **Sikló** (daily 7.30am–10pm, closed every other Monday; 650Ft up, 550Ft down; Budapest Card not valid on this route), a nineteenth-century **funicular** that takes you down to the river and the Lánchíd. Constructed on the initiative of Ödön Széchenyi, whose father built the bridge below, it was only the second funicular in the world when it was inaugurated in 1870, and functioned without a hitch until wrecked by a shell in 1945. The wooden carriages, replicas of the originals, are now lifted by an electric winch rather than a steam engine; they're divided into three sections at different heights to give as many people as possible a view (the bottom compartment gives the most unimpeded views). Capacity is very limited, however, so in summer you can expect to queue to go up. In the small park at the foot of the Sikló stands **Kilometre Zero**, a zero-shaped monument from where all distances from Budapest are measured.

The Széchenyi Lánchíd

The majestic **Lánchíd** (Chain Bridge) has a special place in the history of Budapest and in the hearts of its citizens. As the first permanent link between Buda and Pest (replacing seasonal pontoon bridges and ferries), it was a tremendous spur to the country's economic growth and eventual unification, linking the rural hinterland to European civilization so that Budapest became a commercial centre and transport hub. The bridge symbolized the abolition of feudal

Count István Széchenyi (1791–1860) was the outstanding figure of Hungary's Reform era. As a young aide-de-camp he cut a dash at the Congress of Vienna and did the rounds of stately homes across Europe. While in England, he steeplechased hell-for-leather, but still found time to examine factories and steam trains, providing Bernard Shaw with the inspiration for the "odious Zoltán Karpathy" of *Pygmalion* (and the musical *My Fair Lady*). Back in Hungary, he pondered solutions to his homeland's backwardness and offered a year's income from his estates towards the establishment of a Hungarian Academy. In 1830 he published *Hitel* (Credit), a hard-headed critique of the nation's feudal society.

Though politically conservative, Széchenyi was obsessed with **modernization**. A passionate convert to steam power after riding on the Manchester–Liverpool railway, he invited Britons to Hungary to build rail lines and the Lánchíd. He also imported steamships and dredgers, promoted horsebreeding and silk-making, and initiated the dredging of the River Tisza and the blasting of a road through the Iron Gates of the Danube. Alas, his achievements were rewarded by a melancholy end. The 1848 Revolution and the short-lived triumph of the radical party led by his *bête noire*, Kossuth, triggered a nervous breakdown, and Széchenyi eventually shot himself.

privilege, as nobles, hitherto exempt from taxes, were obliged to pay the toll to cross it. It also symbolized civic endurance, having been inaugurated only weeks after Hungary lost the 1849 War of Independence, when Austrian troops tried and failed to destroy it.

However, in 1945, the Wehrmacht dynamited all of Budapest's bridges in a bid to check the Red Army. Their reconstruction was one of the first tasks of the postwar era, and the reopening of the Lánchíd on the centenary of its inauguration (November 21) was heralded as proof that life was returning to normal, even as Hungary was becoming a Communist dictatorship. Today, the bridge is once again adorned with the national coat of arms rather than Soviet symbols. A positive development in recent years has been the closing of the bridge to traffic for up to ten weekends over the summer for popular festivities, notably the **Bridge Festival** (Hídünnep; see p.38) in June.

The idea for a bridge came to **Count István Széchenyi** after he was late for his father's funeral in 1820 because bad weather had made the Danube uncrossable. Turning his idea into reality was to preoccupy him for two decades, and it became the centrepiece of a grand plan to modernize Hungary's communications. Owing to Britain's industrial pre-eminence and Széchenyi's Anglophilia, the bridge was designed by **William Tierney Clark** (who based it on his earlier plan for Hammersmith Bridge in London) and constructed under the supervision of a Scottish engineer, **Adam Clark** (no relation), from components cast in Britain. Besides the technical problems of erecting what was then the longest bridge in Europe (nearly 380m), there was also the attempt by the Austrians to blow it up – which Adam Clark personally thwarted by flooding its chain-lockers. He also dissuaded a Hungarian general from setting it alight in 1849.

Whereas Széchenyi died in an asylum, Clark settled happily in Budapest with his Hungarian wife. After his death, he was buried on the spot that now bears his name, though his remains were subsequently moved to Kerepesi Cemetery. Adam Clark also built the **tunnel** (*alagút*) under Várhegy – another Széchenyi project – which Budapestis joked could be used to store the new bridge when it rained.

The Víziváros

Inhabited by fishermen, craftsmen and their families in medieval times, the **Víziváros** ("Watertown"), between Várhegy and the Danube, became depopulated during the seventeenth century, and was resettled by Habsburg mercenaries and their camp followers after the Turks were driven out. The following century saw the neighbourhood gradually gentrified, with solid apartment blocks meeting at odd angles on the hillside, reached by alleys which mostly consist of steps rising from the main street, **Fő utca**. Some of these are still lit by gas lamps and look quite Dickensian on misty evenings.

If you head north past the **Institut Français** at Fő utca 17 and a former Capuchin church featuring Turkish window arches at no. 30, you come to **Szilágyi Desző tér**, a square infamous for the events that occurred here in January 1945. When Eichmann and the SS had already fled, members of the Fascist Arrow Cross massacred hundreds of Budapest's Jews and dumped their bodies in the river; an inconspicuous plaque commemorates the victims. From here, you can make a brief detour left up Vám utca, just north of the square, to see the **Iron Block**, a replica of a wooden block into which itinerant apprentices once hammered nails for good luck (the original is in a museum).

Batthyány tér

The main square and social hub of the Víziváros, **Batthyány tér** is named after the nineteenth-century prime minister, Lajos Batthyány, but started out as Bomba tér (Bomb Square), after an ammunition depot sited here for the defence of the Danube. Today it is busy with shoppers visiting the supermarket in an old market hall on the western side of the square, and commuters using the underground metro/HÉV interchange. The sunken, two-storey building to the right of the market used to be the *White Cross Inn*, where Casanova reputedly once stayed. Many of the older buildings in this area are sunken in this way owing to the ground level being raised several feet in the nineteenth century to combat flooding.

The twin-towered **Church of St Anne** (Szent Anna templom) on the southern corner of Fő utca is one of the finest Baroque buildings in Budapest. Commissioned by the Jesuits in 1740, it wasn't consecrated until 1805 owing to financial problems, the abolition of the Jesuit order in 1773, and an earthquake. During Communist times there were plans to demolish the building, as it was feared that the metro would undermine its foundations, but these, fortunately, came to nothing. Figures of Faith, Hope and Charity hover above the entrance, and in the middle of the facade St Anne cherishes the child Mary, while God's eye surmounts the Buda coat of arms on its tympanum. The interior is ornate yet homely, the high altar festooned with statues of St Anne presenting Mary to the Temple in Jerusalem, accompanied by a host of cherubim and angels, while chintzy bouquets and potted trees welcome shoppers dropping in to say their prayers.

In the northern corner of the square, the **Church of the St Elizabeth Nuns** is worth a look inside for its fresco of St Florian protecting the faithful during the 1810 fire of Tabán.

Bem tér and around

Fő utca terminates at **Bem tér**, named after the Polish general Joseph Bem, who fought for the Hungarians in the War of Independence, and was revered by his men as "Father". A **statue of Bem** with his arm in a sling recalls him leading them into battle at Piski, crying "I shall recapture the bridge or die! Forward Hungarians! If we do not have the bridge we do not have the country." Traditionally a site for demonstrations, it was here that the crowds assembled prior to marching on Parliament at the beginning of the 1956 Uprising. In the northwest corner, at the junction of Frankel Leó utca, stands a Budapest institution, the *Bambi* – one of the few unreformed café-bars that retains its 1970s furnishing and fierce waitresses.

You can identify the **Király Baths** nearby (Király gyógyfürdő; see p.182 for more details) by the four copper cupolas, shaped like tortoise shells, poking from its eighteenth-century facade. Together with the Rudas, this is the finest of Budapest's Turkish baths, whose octagonal pool, lit by star-shaped apertures in the dome, was built in 1570 for the Buda garrison. The baths' name, meaning "king", comes from that of the König family who owned them in the eighteenth century.

If you approach the baths from the south, you'll pass the hulking Fascist-style **Military Court of Justice** at Fő utca 70–72, where Imre Nagy and other leaders of the 1956 Uprising were secretly tried and executed in 1958. The square outside has now been renamed after Nagy, whose body lay in an unmarked grave in the New Public Cemetery for over thirty years (see p.128), and makes a suitably emollient site for the new Foreign Ministry building.

A century ago, the neighbourhood surrounding Bem tér was dominated by a foundry established by the Swiss ironworker Abrahám Ganz, which grew into the mighty Ganz Machine Works. The original ironworks only ceased operation in 1964, when it was turned into a **Foundry Museum** (Öntödei Múzeum; Tues–Sun 9am–4pm; free). You can still see the old wooden structure and the foundry's huge ladles and cranes *in situ*, together with a collection of cast-iron stoves, tram wheels, lampposts and other exhibits. The museum is located at Bem utca 20, 200m from Bem tér, or barely a block from Margit körút.

Moszkva tér to Rózsadomb

The area immediately north of Várhegy is defined by the transport hub of **Moszkva tér** (Moscow Square), which has kept its name owing to the sheer cost of renaming all the vehicles, maps and signs on which it appears. To the north, the **Mammut mall** (fronted by a statue of the woolly beast) is a magnet for shoppers, while behind the mall is the lively Fény utca **market**, great for fruit, veg and dairy products. Further down Fény utca lies the main attraction of the area, where the site of the former Ganz Machine Works has been transformed into the **Millenaris Park**, with water features, vineyards and plots of corn to represent different regions of Hungary. Kids can be let loose on the fantastic playground, and visitors of all ages can enjoy the performances at the outdoor theatre, indoor and outdoor concerts and the diverse, ever-changing rota of events and exhibitions in the converted factory buildings (☎1/336 4057, ⊛www.millenaris.hu). A free Internet café, eMagyarország (1hr limit), operates in Building C.

The Millenaris Park provides a cultural focal point, augmenting the longstanding tourist attraction of Gül Baba's tomb, on the lower slopes of Rózsadomb. Otherwise, Moszkva tér is the place to catch buses to such destinations as the Cogwheel Railway (see p.123) or the Farkasréti Cemetery (see p.126), as well as trams #4 or #6 to Pest.

Gül Baba's tomb and Rózsadomb

The smoggy arc of **Margit körút** underlines the gulf between the polluted inner city and the breeze-freshened heights of Budapest's most affluent neighbourhood, **Rózsadomb** (Rose Hill). The hill is named after the flowers that were reputedly introduced to Hungary by a revered Sufi dervish, Gül Baba, the "Father of the Roses", who participated in the Turkish capture of Buda but died during the thanksgiving service afterwards. The **Tomb of Gül Baba** (Tues–Sun: May–Sept 10am–6pm; Oct–April 10am–4pm; 400Ft), its octagonal shrine adorned with Arabic calligraphy and Turkish carpets, is fittingly located on Mecset utca (Mosque Street), five minutes' walk uphill from Margit körút via Margit utca. Restored with funds donated by the Turkish government, it's surrounded by a colonnaded parapet with fine views, and is set in a pristine park with rose bushes and marble fountains decorated with ceramic tiles.

The Rózsadomb itself is as much a social category as a neighbourhood, for a list of residents would read like a Hungarian *Who's Who*. During the Communist era this included the top Party *funcionárusok*, whose homes featured secret exits that enabled several ÁVO chiefs to escape lynching during the Uprising. Nowadays, wealthy film directors and entrepreneurs predominate, and the sloping streets are lined with spacious villas and flashy cars.

The area north of the Margit Bridge contains two noteworthy baths, the Neoclassical **Lukács Baths**, harbouring a thermal pool, a small swimming pool and whirlpools, and slightly further north up the road, the modern **Császár Komjádi Pool** (see pp.182–183 for details of both), past a ruined Turkish bath to the left.

Gellért-hegy
and the Tabán

G ELLÉRT-HEGY, a craggy dolomite hill rearing 130m above the embankment, is one area you'd be foolish to miss: it offers a fabulous view of the city and is as much a feature of the city's waterfront pano- rama as Várhegy and the Parliament building. At its foot, the *Gellért Hotel* is famous for its Art Nouveau thermal baths and summer terrace. North of Gellért-hegy, the **TABÁN**, once Buda's artisan quarter, now has more roads than buildings and makes an incongruous setting for one of Budapest's most historic and magical Turkish baths, the **Rudas Baths**.

Transport to the district is plentiful: bus #7 and trams # 47 and 49 go from Pest to Gellért tér and Móricz Zsigmond körtér, while tram #18 from Moszkva tér and tram #19 from Batthyány tér via the Tabán serve the same points.

Gellért-hegy

Surmounted by the Liberation Monument and the Citadella, **Gellért–hegy** makes a distinctive contribution to Budapest's skyline. The hill is named after the Italian missionary Ghirardus (Gellért in Hungarian), who converted pagan Magyars to Christianity at the behest of King Stephen. After his royal protector's demise, vengeful heathens strapped Gellért to a barrow and toppled him off the cliff, where a larger-than-life **statue of St Gellért** now stands astride an artificial waterfall facing the Erzsébet híd, his crucifix raised as if in admonition to motorists.

The Gellért Hotel and Baths

At the foot of the hill, the graceful wrought-iron **Szabadság híd** (Liberty Bridge) links the inner boulevard of Pest to Szent Gellért tér on the Buda side, dominated by the Art Nouveau **Gellért Hotel**. Opened in 1918, it was commandeered as a staff headquarters by the Reds, the Romanian army, and finally by Admiral Horthy, following his triumphal entry into "sinful Budapest" in 1920 – in his eyes it was a decadent, communist and, above all, a Jewish city. During the 1930s and 1940s, the hotel's balls were the highlight of Budapest's

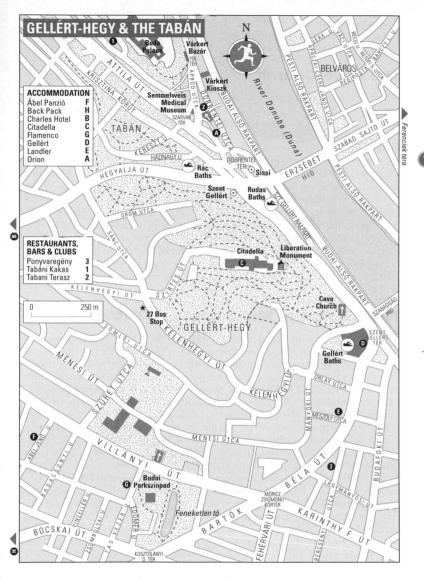

GELLÉRT-HEGY & THE TABÁN

ACCOMMODATION

Ábel Panzió	F
Back Pack	H
Charles Hotel	B
Citadella	C
Flamenco	G
Gellért	D
Landler	E
Orion	A

RESTAURANTS, BARS & CLUBS

Ponyvaregény	3
Tabáni Kakas	1
Tabani Terasz	2

0 — 250 m

★ 27 Bus Stop

social calendar, when debutantes danced on a glass floor laid over its pool. The ostentatious domed **drinking fountain** in front of the hotel has been the source of some controversy: symbolizing the eight springs of Budapest, it was erected without planning permission, and the city authorities toyed with the idea of pulling it down before relenting.

The attached **Gellért Baths** (entered from Kelenhegyi út to the right of the main entrance, though hotel guests can go down in the lift in their bathrobes) are magnificently appointed with majolica tiles and mosaics, and a columned,

Roman-style **thermal pool**, with lion-headed spouts. In the summer visitors can also use the **outdoor pools**, including one with a wave machine, on the terraces behind the main baths. For more details, see p.182.

The Cave Church

On the hillside opposite the *Gellért Hotel* you'll find the **Cave Church** (Szikla-templom; daily 8am–9pm; free), where masses are conducted by white-robed monks of the Pauline order, the only religious order indigenous to Hungary (founded in 1256); its monks served as confessors to the Hungarian kings until Josef II dissolved the order in 1773, though it was re-established 150 years later. The church was created in the 1930s by monks from the nearby Pauline monastery, and functioned until the whole community was arrested by the ÁVO at midnight mass on Easter Monday, 1951, whereupon the chapel was sealed up until 1989. Flickering candles and mournful organ music create an eerie atmosphere during services (daily 8.30–9.30am, 11am–noon, 4.30–6.30pm & 8–9pm), but tourists are only allowed to enter between times. Outside the entrance stands a **statue of St Stephen** with his horse.

From here, you can follow one of the footpaths to the summit – about a twenty-minute climb. The hillside, which still bears fig trees planted by the Turks, was covered in vineyards until a phylloxera epidemic struck in the nineteenth century.

The Liberation Monument and Citadella

Whether you walk up or get there by bus (bus #27 from Móricz Zsigmond körtér to the Busuló Juhász stop, followed by a 10min walk), the **summit** of Gellért-hegy affords a stunning **panoramic view**, drawing one's eye slowly along the curving river, past bridges and monumental landmarks, and then on to the Buda Hills and Pest's suburbs, merging hazily with the distant plain.

On the summit, beside the citadel, stands the **Liberation Monument** (Fel-szabadulási emlékmű) – a female figure brandishing the palm of victory over 30m aloft. There is a famous tale that the monument was originally commissioned by Admiral Horthy in memory of his son István (who was killed in a plane crash on the Eastern Front in 1942), and that, by substituting a palm branch for the propeller it was meant to hold and placing a statue of a Red Army soldier at the base, the monument was deftly recycled to commemorate the Soviet soldiers who died liberating Budapest from the Nazis. While the story may not be true, the monument's sculptor, **Zsigmond Kisfaludi-Strobl**, certainly succeeded in winning approval as a "Proletarian Artist", despite having previously specialized in busts of the aristocracy – and was henceforth known by his compatriots as "Kisfaludi-Strébel" (*strébel* meaning "to climb" or "step from side to side"). The monument survived calls for its removal following the end of Communism, but its inscription was rewritten to honour those who died for "Hungary's prosperity", and the Soviet soldier was banished to the Statue Park on the outskirts of Budapest (p.128).

The **Citadella** behind the monument was built by the Habsburgs to dominate the city in the aftermath of the 1848–49 Revolution; ironically, both its architects were Hungarians. When the historic Compromise was reached in 1867, citizens breached the walls to affirm that it no longer posed a threat to them – though in fact an SS regiment did later hole up in the citadel during World War II. Today it contains a tourist hostel, and an informative outdoor museum relating the hill's history since the Celtic Eravisci lived there two thousand years

△ Statue of Gellért

ago, including panels about St Gellért. Don't bother with the 1944 recreation of a Nazi bunker, which has a couple of wax figures in World War II uniforms and a few photos from the period in a damp concrete cellar, all for 1200Ft.

The Tabán

The **Tabán** district, bordering the northern end of Gellért-hegy, chiefly consists of arterial roads built in Communist times on land left vacant by the prewar demolition of a quarter renowned for its drinking dens and open sewers. Traditionally this was inhabited by Serbs (Rác in Hungarian), who settled here en masse after the Turks were expelled, though, in a typically Balkan paradox, some were present earlier, working in the Ottoman gunpowder factories which may have been the origin of the name Tabán (from *tabahane*, the Turkish for "armoury"). Thankfully, the slum-clearance and motorway building spared Tabán's historic Turkish baths, and its traditions of lusty nightlife are kept alive by summertime concerts in the park.

The Rudas Baths

The relaxing and curative effects of Buda's **mineral springs** have been appreciated for two thousand years. The Romans built splendid bathhouses at Aquincum (see pp.119–120) and, while these declined with their empire, interest in bathing revived after the Knights of St John built a hospice on the site of the present Rudas Baths, near where St Elizabeth cured lepers in the springs below Gellért-hegy. However, it was the Turks who consolidated the habit of bathing (as Muslims, they were obliged to wash five times daily in preparation for prayer) and constructed proper bathhouses which function to this day – though their surroundings and exteriors give little clue to what's inside.

The men-only **Rudas Baths**, in the shadow of Gellért-hegy, harbour a fantastic octagonal pool constructed in 1556 on the orders of Pasha Sokoli Mustapha. Bathers wallow amid shafts of light pouring in from the star-shaped apertures in the domed ceiling, surrounded by stone pillars with iron tie-beams and a nest of smaller pools for parboiling oneself or cooling down; for more details, see p.183.

Walking north from the Rudas Baths, you'll pass the **Drinking Hall** (Ivócsarnok; Mon, Wed & Fri 11am–6pm, Tues & Thurs 7am–2pm), nestling beneath the road to the bridge, which sells inexpensive mineral water from three nearby springs by the tumbler. Regular imbibers bring bottles or jerrycans to fill.

The Rác Baths

Retaining an octagonal stone pool from Turkish times, the **Rác Baths** (Rác Gyógyfürdő) are tucked away beneath Hegyalja út, which leads uphill away from the bridgehead of the Erzsébet híd. At the time of writing, they were closed as part of a major redevelopment, due for completion in 2007, that will turn them into a luxury spa hotel complex. The cuboid **memorial stone** outside the baths commemorates the 51st Esperanto Congress held in Budapest in 1966 – an event that would have been inconceivable in Stalin's day, when Esperanto was forbidden for conflicting with his thesis that the time for an international language had yet to come.

Nearby, on one of the grassy areas that comprise Döbrentei tér, is a seated **statue of Empress Elizabeth** (1837–98), after whom the Erzsébet híd (Elizabeth Bridge) is named. She endeared herself to Hungarians by learning their language and refusing to be stifled by her crusty husband, Franz Josef. Assassinated by an anarchist in Switzerland, she was widely mourned in Hungary and is still fondly known by her nickname, Sissi.

The Semmelweis Medical Museum

Often overlooked by tourists, the **Semmelweis Medical Museum** (Semmelweis Orvostörténeti Múzeum; Tues–Sun: March–Oct 10.30am–6pm, Nov–Feb 10.30am–4pm; ⓦwww.semmelweis.museum.hu; free), at Apród utca 1–3, contains a fascinating collection of artefacts relating to the history of medicine, with mummified limbs from ancient Egypt and a shrunken head used by Borneo witch doctors giving an international dimension to the display. Other exhibits, including a medieval chastity belt, trepanning drills, a lifesize wax model of a dissected female cadaver, and a sewing machine with what looks like a bicycle chain attached, for closing stomach incisions, all give an idea of the centuries of misconceptions and the slow progress of medicine through fatal errors.

Dr Ignác Semmelweis, who lived in this house until he was 5, discovered the cause of puerperal fever – a form of blood poisoning contracted in childbirth, that was usually fatal. While serving in Vienna's public hospitals in the early nineteenth century, he noticed that deaths were ten times lower on the wards where only midwives worked than on the ones attended by doctors and students, who went from dissecting corpses to delivering babies with only a perfunctory wash. His solution was simply to sterilize hands, clothes and instruments between operations, earning him the title "saviour of mothers". The good doctor is buried in the garden.

The museum also contains the 1876 **Holy Ghost Pharmacy**, transplanted here from Király utca, and a collection of portraits, including one of Vilma

Hugonai, Hungary's first woman doctor, and one of Kossuth's sister, Zsuzsanna, who founded the army medical corps during the War of Independence.

Just around the corner is **Szarvas tér** (Stag Square), named after the eighteenth-century *Stag House* inn at no. 1, which functions as a restaurant to this day. In between the museum and the restaurant stands a bust of Dr József Antall, the first democratically elected prime minister of Hungary after the fall of Communism. For many years, while working as the director of the Semmelweis Museum, he had been dreaming of the chance to emerge from the political shadows, and as prime minister he skilfully ran his centre-right coalition to give Hungary a stable start, though his social conservatism was loathed by his opponents. He died in office in 1993.

Past the museum on the riverbank on **Ybl Miklós tér** are two buildings which have had very different fates – both of them designed by Miklós Ybl, the man behind the Opera House and other major works. To the left of the road, the grand facade and terraces of the **Várkert Bazár** stand in deep decay, awaiting a saviour. This was designed as the grand entrance to the Várkert, the park running up to the palace, with shops on either side of the steps. Never recovering from wartime damage, the building is now occupied by a few artists' studios. It's rumoured that the place has been sold to foreign interests for major restoration, though what the place will turn into (yet more luxury flats and shops?) is not known. Some insignificant-looking stones in the gardens behind, which you can get to from Szarvas tér, are actually Turkish gravestones. By the river across the road is the **Várkert Kioszk**, a former pumping station with a highly ornate interior that now hosts a casino, with Ybl's statue standing in front.

8

Óbuda and
Margit sziget

ÓBUDA is the oldest part of Budapest, though that's hardly the impression given by the factories and high-rises that dominate the district today, hiding such ancient ruins as remain. Nonetheless, it was here that the Romans built a legionary camp and a civilian town, later taken over by the Huns. Under the Hungarian Árpád dynasty this developed into an important town, but in the fifteenth century it was eclipsed by Várhegy. The original settlement became known as Óbuda (Old Buda) and was incorporated into the newly formed Budapest in 1873. The small old town centre is as pretty as Várhegy, and has several **museums** worth seeing, but to find the best-preserved Roman ruins you'll have to go to the **Rómaifürdő** district, further out. To the west, there are a pair of interesting **caves** near the valley of Szépvölgy, a visit to which can be combined with the **Kiscelli Museum**, with its interesting collection of furniture and interior furnishings in a former monastery.

In the middle of the Danube northeast of Várhegy and southeast of Óbuda, **MARGIT SZIGET** is a refreshing distance from the noise and pollution of the city centre, but still sufficiently close to feature in its waterfront panorama, and the island is justifiably one of Budapest's most popular parks.

The HÉV provides easy access to riverside Óbuda, while a variety of trams and buses serve Margit sziget. You can also reach both areas on one of the ferries which zigzags up the river from Boráros tér; see p.32 for details.

Óbuda

After its incorporation within the city, **Óbuda** became a popular place to eat, drink and make merry, with dozens of garden restaurants and taverns serving fish and wine from the locality. Some of the most famous establishments still exist around **Fő tér**, the heart of eighteenth-century Óbuda, but, while there's no denying the charm of their Baroque facades and wrought-iron lamps, in many cases they are simply trading on past glories and you'd do better eating elsewhere; see p.162 for our pick of Óbuda's eating places.

There's more to enjoy from a cultural standpoint, with three museums in the vicinity. Directly opposite the Árpád híd HÉV exit at Szentlélek tér 6, the

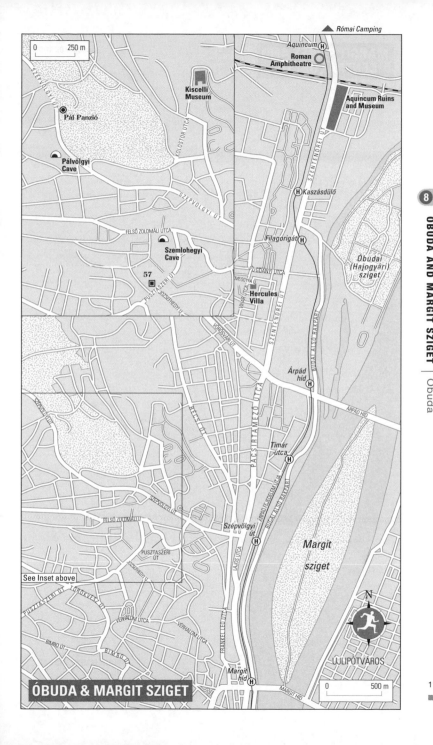

0   250 m

Kiscelli
Museum

Pál Panzió

Pálvölgyi
Cave

KOLOSTOR UTCA

SZÉPVÖLGYI ÚT

FELSŐ ZOLDMÁLI UTCA

Szemlohegyi
Cave

57

PUSZTASZERI ÚT

Aquincum (H)

Roman
Amphitheatre

Aquincum Ruins
and Museum

SZENTENDREI ÚT

(H) Kaszásdűlő

Filagorigát (H)

Óbudai
(Hajogyári)
sziget

PUGDÁNYI UTCA

CMEGYFA U.

VAR UTCA

Hercules
Villa

SZENTENDREI ÚT

BUDAI ALSÓ RAKPART

VÖRÖSVÁRI ÚT

BÉCSI ÚT

PACSIRTAMEZŐ UTCA

Árpád
híd
(H)

ÁRPÁD HÍD

Tímár
utca
(H)

ÁRPÁD FEJEDELEM ÚTJA

BUDAI ALSÓ RAKPART

SZÉPVÖLGYI ÚT

FELSŐ ZOLDMÁLI ÚT

PUSZTASZERI
ÚT

JÓZSEFHEGYI ÚT

See Inset above

Szépvölgyi
út
(H)

LAJOS UTCA

Margit

sziget

SZEMLŐ UTCA

TÖRÖKVÉSZI ÚT

PUSZTASZERI ÚT

VERHALOM UTCA

VERHALOM UTCA

BIMBÓ ÚT

BIMBÓ ÚT

FRANKEL LEO UTCA

N

ÚJLIPÓTVÁROS

Margit
híd
(H)

MARGIT HÍD

ÓBUDA & MARGIT SZIGET

0   500 m

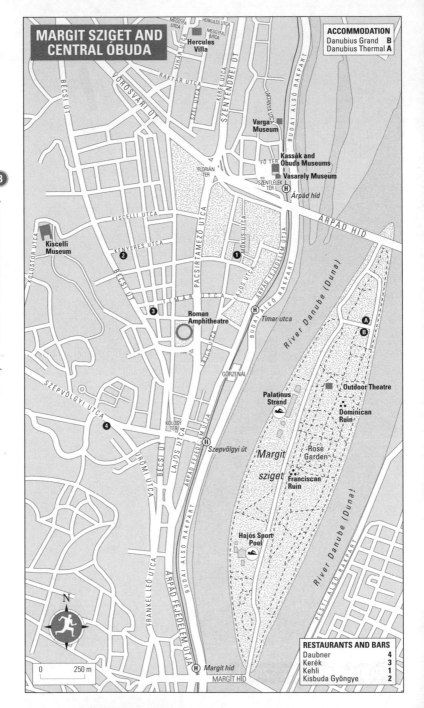

MARGIT SZIGET AND
CENTRAL ÓBUDA

ACCOMMODATION
Danubius Grand **B**
Danubius Thermal **A**

MEGGYFA UTCA
HERKULES UTCA
MEGGYFA UTCA
Hercules
Villa
VIHAR UTCA
RAKTÁR UTCA
SZÉL UTCA
KEREK UTCA
SZENTENDREI ÚT
BUDAI ALSÓ RAKPART
LAJOS UTCA
JACKANYA UTCA

VÖRÖSVÁRI ÚT
BÉCSI ÚT

Varga
Museum

Kassák and
Óbuda Museums
FŐ TÉR
Vasarely Museum
FLÓRIÁN
TÉR
SZENTLÉLEK
TÉR
H *Árpád híd*

ÁRPÁD HÍD

KISCELLI UTCA
PACSIRTAMEZŐ UTCA
ÁRPÁD FEJEDELEM UTJA
BUDAI ALSÓ RAKPART

Kiscelli
Museum
KENYERES UTCA
OLLOSTOR UTCA
2
MÓKUS UTCA
LAJOS UTCA
1

BÉCSI ÚT
MÁRI UTCA
H
River Danube (Duna)
3
Roman
Amphitheatre
LAKTOS UTCA
Tímar utca
A
B

GÖRZENÁL

SZÉPVÖLGYI UTCA

Palatinus
Strand
Outdoor Theatre
Dominican
Ruin

KOLOSY
TÉR
4
H *Szépvölgyi út*
Margit
Rose
Garden
ÚRÖMI UTCA
BÉCSI ÚT
LAJOS UTCA
ÁRPÁD FEJEDELEM UTJA
sziget
Franciscan
Ruin

River Danube (Duna)

Hajós Sport
Pool

N

FRANKEL LEÓ UTCA
ÁRPÁD FEJEDELEM UTJA
BUDAI ALSÓ RAKPART
PESTI ALSÓ RAKPART

0   250 m

H *Margit híd*
MARGIT HÍD

RESTAURANTS AND BARS
Daubner   **4**
Kerék   **3**
Kehli   **1**
Kisbuda Gyöngye   **2**

Vasarely Museum (Tues–Sun 10am–5.30pm; free) displays eyeball-throbbing Op Art works by Viktor Vasarely, one of the founders of the genre, who was born in Pécs in southern Hungary and emigrated to Paris in 1930.

Round on the main square, at no. 1, the Baroque Zichy mansion contains a courtyard seemingly unchanged since Habsburg times, at the far side of which you'll find the small **Kassák Museum** (Tues–Sun 10am–6pm; 150Ft), dedicated to the Hungarian Constructivist Lajos Kassák (1887–1967); featured here is a collection of his paintings, magazine designs and publications, as well as some of his possessions. Kassák was a self-taught artist and publisher who devoted much of his younger life to the socialist cause, publishing work by Cocteau and Le Corbusier. His free avant-garde style had little in common with the postwar Communist regime and he was not allowed to exhibit in his last years.

Back in the courtyard, another door nearby leads into the **Óbuda Museum** (Óbudai Múzeum; Tues–Sun 10am–6pm; 300Ft), a fascinating local history collection with reconstructed living-rooms and workshops, one from the Sváb (German) community on the northern edge of Buda – including a pre-electric washing machine – and one from a good middle-class household where Art Nouveau holds sway. There's also a cute collection of antique toys.

Whatever the weather, you'll see several figures sheltering beneath umbrellas just off Fő tér, life-sized sculptures by Imre Varga; his oeuvre is the subject of the nearby **Varga Museum** at Laktanya utca 7 (Tues–Sun 10am–6pm; 500Ft). While a sense of humour pervades his sheet-metal, iron and bronze effigies of famous personages (including one, now in the Statue Park, of Béla Kun – the leader of the 1919 Communist revolution – addressing a crowd), Varga was also responsible for the sobering Holocaust Memorial in Pest (p.71).

Roman remains

On modern-day Flórián tér, 500m west of Fő tér, graceful columns stand amid a shopping plaza, while the old **military baths** and other finds lurk beneath the Szentendrei út flyover, running off Flórián tér. The largest ruin is the weed-choked, crumbling **amphitheatre** (*amfiteátrum*) at the junction of Pacsirtamező utca and Nagyszombat utca, 800m further south, which once seated up to 16,000 spectators. It can be reached by bus #86 or by walking 400m north from Kolosy tér, near the Szépvölgyi út HÉV stop.

A more elusive relic, however, is fifteen minutes' walk northwest of Flórián tér. Hidden among the blocks of flats at Meggyfa utca 19–21 are the patchy remains of the **Hercules Villa** (Tues–Sun: May–Sept 10am–6pm; late April & Oct 10am–5pm; 100Ft), whose name derives from its third-century AD **mosaic floor**. Originally composed of sixty thousand stones carefully selected and arranged in Alexandria, this depicts the centaur Nessus abducting Deianeira, whom Hercules had to rescue as one of his twelve labours. All that can be seen of it now is a photograph under the largest of the three canopies; the mosaic itself has been moved to the Aquincum Museum up the road (see p.120). The villa was discovered when the neighbouring secondary school was built, and beneath one of the school's walls, the remains of another mosaic, portraying Hercules about to vomit at a wine festival, can still be seen; its best feature is a delightfully rendered tiger.

Rómaifürdő

North of Óbuda, the riverside factory belt merges into the **Rómaifürdő** (Roman Bath) district, a prelude to the leafy suburb of Csillaghegy. Rómaifürdő

△ The Roman ruins at Aquincum

could be ignored but for its **campsite** and **lido** and the ruins of **Aquincum**, which was originally a settlement of camp followers spawned by the legionary garrison. Aquincum eventually became a *municipium* and then a *colonia*, the provincial capital of Pannonia Inferior. The **ruins** of Aquincum (Tues–Sun: May–Sept 9am–6pm; late April & Oct 9am–5pm; 700Ft) are visible from the Aquincum HÉV stop, from where a five-minute walk south under the mainline rail bridge brings you to the site itself. Enough of the foundation walls and underground piping survives to give a fair idea of the layout of Aquincum, with its forum and law courts, its sanctuaries of the goddesses Epona and Fortuna Augusta, and the collegia and bathhouses where fraternal societies met. Its bare bones are given substance by an excellent **museum** (opens at 10am, same ticket) and smaller exhibitions around the site, whose star exhibits are a mummy preserved in natron, a cult-relief of the god Mithras and a reconstructed water-organ.

The caves

In the hills rising to the west are caves that are unique for having been formed by thermal waters rising up from below, rather than by rain water. Two of the sites have been accessible to the public since the 1980s, with guided tours (some English spoken) every hour on the hour, if there are five people. In both cases the starting point is Kolosy tér in Óbuda (accessible by bus #86 from Flórián tér or Batthyány tér, or bus #6 from Nyugati tér in Pest), from where you catch bus #65 five stops to the Pálvölgyi Cave, or bus #29 four stops to the Szemlő-hegyi Cave. As the two caves are ten minutes' walk apart, it's possible to dash from one to the other and catch both tours within two hours, in which case it's worth buying a combined ticket (900Ft).

The **Pálvölgyi Stalactite Cave** (Pálvölgyi cseppkőbarlang; tours hourly Tues–Sun 10am–4pm; 700Ft) at Szépvölgyi út 162 is the more spectacular of the two labyrinths you can visit, and is part of the longest of the cave systems in the Buda Hills; discovered in the 1900s, the Pálvölgyi is still being explored by speleologists. Tours of the stalactites and stalagmites, on which you negotiate hundreds of steps and constricted passages, last about half an hour. The tour starts on the lowest level, which boasts rock formations such as the "Organ Pipes" and "Beehive". From "John's Lookout" in the largest chamber, you ascend a crevice onto the upper level, there to enter "Fairyland" and finally "Paradise", overlooking the hellish "Radium Hall" 50m below.

Quite different is the **Szemlőhegyi Cave** (Szemlőhegyi barlang; tours hourly Mon & Wed–Sun 10am–4pm; 600Ft) at Pusztaszeri út 35, with less convoluted and claustrophic passages and no stalactites. Instead, the walls are encrusted with cauliflower- or popcorn-textured precipitates. Discovered in 1930, the cave has exceptionally clean air, and its lowest level is used as a respiratory sanatorium. After the tour you can view a museum of cave finds and plans from all over Hungary.

For refreshment after the caves you should schedule in a stop at the Daubner patisserie at Szépvölgyi út 29 (close to the bottom of the hill), which does some of the most delicious cakes in the city, and attracts huge queues at weekends. Alternatively, you can combine a visit to the Szemlőhegyi Cave with the Bartok Memorial House (see p.125).

The Kiscelli Museum

On a hillside above Óbuda, fifteen minutes' walk north of the Szemlőhegyi cave, the **Kiscelli Museum** (Tues–Sun: April–Oct 10am–6pm; Nov–March 10am–4pm; 600Ft; ⊛www.btmfk.iif.hu) occupies a former Trinitarian monastery in a beautiful wooded setting at Kiscelli utca 108. The museum's collection includes antique printing presses and the 1830 Biedermeier furnishings of the Golden Lion pharmacy, which used to stand on Kálvin tér. Also on show are carved shop signs, sculptures and graphics by twentieth-century Hungarian artists, and antique furniture exhibited in the blackened shell of the monastery's Gothic church, which makes a dramatic backdrop for operas, performances and fashion shows.

Margit sziget

There's a saying that "love begins and ends on **Margit sziget**", for this verdant island has been a favourite meeting place for lovers since the nineteenth century (though before 1945 a stiff admission charge deterred the poor). A royal game reserve under the Árpáds and a monastic colony until the Turkish conquest, today Margit sziget has two public baths fed by thermal springs, an outdoor theatre and other amenities.

The island was named at the end of the nineteenth century after Princess **Margit** (Margaret), the daughter of Béla IV. Legend has it that he vowed to bring her up as a nun if Hungary survived the Mongol invasion, and duly confined the 9-year-old in a convent when it did. She apparently made the best of it, acquiring a reputation for curing lepers and other saintly deeds, as well as for never washing above her ankles. Beatification came after her death in 1271, and a belated canonization in 1943, by which time her name had already been bestowed on the **Margit híd**, built by a French company in the 1870s. Linking Margit sziget to Buda and Pest, it's an unusual bridge in the form of a splayed-out V, with a short arm joined to the southern tip of the island. In November 1944 it was blown up by the Nazis, killing hundreds of people including the German sappers who had detonated the explosives by mistake. Photos of the result can be seen in the underpass at the Pest end.

The island

There are two entrances to the island, from Árpád híd at the northern end and Margít híd to the south. Trams #4 and #6 stop at the southern entrance to the island, tram #1 stops at the northern entrance and bus #26 runs from Nyugati tér up the island and finishes at the Árpád híd metro (both stations are on the blue metro line). Motorists can only approach from the north of the island, via the Árpád híd, at which point they must leave their vehicles at a paying car park. Near the island entrances you can rent **bikes, pedaloes** and **electric cars** (you should find cheaper ones if you walk further onto the island); they tend to be rather battered, but will get you around the island.

Walking down from the tram stop in the middle of Margít híd, you're greeted by a pointed millennial monument and a huge circular fountain that regularly emits bursts of grand music. On the shore down to the right is a summertime attraction, late-night **open-air bars** such as the *Sark kert* and the *Cha-cha-cha kert*, drawing large crowds. A little further on, behind trees to the left, is the **Hajós Alfréd** swimming pool (known as the "Sport"; daily 6am–6pm; 900Ft), named after the winner of the 100-metre and 1200-metre swimming races at the 1896 Olympics. Hajós was also an architect and designed the indoor pool, but the main attractions here are the all-season outdoor fifty-metre pool and the fresh pastries at the buffet. Another swimming venue, the **Palatinus Strand** (May Mon–Fri 10am–6pm, Sat & Sun 9am–7pm; June–August daily 9am–7pm; 1500Ft), lies nearly a kilometre further north. With a monumental entrance dating from the 1930s, it can hold as many as ten thousand people at a time in numerous open-air thermal pools, complete with a water chute, wave machine and segregated terraces for nude sunbathing.

Off to the east of the road between the two pools are the ruins of a **Franciscan church** from the late thirteenth century, while a ruined **Dominican church and convent** stands in the vicinity of the **Outdoor Theatre** (Szabadtéri Színpad) further north along the main road, which hosts plays, operas, fashion shows and concerts during summer. The café here makes a convenient stop for a beer and a snack, and is easily located by the **water tower** that rises above the complex.

A short way northeast of the tower is a **Premonstratensian Chapel**, whose Romanesque tower dates back to the twelfth century, when the order first established a monastery on the island. The tower's fifteenth-century bell is one of the oldest in Hungary. Two luxury **spa hotels** can be found beyond, across an expanse of lawn: the refurbished fin-de-siècle *Ramada Grand*, with an inviting café and beer terrace, and the modern, less appealing *Thermal*, which replaced the spa damaged during World War II. Beside the latter is a Japanese garden with warm springs that sustain tropical fish and giant water lilies.

The Buda Hills

A densely wooded arc around a sixth of Budapest's circumference, the **BUDA HILLS** are as close to nature as you can get within the city limits. The hills are a favourite place for walking in all seasons, with many trails all marked with the distance or the duration ("ó" stands for hours; "p" for minutes). While some parts can be crowded with walkers and mountain-bikers at the weekend, during the week it's possible to ramble for hours and see hardly a soul. The most rewarding destinations for those with limited time are the "**railway circuit**", using the Cogwheel and Children's railways and the **chairlift**, and the **Bartók Memorial House**. Further south is the **Farkasréti Cemetery**, noted for its architecture as well as the personages buried here.

Moszkva tér is the easiest starting point for all the destinations in the hills: several buses and trams go up to the Cogwheel Railway, and services go to the chairlift and the Farkasréti Cemetery.

The railway circuit

This is an easy and enjoyable way to visit the hills that will especially appeal to kids. The whole trip can take under two hours if connections click, or a half-day if you prefer to take your time. You begin at the lower terminal of the **Cogwheel Railway** (Fogaskerekűvasút), which is two stops from Moszkva tér on tram #18 or #56 or bus #22, #56 and others heading up Szilágyi Erzsébet fasor; alight opposite the cylindrical *Budapest Hotel*, which is beside the terminal. The train was the third such railway in the world when it was inaugurated in 1874, and was steam-powered until its electrification in 1929. Grinding its way along, it runs every ten minutes or so (daily 5am–11pm; BKV fares apply, and BKV passes are valid), its cogs fitting into a notched track, to climb 300m over 3km through the villa-suburb of **Svábhegy**; for the best view, take a window seat on the right-hand side, facing backwards.

From the upper terminal on **Széchenyi-hegy**, it's a minute's walk to the **Children's Railway** (Gyermekvasút). A narrow-gauge line built by youth brigades in 1948, it's almost entirely run by 13- to 17-year-old members of the Scouts and Guides movement, enabling them to get hands-on experience if they fancy a career with MÁV, the Hungarian Railways company. Watching them wave flags, collect tickets and salute departures with great solemnity, you can see why it appealed to the Communists. Trains depart for the 11km, 45-minute journey to Hűvösvölgy every 45–60 minutes (Tues–Sun 9am–5pm, June–Aug also Mon; 250Ft).

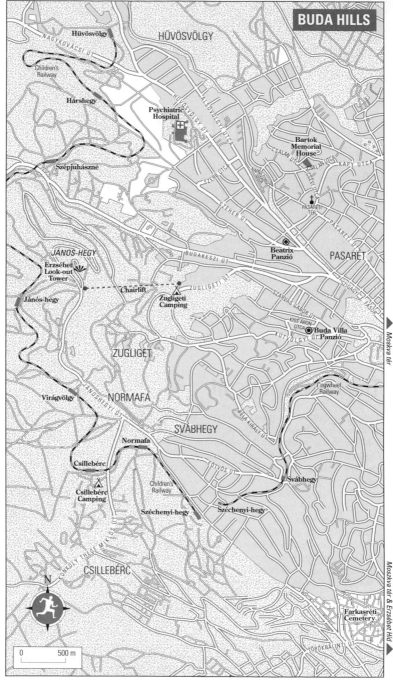

HÜVÖSVÖLGY

Hüvösvölgy

NAGYKOVÁCSI ÚT

Children's
Railway

Hárshegy

Psychiatric
Hospital

Bartok
Memorial
House

CSALÁN ÚT   KÁPY UTCA

CSALÁN UTCA

Szépjuhászné

SZERB UTCA

NAPHEGY

SZEHER ÚT

PASARÉTI
TÉR

PASARÉTI ÚT

JÁNOS-HEGY

Erzsébet
Look-out
Tower

BUDAKESZI ÚT

Beatrix
Panzió

PASARÉT

Chairlift

János-hegy

ZUGLIGETI ÚT

Zugligeti
Camping

SZARVAS GÁBOR ÚT

SZIGLIGET FASOR

KISS ÁRON
UTCA   Buda Villa
Panzió

KÚTVÖLGYI ÚT

ZUGLIGET

Virágvölgy

JÁNOSHEGYI ÚT

NORMAFA

SVÁBHEGY

BÉLA KIRÁLY ÚT

Cogwheel
Railway

Normafa

EÖTVÖS ÚT

Csillebérc

Csillebérc
Camping

Children's
Railway

Svábhegy

TÖRÖK TESE MIKLÓS ÚT

Széchenyi-hegy

Széchenyi-hegy

Moszkva tér

Moszkva tér & Erzsébet Híd

CSILLEBÉRC

N

Farkasréti
Cemetery

TÖRÖKBÁLINT

0   500 m

The first stop, **Normafa** (more quickly reached on bus #21 from Moszkva tér), is a popular excursion centre with a modest **ski-run**. Its name comes from a performance of the famous aria from Bellini's *Norma* given here by the actress Rozália Klein in 1840. Across the road, the humble *Rétes büfé* serves delicious strudel and coffee every day of the year including holidays.

Alighting at **János-hegy**, three stops on, you can either strike out down through woods to the town of **Budakeszi**, from where bus #22 takes you back to Moszkva tér, or make the fifteen-minute climb from the station to the top of **János-hegy** (527m), the highest point in Budapest. The **Erzsébet lookout tower** on the summit offers a panoramic view of the city and the Buda Hills. By the buffet below the summit is the upper terminal of the **chairlift** or Libegő, meaning "floater" in Hungarian (May–Sept 9.30am–5pm; Oct–April 9.30am–4pm; closed every other Mon; 450Ft), which takes you down to **Zugliget**, from where #158 buses return to Moszkva tér.

Wild boar, which prefer to roam during the evening and sleep by day, are occasionally sighted in the forests above **Hárshegy**, one stop before the terminus at Hűvösvölgy. **Hűvösvölgy** (Cool Valley), also linked directly to Moszkva tér by #56 and #56E buses, is a rapidly expanding suburb spreading out into the hills and valleys beyond.

The Bartók Memorial House and Napraforgó utca

The **Bartók Memorial House** (Bartók Béla Emlékház; Tues–Sun 10am–5pm; 500Ft; @www.bartokmuseum.hu) at Csalán utca 29, in a leafy suburb below Látó-hegy, was the residence of Béla Bartók, his wife and two sons from 1932 until their emigration to America in 1940, by which time Bartók despaired of Hungary's right-wing regime. It can be reached by taking bus #29 from the Szemlőhegyi Cave to the Nagybányai út stop, which leads to Csalán utca, or bus #5 from Március 15 tér in Pest or Moszkva tér to the Pasaréti tér terminus, and then a ten-minute walk uphill (take the first left along Csévi utca).

The museum has an extensive range of Bartók memorabilia, including some of his original furniture and possessions; displays may include such items as the folk handicrafts he collected during his ethno-musical research trips to Transylvania with Zoltán Kodály, and the shirt cuff on which Bartók wiped his pennibs when composing scores. The villa was closed in 2005 for major renovation, and should be open by the time you read this. Chamber music **concerts** are held here from September until May (@1/394 2100 for information).

Before you return to Moszkva tér, it's worth a brief detour to see the delightful **Napraforgó utca housing estate**, built in 1931. Its 22 houses – designed by as many architects – embody different trends in Modernist architecture, from severe Bauhaus to folksy Arts and Crafts-style. The estate is signposted from **Pasaréti tér**, near the #5 bus terminus; follow Pasaréti út till you reach a playing field and cross the bridge on the left. For refreshment afterwards, head for the café in the listed 1930s **bus shelter** on Pasaréti tér. The shelter's curving horizontal form contrasts with slender vertical lines of the Franciscan church of Szent Antal across the road – both were designed the architect Géza Rimanóczy as a single project for the square.

Farkasréti Cemetery

Two kilometres west of Gellért-hegy in the hilly XI district is the **Farkasréti Cemetery** (Farkasréti temető; Mon–Fri 7am–9pm, Sat & Sun 9am–5pm; free), easily reached by riding tram #59 from Moszkva tér to the penultimate stop or by catching bus #8 from Március 15 tér in Pest – the mass of flower stalls and stone mason workshops indicate when you've arrived. Of the many poets, writers and musicians buried in the "Wolf's Meadow Cemetery", the best known is **Béla Bartók**, whose remains were ceremonially reinterred in 1988 following their return from America, where the composer died in exile in 1945. His will forbade reburial in Hungary so long as there were streets named after Hitler or Mussolini, and the return of his body was delayed for decades to prevent the Communists from capitalizing on the event. In 1998 the Hungarian-born conductor **Sir Georg Solti** was buried alongside Bartók, having forged a career abroad since he left Hungary in 1939 to meet Toscanini and thus escape the fate of his Jewish parents. The cemetery also contains the grave of **Mátyás Rákosi**, Hungary's Stalinist dictator, who died in exile in the USSR, as well as many wooden grave markers inscribed in the ancient runic Székely alphabet.

However, the real attraction is the amazing **mortuary chapel** by Imre Makovecz – one of his finest designs – whose wood-ribbed vault resembles the throat and belly of a beast. Be discreet, however, for the chapel is in constant use by mourners. Visitors keen to see more of Makovecz's work could pay a visit to Visegrád (p.139), an hour's journey north of the capital.

The city limits

W hile the centre of Budapest is hardly short of attractions, it would be a shame to overlook some of the ones further out towards or just beyond the city limits. In Pest, the **Railway History Park** – where visitors can drive steam trains – is popular with Hungarian tourists, while the **New Public Cemetery** completes the roll-call of illustrious Hungarian dead begun at Kerepesi. In Buda, the **Statue Park**, with its exiled Communist memorials, is the prime outlying destination for foreigners; the **Nagytétényi Castle Museum** is strictly for lovers of antique furniture or stately homes. You can reach any of them from the city centre within an hour.

Railway History Park

One of the best sights further out in Pest is the **Hungarian Railway History Park**, sometimes called the Hungarian Railway Museum (Magyar Vasúttörténeti Park; Tues–Sun: April–Oct 10am–6pm; Nov–March 10am–3pm; 900Ft, family 1800Ft, cameras 200Ft, videocameras 800Ft; ⓦwww.lokopark .hu), in the freight yards of the XVI district. Its sheds and sidings house over seventy kinds of locomotives and carriages from 1900 onwards, and between April and October (10am–4pm) you can even **drive** a steam train (1000Ft) or a luggage cart (300Ft) – wear old clothes. Many of the staff are ex-employees of MÁV (Hungarian State Railways), proud of a tradition inherited from the Royal Hungarian Railways. After the thrill of the engines, the museum above the information centre is less impressive, with displays labelled in Hungarian only, and similarly the books, videos and MÁV souvenirs in the shop on the ground floor are disappointing.

From April to October, the ticket price includes travel to the museum **by special train** (*különvonat*) from Nyugati Station (9.45am, 10.45am, 1.45pm & 3.45pm); since this means travelling in an old diesel-powered car, it will appeal more to enthusiasts who don't mind being choked by the fumes for half an hour or more. Tickets are available from the MÁV Nosztalgia office next to platform 10 in the station. Otherwise, the park gates at Tatai út 95 are a short walk from the Rokolya utca stop, which is a longish ride by bus #30 from Keleti Station or Hősök tere.

New Public Cemetery

The **New Public Cemetery** (Új köztemető; daily 8am–dusk; free; tram #28 or #37 from Népszínház utca near Blaha Lujza tér) is located in the X district beyond the breweries of Kőbánya, near the end of one of the longest tram rides in Budapest. It's the largest cemetery in Budapest, reflecting the city's growth in the latter half of the nineteenth century. Its significance lies in the fact that it was here that Imre Nagy and 260 others, executed for their part in the Uprising, were secretly buried in unmarked graves in 1958. Any flowers left at **Plot 301** were removed by the police until 1989, when the deceased received a state funeral on Hősök tere. The plot is 2km from the main gates on Kozma utca; minibuses shuttle back and forth every twenty minutes. Near the graves, an ornate wooden gateway and headposts mark a mass grave now designated as a **National Pantheon** – as opposed to the Communist pantheon in Kerepesi (see p.88).

In the adjacent **Jewish cemetery** (Mon–Fri & Sun 8am–2pm), where famous rabbis and Ernő Szép (author of *The Smell of Humans*, a powerful memoir of the Holocaust) are buried, the finest tomb is that of **Sándor Schmidl**, with a magnificent blue Art Nouveau tiled design by Lechner and Lajta. The gates to the Jewish cemetery are 700m up the road from the New Public Cemetery; tram #37 runs past.

Statue Park

Easily the most popular site on the outskirts, the **Statue Park** (Szoborpark; daily 10am–dusk; 600Ft; ☎1/424 7500, ⊛www.szoborpark.hu) brings together 42 of the monuments that once glorified Communist Budapest. The park is situated way out beside Balatoni út in the XXII District, 15km to the southwest of the city centre; getting there involves taking a red-numbered bus #7-173 from Ferenciek tere to Etele tér, and then a yellow Volán bus from stand 7 or 8 towards Diósd, which takes twenty minutes to reach the park. More expensive but simpler is the special Statue Park bus that leaves from in front of *Le Meridien* hotel by Deák tér at 11am daily throughout the year, with an additional service at 3pm in July and August (2450Ft including entry to the park – tickets from the Volánbusz ticket office across the road from the *Meridien*).

The Statue Park's outsized gate is clearly visible from the highway, its bogus Classical facade framing giant statues of Lenin, Marx and Engels. Lenin's once stood beside the Városliget, while Marx's and Engels' are carved from granite quarried at Mauthausen, a Nazi concentration camp in Austria, later used by the Soviets. Inside the grounds you'll encounter the Red Army soldier that guarded the foot of the Liberation Monument on Gellért-hegy, and dozens of other statues and memorials, large and small. Here are prewar Hungarian Communists like Béla Kun (secretly shot in Moscow on Stalin's orders) and Jenő Landler (afforded a place in the Kremlin Wall); Dimitrov, hero of the Comintern; and the Lenin statue from outside the Csepel ironworks. Artistically, the best statues are the **Republic of Councils Monument** – a giant charging sailor based on a 1919 revolutionary poster – and Imre Varga's **Béla Kun Memorial**, with Kun on a tribune surrounded by a surging crowd of workers and soldiers (plus a bystander with an umbrella).

Budapestis fondly remember the statue of Captain Ostapenko, which once stood on the highway to Vienna, where hitch-hikers would arrange to meet their friends (a locality still known as "Ostapenko"), while the decision to move to the park the monument commemorating the Hungarian contingent of the International Brigade in the Spanish Civil War (three robotic figures with fists clenched to their heads) provoked a heartfelt debate that few of the others engendered.

Among the **souvenirs** on sale by the entrance are small Lenin and Stalin candles, cans of air from "the last breath of socialism", and selections of revolutionary songs, which can be heard playing from a 1950s' radio set. There's also an informative English-language brochure (600Ft).

Nagytétényi Castle Museum

Reaching the **Nagytétényi Castle Museum** (Nagytétényi Kastélymúzeum; Tues–Sun 10am–6pm; free, 400Ft for temporary displays; cameras 400Ft, video-cameras 1000Ft; @www.nagytetenyi.hu) involves a lengthy journey by bus #3 from Móricz Zsigmond körtér (30–45min). Get off at the Petőfi utca stop in the XXII district, cross the road and follow Hugonnay utca down past the children's playground to the *kastély*. Though rendered as "castle" in English, "*kastély*" generally signifies a manor house or chateau without fortifications, which Hungarian nobles began building after the Turks had been expelled – in this case by converting an older, ruined castle into a Baroque residence. Nowadays, its 28 rooms on two floors display furniture from the Gothic to the Biedermeier epochs, owned by the Applied Arts Museum; the most outstanding exhibit is a walnut-veneered refectory from Trencsen Monastery. In July and August, **historical dances** and **concerts** are held in the grounds (☎1/207-0005 for details).

Excursions from Budapest

The attractions covered in this chapter are all within an hour or so of Budapest, and appear on the "Budapest and around" map at the end of this book. Foremost among them are the sites on the picturesque **Danube Bend**: the artists' colony and historic Serbian settlement of **Szentendre**; the cathedral town of **Esztergom**, where the Danube forms the border between Hungary and Slovakia; and the medieval ruins at **Visegrád** – but don't overlook the former Habsburg palace at **Gödöllő**.

You can get to Szentendre and Gödöllő on the **HÉV**, though note that for travel beyond the city limits, you must punch additional tickets according to the distance travelled. Alternatively, you can purchase a ticket that covers the whole journey at a station ticket office or from the conductor on board. Another option is to use one of the Danube **boats**, which sail from Vigadó tér in Budapest between April and September; two go daily to Szentendre, one of them nonstop, and one goes daily to Visegrád and Esztergom. From May to September there are also steam trains to Esztergom and Nagymaros (a ferry ride from Viségrad) on alternate Saturdays; check wwww.mavnosztalgia .hu for more. For details of buses and trains to Esztergom and Visegrád, see the respective accounts.

Szentendre

SZENTENDRE (St Andrew), 20km north of Budapest, is the most popular tourist destination in the vicinity of the capital and the easiest to reach. Despite a rash of souvenir shops, the centre remains a delightful maze of houses in autumnal colours, with secretive gardens and lanes winding up to hilltop churches. Szentendre's location on the lower slopes of the **Pilis range** is not only beautiful, but ensures that it is one of the sunniest places in Hungary, making it a perfect spot for an artists' colony – though most of the artists there today seem to be turning out tourist tat.

Before the artists moved in, Szentendre's character had been forged by waves of refugees from Serbia. The first followed the catastrophic Serb defeat at Kosovo in 1389; the second, the Turkish recapture of Belgrade in 1690, causing

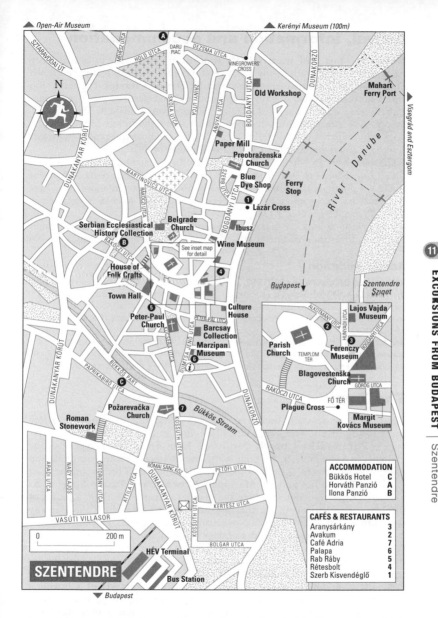

N

Old Workshop

Mahart Ferry Port

Paper Mill

Preobraženska Church

Blue Dye Shop

Ferry Stop

Lázár Cross

Serbian Ecclesiastical History Collection

Belgrade Church

Ibusz

Wine Museum

House of Folk Crafts

Town Hall

Culture House

Peter-Paul Church

Barcsay Collection

Marzipan Museum

River Danube

Budapest

Szentendre Sziget

Lajos Vajda Museum

Parish Church

Ferenczy Museum

Blagovestenška Church

Plague Cross

Margit Kovács Museum

Požarevačka Church

Café Adria

Bükkös Stream

Roman Stonework

ACCOMMODATION
Bükkös Hotel	C
Horváth Panzió	A
Ilona Panzió	B

CAFÉS & RESTAURANTS
Aranysárkány	3
Avakum	2
Café Adria	7
Palapa	6
Rab Ráby	5
Rétesbolt	4
Szerb Kisvendéglő	1

HÉV Terminal

SZENTENDRE

Bus Station

30,000 Serbs and Bosnians to flee. Six thousand settled in Szentendre, which became the seat of the Serbian Church in exile. Prospering through trade, they replaced their wooden churches with stone ones and built handsome town houses, but as Habsburg toleration waned and phylloxera (vine-blight) and floods ruined the local economy they trickled back to Serbia, so that by 1890 less than a quarter of the population was Serb. About seventy families of Serbian descent remain today.

Arrival, information and accommodation

Szentendre's **bus and train (HÉV) stations** are next door to one another, ten minutes' walk south of the town centre. Local buses run to the centre via Dunakanyar körút. There are three docks for **Danube ferries**. The ferry stop 100m north of the Lázár Cross is for nonstop Budapest services that feature a pretty dire commentary (1400Ft; 1hr 30min from Budapest, 55min back). Stopping boats to and from Budapest, which take only slightly longer, use the dock 600m further north (900Ft). The dock for the boat to Szentendrei sziget is located 200m north of the Lázár Cross (hourly; 140Ft).

The busy but very helpful **Tourinform** office is at Dumsta Jenő utca 22 (June–Aug Mon–Fri 9am–7pm, Sat & Sun 9am–6pm; Sept–May Mon–Sat 9.30am–4.30pm, Sun 10am–2pm; ☎26/317-965, ⊛www.szentendre.hu). There is a currency exchange machine on Fő tér. **Internet access** is available at Game Planet, Petőfi utca 1 (daily 10am–10pm).

If you want to **stay** the night in Szentendre, you'll find plenty of "Zimmer frei" signs advertising vacancies, as well as several hotels and pensions.

Accommodation

Bükkös Hotel Bükkös part 16 ☎26/312-021, ℗310-782. Comfy rooms with TV, phone and minibar, in an idyllic location by a stream lined with weeping willows. Rooms from 11,600Ft.

Horváth Panzió Daru piac 2 ☎ & ℗26/313-950, ⊛www.option.hu/horvath. Small pension in the quieter, northern part of the old town,

with its own small bar. The en-suite double rooms are furnished with traditional folk crafts. Doubles from 9000Ft.

Ilona Panzió Rákóczi utca 11 ☎ & ℗26/313-599. Ideally located pension, tucked away a couple of minutes' walk from the centre of town, with a breakfast terrace. Rooms – on the small side – start at around 9000Ft.

The Town

Heading along Kossuth utca from the HÉV and bus stations, just before the Bükkos stream, you'll encounter the first evidence of a Serbian presence – **Požarevačka Church** (Sat & Sun 11am–5pm; 200Ft). Typical of the churches in Szentendre, it was built in the late eighteenth century to replace an older wooden structure. Beyond the stream, Dumtsa Jenő utca continues past the Tourinform office and the **Marzipan Museum and Pastry Shop** at no. 12 (daily 9am–7pm; 350Ft), where the marzipan creations include a model of the Hungarian Parliament. Further up the street on the right is the **Barcsay Collection** (Tues–Sun: March–Nov 10am–6pm; Dec–Feb 1–5pm; 400Ft), a museum housing drawings and paintings by Jenő Barcsay (1900–88), whose dark prewar canvases give way to more abstract works after the war, avoiding the strictures of the regime. His anatomical drawings at the end of the display confirm his skill as a draughtsman. A little further on, the road is crossed by Péter-Pál utca, where a left turn brings you to the **Peter–Paul Church**, a yellow and white Baroque church built in 1708. Its original furnishings were taken back to Serbia after World War I, and the church is now Roman Catholic. Organ recitals take place at the church regularly; ask at Tourinform for details. From here, or from the last uphill stretch of Dumtsa Jenő utca, it's just a block to the main square.

Around Fő tér

Beyond the church, **Fő tér** swarms with tourists and horse-drawn carriages, with diverging streets and alleys leading to various galleries and museums. At the centre of the square stands the **Plague Cross**, its triangular marble base decorated by icons, which was erected by the merchants' guild after Szentendre escaped infection in 1763. From here, diverging streets and alleys lead to an assortment of galleries and museums around the square, as well as to the many tourist shops, especially down Bogdányi utca.

On the north side of the square is the Church of the Annunciation, or **Blagoveštenska Church** (Tues–Sun 10am–5pm; 200Ft), the most accessible of the Orthodox churches in the town. Painted by Mihailo Zivkovia (1776–1824) of Buda in the early eighteenth century, the church's icons evoke all the richness and tragedy of Serbian history. Look out for the tomb of a Greek merchant of Macedonian origin to the left of the entrance, and the rococo windows and gate facing Görög utca.

Next door, a portal carved with emblems of science and learning provides the entrance to a former Serbian school, now the **Ferenczy Museum** (Tues–Sun: March–Nov 10am–6pm; Dec–Feb 9am–5pm; 400Ft). It exhibits paintings by the Impressionist Károly Ferenczy, and by his eldest son Valér and younger twins Nóemi and Béni, who branched out into Expressionism, textiles and bronzeware.

Down a sidestreet from the church, at Vastagh György utca 1, is by far the most popular of the town's galleries, the **Margit Kovács museum** (daily: March–Nov 10am–6pm, Fri–Sun open till 8pm; Dec–Feb 9am–5pm; 600Ft; ticket also gets you in free to one other museum in town). This is a wonderful collection that never fails to delight, the themes of legends, dreams, religion, love and motherhood giving Kovács' graceful sculptures and reliefs universal appeal. Her expressive statues with their big eyes aren't particularly well known abroad, but in Hungary, Kovács, who died in 1977, is honoured as the nation's greatest ceramicist and sculptor.

North of Fő tér

Back on Fő tér you can ascend an alley of steps to gain a lovely view of Szentendre's rooftops and gardens from **Templom tér**, where **craft fairs** are frequently held to help finance the restoration of the Catholic **parish church**. Of medieval origin, with Romanesque and Gothic features, it was rebuilt in the Baroque style after falling derelict in Turkish times. The frescoes in its sanctuary were collectively painted by the town's artists' colony.

North of Templom tér, the burgundy spire of the Orthodox episcopal cathedral or **Belgrade Church** (April–Oct daily 10am–5pm; 400Ft) rises above a walled garden on Alkotmány utca. The entrance to the grounds is from the corner of Alkotmány utca and Pátriárka utca. Built during the late eighteenth century, it has a lavishly ornamented interior with icons depicting scenes from the New Testament and saints of the Orthodox Church. The old tombstones with Cyrillic inscriptions in the churchyard bear witness to a tale of demographic decline, echoed by the **Serbian Ecclesiastical History Collection** (mid-March to Oct Wed–Sun 10am–4pm; Nov to mid-March Fri–Sun same hours; 200Ft) in the episcopal palace (April–Oct Wed–Sun 10am–5pm; 400Ft), whose outstanding hoard of icons, vestments and crosses comes from churches in Hungary that fell empty after the Serbs returned to the Balkans and the last remaining parishioners died out.

From the Belgrade Church you can follow Alkotmány utca back down towards the main square. Just before you get there, you pass two more museums hiding in Hunyadi utca on your left. The **Lajos Vajda Museum** at no. 1 (Tues–Sun: March–Nov 10am–6pm; Dec–Feb 1–5pm; 400Ft) commemorates the work of a Szentendre painter who died in the Holocaust. Vajda's early work reveals Cubist and constructivist influences, while his later charcoal works seem to foretell the approaching torment. Although the museum is housed in a wealthy bourgeois villa, the artist himself was poor – as you can see from the materials he worked with. Downstairs is an excellent display of works by artists of the "European School", including Bálint Endre and Jenő Barcsay. This group formed after the war but was quickly stopped by the Communists.

Bogdányi utca, leading northeast from Fő tér, is packed with stalls attended by shop assistants dressed up in folk gear. The **Wine Museum** at no. 10 (daily 10am–10pm; 100Ft, plus 1600Ft for wine tasting) is really there to lure people into the *Labirintus* restaurant, but otherwise does a fair job of describing Hungary's wine-making regions using maps, wine-bottle labels and other artefacts.

A little further along, Bogdányi utca opens onto a square, at the far corner of which stands the small iron **Lázár Cross**, easy to miss behind the parked cars here. It honours King Lázár of Serbia, whom the Turks beheaded after the battle of Kosovo in revenge for the death of Sultan Murad. His body was brought here by the Serbs and buried in a wooden church. When the relic was taken back to Serbia in 1774, the place was marked by a cross in his memory. Horse-drawn carriages can be rented here (and along Dunakorzó) between March and October for trips round the town; prices start at 1500Ft per person for half an hour, though it's possible to bargain them down. Further on, the Kovács **Blue Dye Shop** at no. 36 showcases a traditional style of folk dyeing that was once popular with ethnic Germans and is now fashionable with Hungarians. The **Preobraženska Church**, a few steps further along Bogdányi utca, was erected by the tanners' guild in 1741–76, and its stoutness enhanced by a Louis XVI gate the following century. The church is chiefly notable for its role in the Serbian festival on August 19, when it hosts the Blessing of the Grapes ceremony, recalling Szentendre's former role as a wine-producing centre. This is followed by a traditional procession round the church and further celebrations in the town square and elsewhere.

At the far end of Bogdányi utca, five minutes' walk further on, is another cross, the **Vinegrowers' Cross**, raised by a local guild and fittingly wreathed in grapevines.

The Village Museum

The fantastic **Szentendre Village Museum** (Szabadtéri Néprajzi Múzeum; March–Oct Tues–Sun 9am–5pm; Tues–Fri 600Ft, weekends 800Ft, festivals 1200Ft; ☎26/502-500, @www.skanzen.hu) is easily the most enjoyable local attraction. Hungary's largest open-air museum of rural architecture (termed a *skanzen*, after the first such museum, founded in a Stockholm suburb in 1891) is sited in rolling countryside 4km west of town, beside Sztaravodai út, and can be reached by buses from stand 7 of the bus terminal near the HÉV station, though they're quite infrequent after noon. Get off when you see the spires in a field to the right, and you'll find the entrance 100m off the road. You can buy an excellent **book** on the contents of the museum at the entrance, which guides you round building by building, and has maps both of the museum and of the villages.

It takes at least two hours to tour the naturalistic village ensembles transported here from five ethnographic regions of Hungary. Each building has its warden who can explain everything in great detail, though usually only in Hungarian. Downhill to the right from the entrance, a village from the backward **Upper Tisza** region reveals that the homes of the poorest squires were barely superior to those of their tenants, yet rural carpenters produced highly skilled work,

△ Folk craft displays at the Szentendre Village Museum

such as the circular "dry mill", the wooden bell tower, and the Greek Catholic church (on a hilltop beyond).

As you walk up past the Calvinist graveyard, where the grave markers from four villages include striking boat-shaped markers from eastern Hungary, signs point you to the remains of the third-century Roman village, and on to the **Western Transdanubia** section. Here there's a school with its old benches with slates for writing on, a towel and basin for washing, and behind the door are children's little home-spun bags. By contrast, the next section, originating from the ethnic German communities of the Kisalföld (Little Plain) in **Northwest Transdanubia**, seems far more regimented. Neatly aligned and whitewashed, the houses are filled with knick-knacks and embroidered samplers bearing homilies like "When the Hausfrau is capable, the clocks keep good time". The next region, still under construction at the time of writing, is **The Great Hungarian Plain**. The house from Süsköd has a beautiful facade, with the visitors' room or "clean room" laid out for Christmas celebrations with a nativity crib and a church-shaped box. In the fields stands a windmill, built in 1888 and with its sails still operating. The **Bakony and Balaton-Uplands** section, located near the hilly part of the museum to the north, has perhaps the most interesting constructions, including a fire station, a working watermill and a Catholic church.

Demonstrations of folk dancing and traditional crafts such as weaving, pottery and basket-making take place at the museum most Sundays as well as on public holidays; check at the museum or at the Tourinform office for precise dates of events. Local **festivals** are also celebrated here, such as the wine festival in September, when folkloric programmes and grape-pressing take place. The huge *Jászárokszállás* **restaurant** (daily 10am–10pm) inside the museum serves up dishes and wines from the various regions.

Eating and drinking

Like most things in Szentendre, **restaurants** tend to be pricey by Hungarian standards, and crowded during the summer. Tour groups tend to make for the ones on Fő tér, but there are more agreeable alternatives away from the main square. Likewise, there are some choice **drinking** options on the fringes of the centre. *Café Adria* at Kossuth utca 4 (daily 10am–10pm) is a lovely Balkan themed café by the Bükkös stream, while *Avakum*, a cool cellar café at Alkotmány utca 14 (daily 8am–10pm) is a good place to escape the heat and enjoy a refreshing cup of tea or glass of wine.

Restaurants

Aranysárkány Alkotmány utca 1a
☎26/3110670. The "Golden Dragon", a minute's walk up from Fő tér, is a smart Hungarian restaurant with air-conditioning – useful as it's got an open kitchen. One of the pricier options in town. Booking is advisable. Daily noon–10pm.

Palapa Dumsta Jenő utca 14a. Brilliant Mexican restaurant/bar with quality food and unusually attentive service. Add to this regular live music in the courtyard and some fine cocktails and you've got the most enjoyable place to eat in town. Arrive early to bag a table. Daily 11am–midnight.

Rab Ráby Kucsera utca 1a. This old restaurant is similar to the *Aranysárkány* but more traditionally Hungarian in style and a touch cheaper. Daily noon–11pm.

Rétesbolt Bercsényi utca. Snack-type place with pizzas, hot dogs and delicious strudels. Daily 9am–6pm.

Szerb Kisvendéglő Dunakorzó 4. Serbian restaurant with typically meaty and filling dishes such as *pljeskavica* and *cevapi,* lamb and beef burgers and meatballs served in thick soft pittas. Daily 10am–midnight.

Visegrád

As you approach **VISEGRÁD**, 23km north of Szentendre, from the south, the hillsides start to plunge and the river twists shortly before you first catch sight of the citadel and ramparts of the ancient fortified site whose Slavic name means "High Castle". The view hasn't changed much since 1488, when János Thuroczy described its "upper walls stretching to the clouds floating in the sky, and the lower bastions reaching down as far as the river". At that time, courtly life in Visegrád was nearing its apogee and the palace of King Mátyás and Queen Beatrice was famed throughout Europe. The papal legate Cardinal Castelli described it as a "paradiso terrestri", seemingly unperturbed by the presence of Vlad the Impaler, who resided here under duress between 1462 and 1475. Today, Visegrád is a mere village, with most local activity centred on the ferry and the church. The three main **historical sites** all lie north of the centre: the Royal Palace and Solomon's Tower down near the river, and the citadel perching on top of the hill above. All the river sites are within easy walking distance, but you might prefer taking a bus up to the citadel.

The main event in town each year (usually during the second weekend in July) is the **International Palace Games**, a series of rousing medieval pageants with jousting and archery tournaments, craft workshops and considerable amounts of eating and drinking, most of which takes place within the grounds of the Royal Palace. For more information, contact Tourinform in Szentendre (see p.132).

The Town

The **layout** of the ruins dates back to the thirteenth century, when Béla IV began fortifying the north against a recurrence of the Mongol invasion, while the construction of a royal palace below the hilltop citadel was a sign of greater security during the reign of the Angevins. However, its magnificence was effaced by the Turkish conquest, and later mud washing down from the hillside gradually buried the palace entirely. Later generations doubted its existence until the archeologist János Schulek unearthed one of the vaults in 1934, at Fő utca 23. While at a New Year's Eve party, after he had been in Visegrád for some time hunting for the lost palace without success, the wine ran out and Schulek was sent to get some more from the neighbours. An old woman told him to go down to the wine cellar, and there he found clues in the stones that convinced him the palace was here.

Now largely excavated and tastefully reconstructed, the **Royal Palace** spreads over four levels or terraces at Fő utca 27–29 (Tues–Sun 9am–5pm; free), ten minutes' walk from the centre. Founded in 1323 by the Angevin king Charles Robert, it was the setting for the Visegrád Congress of 1335, attended by the monarchs of Central Europe and the Grandmaster of the Teutonic Knights. Although nothing remains of this palace, the **Court of Honour** constructed for his successor Louis, which provided the basis for additions by kings Sigismund and Mátyás, is still to be seen on the second terrace. A pilastered **Renaissance loggia** surrounds a replica of the famous **Hercules Fountain**, which cools the tiled, gilded uppermost storey, overlooking the court. Other, cross-vaulted chambers have been reconstructed, and on the third terrace, where Mátyás and Beatrice resided, stands a copy of the **Lion Fountain**, bearing his raven crest and surrounded by dozens of sleepy-looking lions.

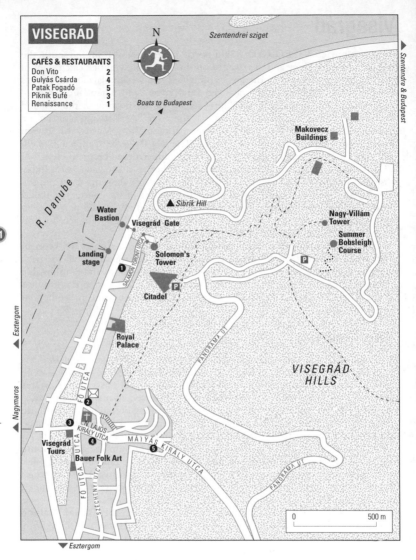

VISEGRÁD

N

Szentendrei sziget

Szentendre & Budapest

CAFÉS & RESTAURANTS	
Don Vito	2
Gulyás Csárda	4
Patak Fogadó	5
Piknik Bufé	3
Renaissance	1

Boats to Budapest

R. Danube

Makovecz Buildings

▲ *Sibrik Hill*

Water Bastion

Visegrád Gate

Nagy-Villám Tower

Summer Bobsleigh Course

Landing stage

Solomon's Tower

Citadel

Royal Palace

VISEGRÁD HILLS

◄ *Esztergom*

◄ *Nagymaros*

FŐ UTCA

SALAMON TORONY UTCA

PANORÁMA ÚT

SZT. LAJOS KIRÁLY UTCA

MÁTYÁS KIRÁLY UTCA

Visegrád Tours

Bauer Folk Art

FŐ UTCA

SZÉCHENYI UTCA

PANORÁMA ÚT

0   500 m

▼ *Esztergom*

11

Five minutes' walk north along Fő utca, just after it rejoins the main highway, you can take a right onto Salamon torony utca, which climbs up through the gate of the old castle fortifications to reach **Solomon's Tower** (Tues–Sun 9am–4.30pm; free). Named after an eleventh-century Hungarian king, this mighty hexagonal keep is buttressed on two sides by unsightly concrete slabs. The **Mátyás Museum** on the ground and first floors exhibits finds from the palace, including a copy of the white Anjou Fountain of the Angevins and the red marble *Visegrád Madonna*, a renaissance masterpiece that shows many similarities to the works of Tomaso Fiamberti nearby. The next two floors present the history of Visegrád up to the Turkish occupation. It's worth climbing to the top for the view of the lines of fortification running down from the citadel on both sides, meeting at the Water Bastion by the river. However, neither this nor the **ruined Roman fort** to the north atop Sibrik Hill are worth a special detour, so you might want to save your energy for the climb to Visegrád's citadel.

The citadel

From the exit at the rear of Solomon's Tower, it's forty minutes' walk up a steep path through the woods to the hilltop **citadel** (mid-March to mid-Nov daily 9.30am–6pm; rest of the year Sat & Sun 10am–3pm; closed when it snows, as the battlements are too slippery; 550Ft including all displays) – look out for signs up to the right after ten to fifteen minutes. It is a slightly easier walk if you go from the centre of town via the "Calvary" **footpath** (signposted "Fellegvár" and marked by a red cross on the way), which takes its name from the calvary of reliefs that you follow on your way up; it heads up to the left off Nagy Lajos Király utca, 50m behind the church. There are also three buses a day (April–Sept 9.30am, 12.30am & 3.30pm), which stop at both the boat and the ferry stations on the river side of the road, and follow the scenic Panorama Route uphill. Though only partly restored, the citadel is mightily impressive, commanding a superb view of the Börzsöny Mountains on the opposite bank of the Danube. Besides two **museums** devoted to medieval hunting, fishing, punishment and torture, there are outdoor displays of **archery** and **falconry** in the summer.

The Visegrád Hills

Thickly wooded and crisscrossed with paths, the **Visegrád Hills** are a popular rambling spot. From the car park near the citadel, it's a four-hundred-metre walk up the main road to another car park, from where you can follow a signposted path off to the left, leading to the **Nagy-Villám observation tower** (*kilátó*; 10am–5pm: April–Oct daily; Nov–March Sat & Sun; 100Ft). Sited at the highest point on the Danube Bend, it offers wonderful views as far as Slovakia. Back down by the car park is the **bobsleigh course** (Nyári Bob), where for 280Ft you can race down a one-kilometre run (April–Oct daily 9am–7pm; Nov–March Sat & Sun 10am–4pm; ☎26/397-397), except on rainy days, when the brakes are rendered ineffective.

A kilometre north of the tower lies Mogyoró-hegy and a collection of wooden **buildings by Imre Makovecz**. As a promising architect in the Kádár years, Makovecz was branded a troublemaker for his outspoken nationalism, banned from teaching and "exiled" to Visegrád's forestry department in 1977. Here he refined his ideas over the next decade, acquiring a following of students for whom he held summer schools on how to construct temporary buildings using low-technology methods and raw materials such as branches and twigs. The Cultural House near *Jurta Camping* is an excellent example, with a turfed roof and a light, homely interior, while the oesophagus-like crypt of the Farkasréti Cemetery in Budapest represents his apotheosis. Makovecz also designed the much admired Hungarian Pavilion at the 1992 Expo in Seville, with its seven towers representing the seven Magyar tribes. Though he has won a considerable amount of praise abroad, his generous use of wood does not appeal to all environmentalists, and his dabbling in right-wing politics turns his idea of a return to the "real" Hungarian style of building, once a righteous tool against the old regime, into something less appealing.

Practicalities

Boats from Budapest (1090Ft; 3hr 20min to Viségrad, 2hr 30min back to Budapest) and Esztergom (790Ft; 2hr) land at Visegrád just below Solomon's Tower, little more than fifteen minutes' walk north of the centre. You can also travel by **train** from Nyugati Station to Nagymaros–Visegrád on the Szob line, and then catch one of the hourly ferries across to Visegrád, which dock further to the south. **Buses** make two stops in Visegrád – there is no bus station here – by the ferry and boat stations.

Two of the best **restaurants** in Visegrád are up on the road towards the citadel. The *Gulyás Csárda* at Nagy Lajos Király utca 4 is a well-established Hungarian restaurant serving good food at reasonable prices; the *Patak Fogadó*, a few hundred metres further on at Mátyás király utca 92, is more stylish, with better food. Other options include the medieval-themed *Renaissance*, at Fő utca 9, where you can feast on suckling pig, while wearing a cardboard crown, and be serenaded by a pantalooned man with a lute. *Don Vito*, next to the church at Fő utca 83, is always heaving, due to their impressive stone-baked pizzas. For a simple quick fill, the self-service *Piknik Büfé* just across the road on Rév utca does the job.

Esztergom

Beautifully situated in a crook of the Danube facing Slovakia, **ESZTERGOM** is dominated by its basilica, whose dome is visible for miles around – a richly symbolic sight, as it was here that Prince Géza and his son Vajk (the future king and saint Stephen) brought Hungary into the fold of Christendom. Even after the court moved to Buda following the Mongol invasion, Esztergom remained the centre of Catholicism until the Turkish conquest, and resumed this role in the 1820s. Though the Church was persecuted during the Rákosi era, from the 1960s onwards the Communists settled for a modus vivendi, and during the 1990s it regained much of its former influence. Esztergom itself makes an ideal day-trip, combining historic monuments and small-town charm in just the right doses.

Arrival, information and accommodation

If you arrive by bus from Visegrád, it's best to get off near Basilica Hill or in the centre rather than travelling on to the **bus station** on Simor János utca, where services from Budapest terminate. From the **train station**, 1km further south, buses #1 and #5 run into the centre. Ferries from Budapest (1490Ft; 5hr 30min from Vigadó tér, 4hr back) tie up on the Danube embankment of Prímás sziget, fifteen minutes' walk from the centre. **Slovakia** is just across the Mária Valéria Bridge, you can walk or drive there and back quite easily (remember to carry your passport with you).

For **information**, head for Gran Tours, on the corner of Rákóczi tér (June–Aug Mon–Fri 8am–6pm, Sat 9am–noon; Sept–May Mon–Fri 8am–4pm; ☎33/413-756). They also change money, as does the K&H bank opposite. There's **Internet access** at Solva (Mon–Fri 8am–4pm), just round the corner from Gran Tours.

You can **stay** in Esztergom at the outstanding *St Kristóf Panzió*, Dobozi Mihály utca 11 (☎ & ☎33/414-153, ✉kristoph@elender.hu; 12,000Ft), boasting

BARS & RESTAURANTS
Anonim 2
Csülök Csárda 3
Gambrinus
 Maláta Bar 4
Olagz 5
Phillippe 7
Prímás Pince 1
Szálma Csárda 6

ACCOMMODATION
Platán Panzió **C**
Ria Panzió **B**
St Kristóf Panzió **A**

SZENTGYÖRGYMEZŐ

DOBOZI MIHÁLY UTCA Ⓐ

N

ISKOLA UTCA

VAREOK UTCA

BÁNOM

SZENT
ISTVÁN
TÉR

Basilica

Dark
Gate

Ⓞ

MAJER ISTVÁN UTCA

BASA UTCA

Cat
Stairs

Castle Museum

Rondella

BATTHYÁNY UTCA

VASVÁRI PÁL UTCA

River Danube

BERÉNYI UTCA

Ⓞ

VÍZIVÁROS

Ⓑ

Ⓞ

Christian
Museum

Bálint Balassi Museum

PÁZMÁNY UTCA

TÖRÖK UTCA

SZENT
TAMÁS-HEGY

Chapel

Štúrovo (Slovakia) ▲

Budapest ▲

Vízivaros
Parish
Church

SÁNDOR SZENTÍ TÉRE

BAJCSY-ZSILINSZKY UTCA

ATTILA
TÉR

Ⓗ

Technika Háza

IMAHÁZ UTCA

Museum
of the
Danube

Mária
Valéria
Bridge

NAGY DUNA SÉTÁNY

Outdoor
Pool

KIS-DUNA SÉTÁNY

VÖRÖSMARTY UTCA

KÖLCSEY UTCA

Customs
House

TÁNCSICS MIHÁLY UTCA

LŐRINCZ UTCA

Ⓞ

PETŐFI UTCA

SIMOR JÁNOS UTCA

PRÍMÁS

SZIGET

Kis-Duna

Ⓒ

RÁKÓCZI
TÉR

Ⓞ

Ferry Port

Sports
Centre

HERLISCHER ÚT

Gran Tours

Ⓞ
@

KOSSUTH LAJOS UTCA

Ibusz

SZÉCHENYI
TÉR

ARANY JÁNOS UTCA

DEÁK UTCA

Market

0   100 m

ESZTERGOM

Town Hall

Bus & Train Stations ▼

spacious, air-conditioned rooms and apartments, a lovely garden and a splendid restaurant. *Ria Panzió* at Batthány utca 11–13 (☎33/313-115, ✆www.riapanzio .com; rooms from 10,500Ft) is a comfortable pension with spotless rooms in two buildings, and a beer garden and bike rental. The cheapest pension in town is *Platán Panzió*, Kis-Duna sétány 11 (☎ & ✆33/411-355; 6000Ft), pleasantly located opposite Prímás sziget, close to the centre of the lower town.

The Town

Built upon the site of the first cathedral in Hungary, where Vajk was crowned as King Stephen by a papal envoy on Christmas Day 1000 AD, Esztergom's **Basilica** is the largest in the country, measuring 118m in length and 40m in width, and capped by a dome 100m high. Liszt's *Gran Mass* (Gran being

141

When the much-travelled body of **Cardinal József Mindszenty** was finally laid to rest with state honours in May 1991, it was a vindication of his uncompromising heroism – and the Vatican realpolitik that Mindszenty despised. As a conservative and monarchist, he had stubbornly opposed the postwar Communist takeover, warning that "cruel hands are reaching out to seize hold of our children, claws belonging to people who have nothing but evil to teach them". Arrested in 1948, tortured for 39 days and nights, and sentenced to life imprisonment for treason, Mindszenty was freed during the Uprising and took refuge in the US Embassy, where he remained for the next fifteen years – an exile in the heart of Budapest.

When the Vatican struck a deal with the Kádár regime in 1971, Mindszenty had to be pushed into resigning his position and going to Austria, where he died in 1975. Although his will stated that his body should not return home until "the red star of Moscow had fallen from Hungarian skies", his reburial occurred some weeks before the last Soviet soldier left, in preparation for the pope's visit in August of that year. Nowadays the Vatican proclaims his greatness, without any hint of apology for its past actions.

the German name for Esztergom) was composed for its completion in 1869. Admission (daily 7am–6pm) is free, but tickets are required for the spooky **crypt** (*krypta*; daily 9am–5pm; 100Ft), where Cardinal Mindszenty (see box above) is buried; the **cupola** (May–Oct daily 9am–5pm; 200Ft), reached by three hundred steps and offering a superb view of Esztergom; and the collection of bejewelled croziers and kitsch papal souvenirs in the **treasury** (*kincstár*; daily: March–Oct 9am–4.30pm; Nov & Dec 10am–3.30pm; 400Ft). The last is at the back of the nave, whose main altarpiece was painted by the Venetian Michelangelo Grigoletti, based on Titian's *Assumption* in the Frari Church in Venice. Don't miss the red and white marble **Bakócz Chapel** (below the relief of Christ on a donkey), whose Florentine altar was salvaged from the original basilica that was destroyed by the Mongols.

The Castle Museum

On higher ground 30m south of the basilica are the red-roofed, reconstructed remains of the palace founded by Prince Géza, now presented as the **Castle Museum** (Tues–Sun 10am–6pm; 400Ft). A royal seat for almost three hundred years, it was here that Béla III entertained Philip of France and Frederick Barbarossa on their way to the Third Crusade. The Renaissance prelate János Vitéz made it a centre of humanist culture, where Queen Beatrice spent her widowhood. Although it was sacked by the Turks and twice besieged before they were evicted in 1683, enough survived to be excavated in the 1930s.

Though foreigners are expected to join a tour in Hungarian, you can slip away to the rooms displaying visualizations of the palace in various epochs to reach the royal suite ahead of the crowd. Traces of the frescoes that once covered every wall can be seen in the vaulted living hall from Béla III's reign, from which stairs ascend to the study of Archbishop Vitéz – known as the **Hall of Virtues** after its allegorical murals. Beyond lies the **royal chapel**, whose Gothic rose window and Romanesque arches were executed by craftsmen brought over by Béla's French wives, while the rooftop offers a panoramic view of Esztergom and the river.

During June and July, **plays** and **dances** are staged in the **Rondella** bastion on the hillside. Descending the hillside after your visit, notice the monumental

Dark Gate – a tunnel built in the 1820s as a short cut between church buildings on either side of the hill and later exploited by the Soviet army, which maintained a base there until 1989 – and the former primate's wine cellars, now the *Prímás Pince* restaurant.

The Víziváros and Prímás sziget

The **Cat Stairs** cut into the side of the hill lead down from ramparts of the basilica, and it's an unrelenting but breathtaking climb down to the **Víziváros**, a small district of Baroque churches and seminaries where practising choirs are audible along the streets. Turning into Pázmány utca, you come to the **Bálint Balassi Museum** at no. 13 (Tues–Sun 9am–5pm; 100Ft), which mounts temporary historical exhibitions rather than dwelling on the romantic poet Bálint Balassi (1554–94), who died trying to recapture Esztergom from the Turks. This half-crazed philanderer was famous for sexually assaulting women and then dedicating verses to them – behaviour that resulted in him being beaten unconscious on several occasions.

Beyond the Italianate Baroque **Víziváros Parish Church**, the old Primate's Palace at Berényi utca 2 houses the **Christian Museum** (Tues–Sun 10am–6pm; 250Ft), Hungary's richest hoard of religious art, featuring the largest collection of Italian prints outside Italy; Renaissance paintings and wood carvings by German, Austrian and Hungarian masters; and a wheeled, gilded catafalque once used in Easter Week processions.

From the church you can cross a bridge onto **Prímás sziget**, a popular recreational spot. A little way south of the landing stage for ferries to Štúrovo is the reconstructed **Mária Valéria Bridge** that connects the two towns. Blown up by retreating Germans at the end of World War II, the bridge was left neglected until an agreement to rebuild the bridge was finally signed in 1999, after years of protracted negotiations between Hungarian and Slovakian ministers. The renovated **Customs House** has a free exhibition on the history of the bridge.

The lower town

While Rákóczi tér, with its supermarkets and banks, is the de facto centre of the **lower town**, its most attractive feature is the **Kis–Duna sétány**, a riverside walk lined with weeping willows and villas, popular with promenaders. Inland, civic pride is manifest in the brightly painted public buildings on **Széchenyi tér**, including a town hall with rococo windows that once belonged to Prince Rákóczi's general, János Bottyán, whose statue stands nearby.

To end with an overview of the lower town, walk up Imaház utca past a flamboyant, Moorish-style edifice that was once Esztergom's synagogue and is now a science club, or **Technika Háza**. Shortly afterwards you'll find a flight of steps leading to **Szent Tamás-hegy** (St Thomas's Hill), a rocky outcrop named after the English martyr Thomas à Becket. A **chapel** was built here in his honour by Margaret Capet, whose English father-in-law, Henry II, prompted Thomas's assassination by raging "Who will rid me of this turbulent priest?" Even after her husband died and Margaret married Béla III of Hungary, her conscience would not let her forget the saint. The existing chapel (postdating the Turkish occupation) is fronted by a trio of life-size statues representing Golgotha.

Eating and drinking

Restaurants near the tourist sites are geared to coach parties and a fast turnover, though none of them is so bad or expensive that you feel compelled to look elsewhere. Indeed, it's hard to resist a meal in the cavernous cellars of the *Prímás Pince* (daily 10am–10pm), beneath Basilica Hill. On Prímás sziget, the terraced rustic-style *Szálma Csárda* (daily noon–9pm) near the Budapest ferry-dock serves fish, poultry and game in large portions. In the Víziváros, *Anonim* at Berényi utca 4 (Tues–Sun noon–10pm) specializes in exotically sauced game dishes, while the *Csülök Csárda* (daily noon–midnight), next to the *Ria Panzió*, serves up large portions of moderately priced Hungarian food, and is popular with locals and tourists alike. There's Belgian cooking at *Phillippe*, Széchenyi tér 16 (Wed–Sun noon–11pm), a stylish place serving wild boar sausages, or for something a little less complicated, try the good-value pizzas at *Olagz*, Lőrincz utca (daily 11am–11pm). Almost any of these restaurants are feasible **drinking** spots, as are the **pavement cafés** between Rákóczi tér and Széchenyi tér, which are also good for sandwiches, cakes and ices – though only the *Gambrinus Maláta Bar* at Vörösmarty utca 3 (Mon–Thurs & Sun 11am–2am, Fri & Sat till 3am) could be described as trendy, an intimate tangle of varnished branches with dance music on the jukebox.

Gödöllő

The small town of **GÖDÖLLŐ** boasts a former Habsburg summer palace and a famous artists' colony, but being 30km northeast of Budapest rather than on the Danube Bend, it gets far fewer tourists than Szentendre, despite a reliable train service that enables visitors to enjoy an evening concert and return to the capital afterwards.

The Royal Palace of Gödöllő

The **Royal Palace** (Gödöllői Királyi kastély; Tues–Sun: Feb, March, Nov & Dec 10am–5pm; April–Oct 10am–6pm; 600Ft; last tickets 1hr before closing; ⓦwww.kiralyikastely.hu) was commissioned by a confidante of Empress Maria Theresa's, Count Antal Grassalkovich, and designed by András Mayerhoffer, who introduced the Baroque style of mansion to Hungary in the 1740s. The palace suffered as a result of both world wars, being commandeered as a GHQ first by the Reds and then by the Whites in 1919–20, and pillaged by both the Nazis and the Red Army in 1944. One wing was later turned into an old people's home, while the rest was left to rot until a few years ago, when the restoration of the palace finally began.

So far 26 rooms have been opened, most recently the Royal Theatre and the little Royal Pavilion in the gardens. The formal state rooms, reached by a grand staircase, precede the private apartments used by Emperor Franz Josef and his wife Sissi – his decorated in grey and gold, hers draped in her favourite colour, violet. Sissi stayed two thousand nights here, preferring it to Vienna. While her possessions are reverentially displayed right down to a nail from her horse's shoe, there's no sign to identify the secret staircase that she had installed for some privacy in a relentlessly public life.

A fifty-minute guided **tour** in English costs 2000Ft per person, or you could explore on your own, armed with the English-language *Guide to Gödöllő*, sold at the palace bookshop. Regular musical and cultural programmes are staged within the palace throughout the year, including open-air classical concerts in the Ornamental Yard during the summer – check with the Tourinform office inside the palace for details.

Town Museum

The delightful **Town Museum of Gödöllő** at Szabadság tér 5 (Gödöllői Városi Múzeum; Tues–Sun 10am–6pm; 300Ft) focuses heavily on the **Gödöllő Artists' Colony**. Founded in 1901, the colony was inspired by the English Pre-Raphaelites and the Arts and Crafts movement of William Morris and John Ruskin, whose communal, rural ethos it took a stage further. Members included Aladár Körösfői Kriesch, who wrote a book about Ruskin and Morris; Sándor Nagy, whose home and workshop may eventually become a separate museum; and the architect Károly Kós. Though the colony dispersed in 1920, its stamp on the decorative arts persisted until the 1950s, while Kós's work has been a major influence on Imre Makovecz and his protegés, who dominate today's architectural scene. The museum, captioned in English throughout also has a terrific exhibition of regional history, including mock-up rooms illustrating the life of the Gödöllő estate, and a room of exhibits from New Guinea donated by the local naturalist and explorer Ferenc Ignácz.

Practicalities

Arriving by HÉV train, get off before the terminal at the Szabadság tér stop, which is bang in the centre of town opposite the palace. You can get **information** from the extremely well-informed Tourinform booth inside the palace near the ticket office (same hours as palace; ☎28/415-402, ⊛www.gkrte.hu). The *Galéria Panzió*, Szabadság tér 8 has a sublime **restaurant** offering over a hundred moderately priced dishes, with exotic choices such as deer stew and shark on the menu (daily 11am–11pm; ☎28/418-691).

Listings

Listings

Accommodation

I n recent years Budapest **accommodation** has improved markedly in terms of availability, but has also become much more expensive. Predictably, the heaviest demand and highest prices occur over summer, when the city feels like it's bursting at the seams. Christmas, New Year, the Spring Festival in March/April and the Grand Prix in August are also busy periods, with rates marked up as much as twenty per cent in some hotels. Even so, it should always be possible to find somewhere that's reasonably priced, if not well sited.

Budget travellers will find most **hotels** expensive even during low season (Nov–March, excluding New Year). **Pensions** are cheaper yet often much the same as small hotels, with en-suite bathrooms and other mod cons. If you're on a tight budget, your safest bet is a **private room**. Though its location might not be perfect, the price should be reasonable. However, there are ever fewer of these around, as fewer people are seeking an extra bit of cash by letting rooms.

Hostels vary in price: some represent the cheapest accommodation in the city, while others are more expensive than private rooms. Another inexpensive option are **campsites**, where tent space can usually be found, even if all the **bungalows**, which some have, are taken.

Accommodation rates are often quoted in **euros**, but you pay in forint. In reviews overleaf, the prices given usually refer to double rooms in high season, and include taxes where applicable.

Hotel booking agencies

American Express V, Deák Ferenc utca 10 (Mon–Fri 9am–5.30pm, Sat 9am–2pm; ☏1/235-4330). Handles hotel bookings, with a $20 service fee for non-cardholders.

Express V, Semmelweis utca 4 (Mon–Thurs 8.30am–4.30pm, Fri 8.30am–3pm; ☏1/327-7092, ⓦwww.express-travel.hu). Books hotels.

Ibusz V, Ferenciek tere 10, on the corner of Petőfi Sándor utca (Mon–Fri 8.15am–5pm; ☏1/485-2716); V, Vörösmarty tér 6, facing the British Embassy (Mon–Fri 8.15am–5pm; ☏1/317-0532); VII, Dob utca 1 (Mon–Fri 8am–4pm; ☏1/322-7214); ⓦwww.ibusz.hu. Handles all forms of accommodation.

Vista Visitor Center VI, Paulay Ede utca 7 (Mon–Fri 9am–8pm, Sat 9am–6pm; ☏1/429-9950, ⓦwww.vista.hu). Books hotels and apartments.

ⓦ**www.hotels.hu** Site listing most of Hungary's hotels and pensions, and handling reservations.

Hotels and pensions

The greatest choice of hotels can be found in **Pest**, where there's also more in the way of restaurants and nightlife – and more traffic noise, too. The prime spots are along the river bank, with views across to Várhegy; having said that, all the really grand hotels were destroyed during World War II, and their replacements don't have quite the same elegance. Staying out of the centre is a viable option, since most places are within reach of a metro station.

Star ratings give you a fair idea of standards, though facilities at some of the older three-star places don't compare with their Western equivalents, even if room prices are similar. Almost all hotels reduce their rates out of season.

Both hotels and pensions are in high demand, so it's sensible to **book** before leaving home or through an airport tourist agency on arrival.

The Belváros

For locations, see the map on p.48.

Hotel Art (Best Western) V, Királyi Pál utca 12 ☎1/266-2166, ⑩www.bestwestern.com. A small hotel in a quiet backstreet. Rooms are quite cramped, but have a/c, minibar, phone and TV, though only Hungarian and German channels. Sauna, fitness room and laundry service. Doubles €120.

Astoria V, Kossuth utca 19 ☎1/889-6000, ⑩www.danubiusgroup.com/astoria. A four-star vintage hotel which gave its name to the major junction in central Pest on which it's located. Good-sized rooms have a sofa, safe, minibar, phone and TV; half have baths while the rest have showers. As well as a wonderful coffee house (see p.163), the hotel has a restaurant complete with Hungarian gypsy band. Doubles from €115.

ELTE Peregrinus Vendégház V, Szerb utca 3 ☎1/266-4911, ⑩www.peregrinushotel.hu. Friendly place in a quiet backstreet in central Pest with 25 rooms, complete with minibar and TV. Rooms are spacious, unlike the bathrooms. It belongs to the university, and all rooms have writing tables to meet the needs of academic visitors. Buffet breakfast included in the €110 price.

Kempinski Corvinus V, Erzsébet tér 7–8 ☎1/429-3777, ⑩www.kempinski-budapest.com. A flashy, smug five-star establishment on the edge of the Belváros, which counts Madonna and Michael Jackson among past guests. Tastefully furnished rooms offer every luxury, right down to a phone extension in the bathroom. Swimming pool, sauna, solarium, fitness room and underground garage. Rooms from €320 excluding breakfast.

Marriott Budapest V, Apáczai Csere János utca 4 ☎1/266-7000, ⑩www.marriott.com. There's a view of the Danube from every room in this five-star hotel. Facilities include a sauna, squash court, parking and baby-sitting service. Doubles from €280 excluding breakfast.

🏃 **Le Meridien V, Erzsébet tér 9–10** ☎1/429-5500, ⑩www.lemeridien-budapest.com. Originally built for the Adria insurance company at the turn of the twentieth century, this building housed the police headquarters in the Communist years until it was totally gutted and reopened as a luxury hotel in 2000 – a welcome rival for the *Kempinski* next door. The hotel is magnificently furnished throughout, and its well-equipped rooms are perhaps the most tasteful in the city. Parking and swimming pool. Rooms from €480.

Lipótváros and Újlipótváros

🏃 **Four Seasons V, Roosevelt tér 5–6** ☎1/268-6000, ⑩www.fourseasons.com/budapest. See map, p.56 A magnificent restoration of this Budapest landmark (see map, p.55) has produced a new level of luxury in the city; the rooms all have Art Nouveau-style fittings (even down to the beautiful radiators) and are excellently equipped. Rooms overlooking the Danube naturally have the best aspect. Both the restaurants are excellent – the *kávéház* is cheaper than the *Páva* but still a very good option – and the service throughout the hotel is superlative. Underground garage. Standard rooms from €300.

Terézváros and Erzsébetváros

For locations, see the map on p.66.

🏃 **Andrássy VI, Andrássy út 111** ☎1/462-2100, ⑩www.andrassyhotel.com. Housed in a stunning, newly refurbished Bauhaus building, the *Andrássy* offers five-star accommodation without the corporate feel. All double rooms have balconies and mod cons. Smaller (single) rooms actually sleep two, since they come with double beds, as well as a massage shower but no balcony. There's well-priced quality food in the *Zebrano* restaurant, Wi-Fi access in the lobby, and the hotel enjoys a good location between the City Park and the Belváros. Doubles start at €260, singles at €225.

Béke Radisson VI, Teréz körút 43 ☎1/889-3900, ⓦ**www.danubiushotels.com/beke.** Facilities at this refurbished vintage hotel include a sauna, pool, business centre, underground garage, restaurant and an excellent coffee house. Rooms have minibar, TV and safe, and go from €150.

Benczúr Hotel VI, Benczúr utca 35 ☎01/479-5650, ⓦ**www.hotelbenczur.hu.** Modern, functional hotel on a leafy street off Andrássy út, with a nice garden at the back and parking in the yard (850Ft extra). Rooms in one wing of the building come with bath, TV and phone, while those in the other wing have showers and fewer frills. Pope John Paul II was a guest here, according to the hotel website, but it doesn't say which grade of room he went for. Doubles from €105.

Corinthia Grand Royal VII, Erzsébet körút 43–49 ☎1/479-4000, ⓦ**www.corinthiahotels.com.** Pleasant new five-star hotel on the main boulevard, with over four hundred comfortable rooms and two good restaurants. This was once one of the grand prewar hotels, but for forty years the building was used as offices, while the ballroom acted as the very grand Red Star cinema. The rebuilding – only the facade is original – has been beautifully executed, using original drawings; even the gorgeous ballroom (except for the chandeliers) is totally reconstructed. The hotel will have its own pool when work is complete. Standard doubles start at €280.

Délibáb VI, Délibáb utca 35 ☎1/342-9301, ⓦ**www.hoteldelibab.hu.** Simply furnished but pleasant, the *Délibáb* stands right on Hősök tere, within walking distance of the sights on Andrássy út and the City Park, and has excellent transport links too. No a/c. Rooms from €85.

🦾 **K&K Opera VI, Révay utca 24** ☎1/269-0222, ⓦ**www.kkhotels.com.** Bright, modern and fully a/c four-star hotel right by the Opera House, with underground parking. Rooms – all with minibar, TV, safe and phone – are pleasantly furnished. Doubles from €225, including buffet breakfast.

Medosz Hotel VI, Jókai tér 9 ☎1/374-3000, ⓦ**www.medoszhotel.hu.** Overlooking a square near Oktogon is this pleasant hotel, in a simple modern block that formerly served as a trade union hostel. Small, bright rooms with bath and TV make this good value for the location. Doubles cost around €60, including breakfast.

Radio Inn VI, Benczúr utca 19 ☎1/342-8347, ⓦ**www.radioinn.hu.** Spacious apartments complete with kitchen, living room and TV. Situated in a leafy street, by the Chinese and Vietnamese embassies, with a pleasant garden. From €85.

Józsefváros and Ferencváros

For locations, see the map on p.84.

Anna VIII, Gyulai Pál utca 14 ☎1/327-2000, ⓦ**www.hotels.hu/annahotel.** Located in a quiet street, this hotel offers small, basic rooms – twin beds only – with TV and shower, and off-street parking. Prices start at €95.

🦾 **Mercure Museum VIII, Trefort utca 2** ☎1/485-1080, ⓦ**www.mercure-museum.hu.** A new hotel housed in an imaginatively transformed Pest apartment block, with the restaurant in the glass-roofed courtyard. Rooms are small but well-equipped, with en-suite bathroom, hairdryer, satellite TV and minibar. Off-street parking available. Prices from €120.

Nemzeti Hotel VIII, József körút 4 ☎1/477-2000, ⓦ**www.mercure-nemzeti.hu.** Small but elegant rooms in an Art Nouveau-style building overlooking the busy Blaha Lujza tér. Rooms facing onto the square have double glazing but the courtyard ones are still quieter. The glass-roofed restaurant and the staircase are both magnificent. Doubles from €145.

Várhegy and the Víziváros

For locations, see the map on pp.93 and 94.

🦾 **Art'otel I, Bem rakpart 16–19** ☎1/487-9487, ⓦ**www.artotel.hu.** The first boutique hotel in the city combines eighteenth-century buildings – comprising beautiful, spacious rooms with original doors and high ceilings – with a modern wing overlooking the river, offering marvellous views. Rooms are well equipped (bright red dressing gowns are among the items provided). There's a Wi-Fi network all round the hotel, and the business centre offers Internet use. Doubles start at €210.

Astra I, Vám utca 6 ☎1/214-1906, ⓦwww
.hotelastra.hu. Small hotel in a converted
300-year-old building at the foot of the castle near Batthyány tér. Twelve well-furnished
rooms with minibar and a/c, from €110.
Burg I, Szentháromság tér 7 ☎1/212-0269,
ⓦwww.burghotelbudapest.com. All rooms in
this small hotel right opposite the Mátyás
Church have en-suite bathrooms, a/c, minibar and TV. Doubles from €120.
Carlton I, Apor Péter utca 3 ☎1/224-0999,
ⓦwww.carltonhotel.hu. Four-star hotel well
situated by the Chain Bridge, below Castle
Hill. The modern interior is comfy enough
but slightly lacking in atmosphere. Parking
available. Doubles from €110.
Hilton Budapest I, Hess András tér 1–3 ☎1/889-
6600, ⓦwww.danubiusgroup.com/hilton. By
the Mátyás Church in the Vár, with superb
views across the river, this hotel incorpo-
rates the remains of a medieval monastery
and hosts summertime concerts in the
former church. Luxurious to a fault. Standard doubles from €140; excellent special
offers available.
Kulturinnov I, Szentháromság tér 6 ☎1/224-8105,
ⓦwww.mka.hu. Well positioned for sightseeing, in a neo-Gothic building right by Mátyás
Church. The hotel is poorly signed; the
entrance is up on the first floor. The rooms,
spacious and quiet, have a minibar but no
TV, and only half the rooms have a/c – but
the thick walls offer some protection against
the heat. The hotel hosts Hungarian cultural
events, concerts and exhibitions. Breakfast
included. Doubles from €85.
🏃 **Victoria I, Bem rakpart 11** ☎1/457-8080,
ⓦwww.victoria.hu. Small, very friendly
hotel on the embankment directly below the
Mátyás Church. The rooms have excellent
views of the Lánchíd and the river, and are
equipped with minibar, TV and a/c. Sauna
and garage facilities. Doubles €118.

Tabán and Gellért-Hegy

For locations, see the map on p.111.
🏃 **Ábel Panzió XI, Ábel Jenő utca 9**
☎1/209-2537, ⓦwww.abelpanzio.hu.
Perhaps the most appealing pension in
Budapest, a 1913 villa with beautiful Art
Nouveau fittings in a quiet street, twenty
minutes' walk from the Belváros. There are
just ten rooms, so it's essential to book in
advance. Cash discounts available. Doubles
from €75.

Charles Hotel XI, Hegyalja út 23 ☎1/212-9169,
ⓦwww.charleshotel.hu. Friendly place situated on the hill up from the Erzsébet híd on
the main road to Vienna. Rooms come with
cooking facilities, minibar and TV (those facing the inner yard are quieter), and there's a
business room with Internet access. Parking
costs €8. Bikes are available for rent. Doubles from €70.
Flamenco XI, Tas vezér utca 3–7 ☎1/889-5600,
ⓦwww.danubiusgroup.com/flamenco. In the
leafy district behind Gellért Hill, this is a large
modern conference hotel, with two floors at
the top for individual travellers. The rooms
are of a good size, complemented by a pool,
sauna and fitness room downstairs, and Wi-
Fi access in the lobby. Rooms from €100.
🏃 **Gellért XI, Szent Gellért tér 1** ☎1/889-
5500, ⓦwww.danubiusgroup.com/gellert.
Large, light corridors and lots of character
at this well-established hotel. The facade,
especially when floodlit, is magnificent, and
so is the thermal pool, to which residents
have their own lift down (and free entry,
which comes with a bathrobe). A large
number of single rooms are available; all
rooms are en suite. The cheaper rooms
look on to the courtyard and don't have the
views – or the sound of the trams, which
blight the others, in spite of double-glazing.
The beer hall (*söröző*) serves good food,
and the coffee shop is excellent. Rooms
start at €140.

▽ The fountain in fron of the *Gellért*

Orion I, Döbrentei utca 13 ☏1/356-8583, ⓦwww.bestwestern.com/budapest. Small modern place in the Tabán district, just south of the Vár. Rooms have TV and minibar – those at the front can be noisy – and guests can make use of a sauna. Doubles €120.

Óbuda and Margit sziget

Danubius Grand and Danubius Thermal XIII, Margit sziget ☏1/889-4700, ⓦwww.danubiusgroup.com/grandhotel, ⓦwww.danubiusgroup.com/thermalhotel. Both these hotels are at the northern end of the island and provide a very wide range of spa facilities, with mud spas and massages, as well as medical and cosmetic services from pedicures to plastic surgery, and they have Wi-Fi access in the lobby. Prices include access to the thermal baths, pool, sauna, gym and other facilities. The *Grand* is the island's original, *fin-de-siècle* spa hotel; rooms here have balconies and high ceilings, and have been totally refurbished, with period furniture. The *Thermal* is the big modern one, with balconies offering views over the island. Doubles in the *Grand* start at €180, while those in the *Thermal* start at €195.

Pál Panzió III, Pálvölgyi köz 15 ☏1/388-7099. See map, p.117. Eight double rooms in this small, welcoming pension, situated in the hills near the Pálvölgy Stalactite Cave. Doubles from €60.

The Buda Hills

Beatrix Panzió II, Szehér út 3 ☏1/275-0550, ⓦwww.beatrixhotel.hu. Friendly eighteen-room pension in the villa district northwest of Moszkva tér – take tram #56. There's a bar on the ground floor, plus a sauna. Doubles €70.

Budapest II, Szilágyi E. fasor 47 ☏1/889-4200, ⓦwww.danubiusgroup.com//budapest. Cylindrical tower facing the Buda Hills, opposite the lower terminal of the Cogwheel Railway, 500m from Moszkva tér. Rooms come with a/c, TV and minibar, and there's a sauna, fitness room and business centre too. The lobby's decor is rather Seventies, but at least there are excellent views over the city from the upper floors. Doubles from €90.

Buda Villa Panzió XII, Kiss Áron utca 6 ☏1/275-0091, ⓦwww.budapansio.hu. See map, p.124 Up in the hills just above Moszkva tér (catch bus #156) this comfortable little pension has a small garden that's perfect for relaxing in after a day's sightseeing, and a bar in the lounge on the first floor. Doubles from €65, including breakfast.

Hostels

If you don't have a tent, a dormitory bed in a **hostel** is the cheapest alternative. Many hostels also have rooms at much the same price as private accommodation, but often with very basic student furniture. Still, at least there are no surcharges of the sort levied in private rooms for staying fewer than four nights, and the hostels offer 24-hour information from English-speaking staff at the reception desk.

Unless stated otherwise, the hostels listed below are open year-round. Student dormitories are open during July and August only, many of them located in the university area south of Gellért-hegy. You can't be sure of getting a bed in the hostel of your choice in summer without **booking** in advance.

The larger hostels offer transport from Keleti Station to the their premises, which can make arrival less daunting. The Mellow Mood group runs some excellent all-year hostels in the city and also handles some of the university accommodation open during the summer. They have offices in Keleti Station, on the right of the glass doors at the far end as you arrive, and can give you information and make bookings (daily: June–Aug 7am–midnight, Sept–May 7am–8pm; ☏1/413-2062, ⓦwww.mellowmood.hu).

Pest

Astoria City Hostel VII, Rákóczi út 4 ☏1/266-1327, ⓦwww.astoriacityhostel.com. See map, p.66. On the third floor, this is a pleasant new hostel in the heart of the city, with eight-bed dorms and one en-suite double room. The double and one dorm overlook a quiet inner courtyard. Prices includes break-fast and Internet access. Laundry service available. Dorm beds 3000Ft, double room 8000Ft.

Best Hostel VI, Podmaniczky utca 27, first floor ☎1/332-4934, @www.besthostel.hu. **See map, p.66.** Rambling friendly place in a typical, high-ceilinged large Pest apartment, close to Nyugati train station. All the rooms look out onto busy streets, so it isn't quiet. Cooking facilities. Dorm beds 3000Ft, doubles 8400Ft.

Green Bridge V, Molnár utca 22 ☎1/266-6922, @www.greenbridgehostel.com. **See map, p.48.** New, well-situated hostel near the Danube in the Belváros. Run by a young couple, Tünde and Xavier, it's a small, friendly place with rooms of five to eight beds, two double rooms and apartments for groups. Free Internet access and coffee. Beds €10, doubles €45.

Marco Polo VII, Nyár utca 6 ☎1/413-2555, @www.marcopolohostel.com. **See map, p.66.** Well positioned at the edge of the old Jewish quarter, this has pleasant, simply furnished four- and twelve-bed dorms with bunks, as well as 36 double rooms, and a bar in the cellar. IYHF cardholders get a discount. Dorm beds 5000Ft, doubles 19000Ft.

Mellow Mood V, Bécsi utca 2 ☎1/411-1310, @www.mellowmoodhostel.com. **See map, p.48.** Friendly, well-run and very centrally located hostel with 270 beds in doubles and rooms of four, six and eight beds, all overlooking the street. Internet access. You get a lift here if you book at Mellow Mood in Keleti Station. Discount for IYHF cardholders. Dorm beds from 3200Ft.

Museum Guest House VIII, Mikszáth Kálmán tér 4, 1st floor ☎1/318-9508, @www.budapesthostel.com. **See map, p.84.** In the streets behind the National Museum, handy for the bars and cafés in the centre. (They have another operation near Astoria.) There are three spacious dorms, each sleeping seven or eight on mattresses on the floor. Cave trips are organized, and there's free Internet access in the evening. Dorm beds 3000Ft.

Ráday Youth Hostel IX, Ráday utca 43–45 ☎1/218-4766. **See map, p.84.** Near Kálvin tér, with basic student hostel furniture, high-ceilinged rooms of two to six beds or dormitories. Open July & Aug only. Beds 3500Ft.

Red Bus V, Semmelweis utca 14 ☎1/266-0136 @www.redbusbudapest.hu. **See map, p.84.** Friendly and relaxed English-run hostel with rooms of two to five beds, very close to Deák tér. Breakfast and the use of the kitchen is included in the price, and a laundry service is available. See website for special offers; otherwise 3000Ft for dorm beds, 7900Ft for doubles.

Buda

For locations, see the map on p.111.

Back Pack XI, Takács Menyhért utca 33 ☎1/385-8946, @www.backpackbudapest .hu. Charming fifty-bed hostel with a shaded garden, just twenty minutes from the centre (tram #49 or bus #7 to Tétényi út stop). They provide lots of information on the city, sport and fitness, and they also organize cave trips. Dorm beds from 2500Ft, doubles 7000Ft.

Citadella I, Citadella sétány ☎1/466-5794. Breathtaking views of the city from this well-sited hostel inside the hulk of the old citadel, but note that the weekend disco in the neighbouring nightclub sets the whole place shaking. Call in advance to get a bunk, as all but one of the dorms have been converted into doubles. To get here, take bus #27 from Móricz Zsigmond körtér, then it's a 10min walk from the Busuló Juhász stop – you can get round any attempt to charge entry to the citadella by saying you're at the hostel. Doubles cost €55, beds in the fourteen-bed dorm €10.

Landler XI, Bartók Béla út 17 ☎1/463-3621. Tram #47 or #49 from Deák tér. One of the older hostels, housed in the Baross Gábor Kollégium, near the Gellért Baths. Two- and three-bed dorms, with high ceilings. Open July & Aug only. Beds 5000Ft.

Private rooms and apartments

There are **private rooms** throughout the city, many in the sort of locations where a hotel would be unaffordable. Depending on location and amenities, **prices** for a double room range from 5000Ft a night. On the downside, solo travellers will almost certainly have to pay for a double, and rates are thirty percent higher if you stay fewer than four nights (making pensions or hostels more economical for short-staying visitors).

It's easy enough to get a room from one of the touts at the train stations, but it's safer to go through a tourist **agency**, where you book and pay at the counter signposted *fizetővendég*. Ibusz (see box on p.149) handles private rooms, as does the To-Ma Travel Agency at V, Október 6 utca 22 (☎1/353-0819, ⓦwww .tomatour.hu).

Since rooms are rented unseen, it pays to take some trouble over your choice. Your host and the premises should give no cause for complaint, but the location or ambience might. For atmosphere and comfort you can't beat the nineteenth-century blocks where spacious, high-ceilinged apartments surround a courtyard with wrought-iron balconies – most common in Pest's V, VI and VII districts, and the parts of Buda nearest the Vár. It's best to avoid the rundown VIII and IX districts unless you can get a place inside the Nagykörút. Elsewhere – particu-larly in Újpest (IV), Csepel (XXI) or Óbuda (III) – you're likely to end up in a box on the twelfth floor on a *lakótelep* (housing estate). The *Budapest Atlasz* is invaluable for checking the location of sites and access by public transport.

Because many proprietors go out to work, you might not be able to take possession of the room until 5pm. Some knowledge of Hungarian facilitates **settling in**; guests normally receive an explanation of the boiler system and multiple door keys (*kulcs*), and may have use of the washing machine (*mosógép*), which might itself require a demonstration. The agencies on p.149 also have apartments on their .

Camping

Budapest's **campsites** are generally well equipped and pleasant, with trees, grass and sometimes even a pool. They can get crowded between June and September, when smaller places might run out of space. It is illegal to camp anywhere else, and the parks are patrolled to enforce this.

The campsites listed here are all in Buda, since the Pest ones are far out and not very inviting.

Csillebérci Camping XII, Konkoly Thege M. út 21 ☎1/395-6537, ⓦwww.csilleberciszabadido .hu. See map, p.124. Large, well-equipped site up in the Buda Hills, with space for 1000 campers. A range of bungalows is also available. Bus #21 from Moszkva tér to Normafa, then a short walk or bus #90 to the Csillebérc stop. Open all year.

Római Camping III, Szentendrei út 189 ☎1/368-6260. Huge site with space for 2500 campers beside the road to Szentendre in Rómaifürdő (25min by HÉV from Batthyány

tér). They also have wooden bungalows. Higher than average rates include use of the nearby swimming pool. Open year round.

Zugligeti Niche Camping XII, Zugligeti út 101 ☎1/200-8346, ⓦwww.campingniche.hu. See map, p.124. At the end of the #158 bus route from Moszkva tér, opposite the chairlift up to János-hegy, this is a small, terraced ravine site in the woods with space for 260 camp-ers and good facilities, including a pleasant little restaurant occupying the former tram station at the far end. April–Oct.

13

Eating

H ungarian cuisine was born on the plains: good solid meals to last you the day; food you could cook up over a fire. Staples are meat (especially pork), paprika, bread and lard, all washed down with wine or *pálinka*, the harsh Hungarian fruit brandy. Unsurprisingly, Hungarian fare is traditionally heavy and calorific.

Although meat is still an essential ingredient in most meals and you can be assured of a hearty meal in many restaurants, particularly cheaper ones, things do seem to be lightening up a bit when it comes to dining out. In recent years Budapest's culinary scene has been distinguished by the appearance of a number of very good restaurants, offering high quality Hungarian or Mediterranean-style food – even some nouvelle cuisine – and the best in Hungarian wine. There has also been a welcome diversification of late, with many new places offering Chinese and Japanese food, mainly to wealthy tourists and nouveau-riche natives.

For foreigners, though, the archetypal Magyar dish is still goulash – historically the basis of much **Hungarian cooking**. The ancient Magyars relished cauldrons of this *gulyás* (pronounced "gou-yash"), a soup made of potatoes and whatever meat was available, which was later flavoured with paprika and beefed up into a variety of stews, modified over the centuries by various foreign influences, which helped diversify the country's cuisine. Hungary's Slav visitors probably introduced native cooks to yogurt and sour cream – vital ingredients in many dishes while the influence of the Turks, Austrians and Germans is apparent in a variety of sticky pastries and strudels, as well as in recipes featuring sauerkraut or dumplings. There is a lot of fish, too – fish soup is one of the national dishes, a marvellously spicy bouillabaisse in the right hands – but it is worth remembering that landlocked Hungary's fish all come from lakes and rivers, such as the very bony carp to the more palatable catfish – anything else will be imported. For a glossary of **food and drink terms** see p.221.

Restaurant gypsy bands

A traditional accompaniment to a Hungarian meal is the gypsy band, dressed in blue and red waistcoats and displaying astonishing skill – one favourite piece of music imitates the sound of the lark (*pacsirta*). The several big restaurants along the Pest bank of the Danube and many in the Belváros boast these bands, but they are all aimed at tourist coach groups. To get the full charm of this entertainment try the *Rézkakas* in the Belváros or the *Kéhli*, in Óbuda – the latter has a big local following and the atmosphere is great on Friday nights. If you ask for a tune when the primás (the lead violinist in the all-blue waistcoat) comes round the tables, bear in mind that you'll be expected to pay for the privilege.

Hungarian wine

Hungary's **wines** are a delight, thus far under-appreciated in the global market. In general, the country's climate favours whites, especially crisp and floral varieties, but its reds are also delicious and offer more complexity and variation, including light and spicy vintages that are often chilled before drinking as well an emerging number of fine rosés.

In the Communist era **wine production** emphasised quantity over quality, throwing any number of different grapes together and shipping as much as possible to an undemanding Soviet market. Since 1989, however, there has been a huge investment in wine production, especially by foreign concerns in the internationally recognised Tokaj region, but also by native vintners in other regions. These smaller producers have turned their quality around extremely quickly, reviving older grape varieties and introducing new treatments, such as barrique (ageing the wine in small oak barrels).

Although Hungary has twenty official wine regions, the best kinds and producers are concentrated in a few areas. For **reds** seek out Eger in the north (Vilmos Thummerer is a name to look out for), Szekszárd to the south (Ferenc Vesztergombi, Péter Vida, Tamás Dúzsi and others) and Villány near the Croatian border (the long list includes József Bock, Attila Gere and Tiffán and Vylyan). The last two regions also produce excellent **rosés** – those of Bock and Dúzsi are particularly recommended. For **whites**, the best regions are located around Lake Balaton to the southwest of Budapest (Huba Szeremley and Otto Légli), and of course Tokaj, the wine region famed for its incredibly sweet Aszú wines.

The standard of wines served in **restaurants** reflects the improvement in the country's stock over the past fifteen years. Many of the top places get their wines from one source, the Budapest Wine Society, one of the best wine outlets. If you are doing a lot of restaurant dining you might get slightly weary of the same selections and descriptions cropping up, though a few establishments, noted in the reviews, do draw on different suppliers.

A nation of early risers, Hungarians traditionally have a calorific **breakfast** (*reggeli*). Commonly, this includes cheese, eggs or salami together with bread and jam, and coffee; in rural areas it's often accompanied by a shot of *pálinka* (brandy) to "clear the palate" or "aid digestion". A popular development among foreign residents in the city is **Sunday brunch**, giving you as much as you can eat for a fixed price.

Traditionally, Hungarians take their main meal at **lunchtime**. While some restaurants offer a bargain set menu (*napi menü*) of basic dishes, the majority of places are strictly *à la carte*. You'll probably be asked if you want a **starter** (*előétel*) – generally a soup or salad – though nobody will mind if you just have one of the dishes offered as the **main course** (*főétel*) or, alternatively, order just a soup and a starter. Bread is supplied almost automatically, on the grounds that "a meal without bread is no meal". **Drinks** are normally listed on the menu under the heading *italok*.

It's wise to **reserve** a table if you're determined to eat somewhere in particular, though you can usually find an alternative within a couple of blocks. We've included phone numbers where booking is advisable, though of course not all staff will speak English. While some smarter restaurants – especially in hotels – have introduced no-smoking sections, **smoking** is generally accepted.

Despite the emergence of *vegetarianus* restaurants in Budapest, and a growing understanding of the concept, **vegetarians** are still poorly catered to, and it's only in the more upmarket places that the choices become anything close to tempting. Otherwise you can find yourself on a diet of vegetables and cheese fried in breadcrumbs; these are known as *rántott gomba* (mushrooms), *rántott karfiol* (cauliflower), or *rántott sajt* (cheese) *Gomba paprikás* (mushroom paprika stew) is also fine if it is cooked in oil rather than in fat. Alternatively there are eggs – fried (*tükörtojás*), soft-boiled (*lágy tojás*), scrambled (*tojásrántotta*), or in mayonnaise (*kaszínótojás*) – or salads, though Hungary is surprisingly weak in these, given the excellent produce you can see in the shops.

A **note of caution**: waiters in Budapest are known to make "mistakes" with the bill, and foreign visitors are especially easy targets for overcharging. Other more common tactics include offering expensive "specials of the day", hiking up the bill or charging exorbitant amounts for the wine. Insist on a proper menu (including prices for drinks), don't be shy about querying the total, and avoid the seedier tourist joints in the Belváros (see p.39)

Restaurants

Despite the plethora of tourist traps in the Vár, **Buda** offers some excellent eating possibilities. There is no typical style of Buda restaurant: establishments here range from grand villas in the hills to small friendly locals. **Pest** has a much wider range of places, particularly within the Nagykörút. You can generally reckon that the places further from the Belváros or the Vár are likely to be cheaper.

The Belváros

The places reviewed here appear on the map on p.48.

Baraka V, Magyar utca 12–14 ☏1/483-1355, www.barakarestaurant.hu. Stylish and pricey restaurant on two floors, with contemporary decor, an intimate feel and a modern European menu that includes dishes such as caramelized soy chicken breast with cilantro polenta (2400Ft). Attentive service. Mon–Sat 6–11pm.

Károlyi kert V, Károlyi Mihály utca 16 ☏1/328-0240. It's the courtyard setting in the heart of the city, inside the gates of the Petőfi Museum and backing onto the Károlyi garden behind, that makes this so special. The interior is also pleasant, and even nicer when the piano player takes his breaks. Mains are 1700–3500Ft. Daily 11am–midnight.

Papageno V, Semmelweis utca 19 ☏1/485-0161. Small pricey bistro with an experienced chef specializing in pasta dishes. A very good lunchtime place (you'll need to book). Mon–Fri 11.30am–midnight, Sat 12.30pm–midnight.

Rézkakas V, Veres Pálné utca 3 ☏1/318-0038, www.extra.hu/rezkakas. The smart "Golden Cockerel" (as the name translates) is one of the best places to eat in traditional Hungarian style, with an excellent gypsy band playing away in the corner. Popular with foreign visitors, so expect to pay anything from 3000Ft up to 7000Ft for a main course. Daily noon–midnight.

Trattoria Toscana V, Belgrád rakpart 13, ☏1/327-0045, www.toscana.hu. A favourite spot for authentic Italian cuisine at reasonable prices, and with appealing faux Tuscan surroundings. The atmosphere is relaxed despite the smart business clientele. On Sundays a clown offers entertainment for the kids. Daily noon–midnight.

Lipótváros and Újlipótváros

The map on p.56 shows the locations of places reviewed below.

Café Kör V, Sas utca 17 ☏1/311-0053. Buzzy place near the basilica, with a very relaxed feel and good grilled meats, salads and wines. The specials of the day, displayed on a board, are recommended – the roasted pike-perch in garlic is always a favourite. The staff speak English. Main courses 1700–3200Ft. Booking essential. Mon–Sat 10am–10pm.

Csarnok V, Hold utca 11 ☏1/269-4906. Good, down-to-earth Hungarian restaurant specializing in mutton, lamb and bone-marrow dishes for around 1000Ft. Mon–Fri 9am–11pm.

Firkász XIII, Tátra utca 18 ☏1/450-1118. Done

up like a journalists' haunt from the turn of the last century, *Firkász* serves good traditional Hungarian food, with creamed veg stews and the like at excellent prices. Daily noon–midnight.

Govinda V, Vigyázó Ferenc utca 4 ☎1/473-1310. Hare Krishna vegetarian restaurant serving good inexpensive set meals, accompanied by the whiff of soporific incense. Mon–Sat noon–9pm.

Kispozsonyi XIII, Pozsonyi ut 18. Atmospheric (and smoky) local joint with filling Hungarian dishes; its popularity means you may have to wait for a table. The small terrace affords an escape from the fumes in the summer. Mains 800–1400Ft. Daily 10am–midnight.

Lou Lou V, Vigyázo Ferenc utca 4 ☎1/312-4505, ⓦwww.lou-lou.hu. Simply one of the top restaurants in town. The menu has French influences but goes far wider than that, with tantalising dishes such as a delicious lamb steak in an orange and coffee bean sauce. Top Hungarian wines too. No-smoking section. Mon–Fri noon–3pm & 7–11pm, Sat 7–11pm.

Mokka V Sas utca 4 ☎1/328-0081 ⓦwww.mokkarestaurant.hu. Strikingly furnished restaurant clearly aiming at tourists, with service that's overly hands-on and high prices. But don't be put off: the food is excellent, with unusual combinations on the fusion menu such as wild boar in lavender (4000Ft). Daily noon–midnight.

Okay Italia XIII, Szent István körút 20. A lively restaurant, popular with expats and locals alike, serving up very good pasta and pizza at reasonable prices. A second

branch is located on Nyugati tér, diagonally across from the station. Daily noon-midnight.

Via Luna V, Nagysándor József utca 1 ☎1/312-8058. Popular Italian-style restaurant, serving pizzas (from 1400Ft) and good filling salads. Daily noon–11.30pm.

Terézváros and Erzsébetváros

The places reviewed here are marked on the map on p.66.

Al Amir VII, Király utca 17 ☎1/352-1422. Recently refurbished Syrian restaurant offering some of the cheapest and best vegetarian starters and salads in the city – and also a wide range of Middle Eastern meat dishes, with prices starting at 1200Ft. No alcohol. Daily 11am–11pm.

Belcanto VI, Dalszínház utca 8 ☎1/269-2786 ⓦwww.belcanto.hu. Right by the Opera House, this is a smart place whose distinctive feature is that in the course of the evening the waiters join together for bursts of song, making for a lively atmosphere. They serve good international fare, but with prices for mains starting at 3400Ft, this isn't a cheap evening out. Daily noon–3pm & 6pm–midnight.

Bock Bisztró VII, Erzsébet körút 43-49 ☎1/321-0340. Located within the refurbished *Corinthia Grand Hotel*, this new establishment manages to be both classy and relaxed, with friendly staff and delicious food, all at reasonable prices (mains 1900–3200Ft). The Esterházy chicken and smoked duck breast are both recommended. The restaurant takes its name from one of Hungary's top vintners, József Bock, and its stock includes many labels that you won't find elsewhere in the city. Many wines can be ordered by the glass. Unobtrusive live guitar or accordion music in the evenings.

Chez Daniel VI, Szív utca 32 ☎1/302-4039. Fresh ingredients, including fish, are a plus at this French restaurant – one of the best in town, run by idiosyncratic master chef Daniel Labrosse, who is brilliant and friendly when in form – but don't come cheap. In summer things spread out into the very atmospheric courtyard. Booking recommended. Daily noon–10.30pm.

▽ Café Kör

⑬

EATING | Restaurants

Fausto's VII, Dohány utca 5 ☎1/269-6806. One of the best Italian restaurants in town, a very elegant place run by master chef Fausto DiVora. Mon–Sat noon–3pm & 6–11pm.

Feszek VII, Kertész utca 36 ☎1/322-6043. Under new management, so there is hope that the food will at last match the magical setting – in the courtyard of an artists' club on the corner of Dob utca. Most main courses are under 2000Ft.

Goa VI, Andrássy út 8. Fashionable restaurant which slightly overdoes the Eastern feel, but the food is very good, covering a range of cuisines, including Thai and Japanese. Fairly expensive, with mains in the 2700–5000Ft range. Daily noon–midnight.

🏃 **Giero VI, Paulay Ede utca 58.** The food is almost a sideshow at this highly atmospheric cellar restaurant run by a Roma family, who also provide the music. It has just three tables since a third of the space is given over to the musicians, who play for themselves, or their friends, or customers if the band likes them. It's a very relaxed place with a small menu (which may not be that relevant to what they have on the day) and the prices are also flexible – and cheap. The food is sometimes marvellous and fresh, sometimes less so, but that's beside the point. Daily noon–midnight (times flexible).

Il Terzo Cerchio VII, Nagydiófa 3. A cellar restaurant full of elderly Italian blokes watching football, and if that doesn't make it authentic enough, the food is excellent and inexpensive: pizzas from 1100Ft and pasta dishes for around 1800Ft. Daily noon–midnight.

🏃 **Kádár Étkezde VII, Klauzál utca 10.** Diner with delicious home cooking; traditional Budapest Jewish food (non-kosher) on Friday. Mon–Sat 11.30am–3.30pm; closed mid-July to mid-Aug.

King's Hotel VII, Nagy Diófa utca 25–27 ☎1/352-7675. Mehadrin kosher food, which is rare in this city, and it's reasonably good too. You have to pay in advance for Sabbath meals. Daily noon–9.30pm.

Kinnor David VII, Dohány utca. Under new management, and rated by some as the best of the city's kosher establishments. It's ideally placed, right by the main synagogue.

🏃 **Krizia VI, Mozsár utca 12** ☎1/331-8711. Top-class Italian restaurant, one of the best in town, with prices to match. Conveniently located near the Opera. Mon–Sat noon–3pm & 6.30pm–midnight.

Marquis de Salade VI, Hajós utca 43 ☎1/302-4086. Cuisine from all round the world, served up in generous portions. The large basement dining area is decorated with beautiful Persian carpets. Expect a three-course meal with wine to come to 7,000Ft per head. Daily 11am–midnight.

🏃 **Menza VI, Liszt Ferenc tér** ☎1/413-1482. Excellent and moderately priced establishment with stylish retro decor – and retro Hungarian dishes, to – such as *hagymás rostélyos*, braised steak piled high with onions – evoking nostalgic memories among the locals. Daily 10am–midnight.

🏃 **Vörös és Fehér** ("Red and White") **VI, Andrássy út 41** ☎1/413 1545. This wine bar is one of the best restaurants in town – and the waiters know it, and can be rather uppity. Very good tapas-style fare, plus salads and snacks, as well as full meals with an emphasis on seasonal dishes. Also recommended is the steak Andrassy (their take on Tournedos Rossini) for 4200Ft. They're strong on game and do good puddings, too. The food is accompanied by top Hungarian vintages – you can drink most wines by the glass, and the staff can advise on what goes well with what. On the down side, portions are small and hardly cheap. Worth booking. Daily 11am–midnight.

The Városliget

See the map on p.76 for the locations of places reviewed below.

🏃 **Bagolyvár XIV, Állatkerti körút 2** ☎1/468-3110 🌐www.bagolyvar.com. Sister to the *Gundel* (see below), but offering traditional Hungarian family-style cooking at far lower prices. Housed in an intriguing Károly Kós-style building, it aims to recreate the atmosphere of the interwar middle-class home, both in its menu and its service (all the staff are women – reflecting the quaint idea that in those days all women stayed at home). It's an excellent introduction to Hungarian cooking. Mains 1400–3600Ft, with a three-course menu at 3300Ft. Daily noon–11pm.

Gundel XIV, Állatkerti körút 2 ☎1/321-3550, 🌐www.gundel.hu. Budapest's most famous restaurant offers plush surroundings and a fantastically expensive menu. The all-you-can-eat Sunday brunch (4900Ft) is the cheapest way of getting a taste. Smart dress is required, though ties aren't compulsory for Sunday brunch. Booking essential. Daily noon–4pm & 7pm–midnight, Sunday brunch 11.30am–3pm.

Józsefváros and Ferencváros

The places reviewed below are marked on the map on p.84.

Lanzhou VIII, Luther utca 1b ☎1/314-1080. One of the best Chinese restaurants in Budapest, with a large menu of specialities, such as spicy tripe. Popular with the local Chinese community, and excellent value. They have a new, more upmarket, outlet in Fő utca in Buda. Daily noon–11pm.

Múzeum Kávéház VIII, Múzeum körút 12 ☎ 1/267-0375, ⓦwww.muzeumkavehaz .hu. Excellent food in a grand nineteenth-century restaurant near Astoria metro – note the Zsolnay tiles and the frescoes on the ceiling. Rather old-school, with a kitsch singing pianist in the background. Mains from 2500Ft, including an excellent beef steak with ginger and chocolate. Booking essential. Mon–Sat 10am–midnight.

Szahara VIII, József körút 82. Close to the Corvin cinema at Ferenc körút metro station. Bright joint with a wide range of tasty Middle Eastern food, eaten at shared tables. No smoking inside, though there are some tables outside in summer. It's easy to order: just point to the pictures of the food on the menu. Mon–Thurs & Sun 10am–midnight, Fri & Sat 10am–3am.

The Vár and central Buda

For the locations of the places reviewed, see the maps on p.93 and p.94.

Arcade XII, Kiss János alt. utca 38 ☎1/225-1969. Upmarket place with a low-key modern interior and a small terrace serving excellent international cuisine, including a delicious duck breast in maple syrup with walnuts.There's also a good range of top Hungarian wines. A meal will set you back 8,000Ft a head including half a bottle of wine each, unless you go for more expensive corks such as the Gere Kopár. Tues–Sun 11am–11pm.

Carne di Hall II, Bem rakpart 20 ☎1/210-8137, ⓦwww.carnedihall.com. Under the same management as Lou Lou in Pest, and serving food that's just as good, even if the pun in the name (a reference to Carnegie Hall)

doesn't quite work. Service is leisurely. Delicious steaks and chocolate torte. Mains 2000–4500Ft. Daily noon–midnight.

Gusto's II Frankel Leo utca ☎1/316-3970. Near the Buda side of Margit Bridge, this charming little bar serves light meals – as well as very good tiramisu, at moderate prices. Booking essential. Mon–Fri 10am–10pm, Sat 10am–4pm.

Horgásztanya I, Fő utca 27 ☎1/489-0236. An enjoyable fish restaurant that has resisted the forces of modernization, with decor that has remained unchanged for many years, and a regular clientele. Some of the best fish soups in the city are served here for under 2000Ft, in generous portions. Daily noon–11pm.

Márkus Vendéglő II, Lövőház utca 17 ☎1/212-3153. Large portions of traditional Hungarian dishes, such as *jókai bableves* and various stuffed turkey dishes, at this friendly restaurant. Prices are reasonable, with main courses in the 1200–3000Ft range. Menus in English available. Daily noon–midnight.

Rivalda I, Szinhaz utca 5–9 ☎1/489-0236. Unlike so many other places on Castle Hill, the *Rivalda* attracts a loyal local clientele. Prices are fairly steep, but in return you get cooking of a high standard (the chicken with mustard maple syrup and the chocolate gateau are especially recommended) and wacky, theatrically inspired decor. Daily 11.30am–11.30pm.

Tabán

For the locations of the places reviewed, see the map on p.111.

Tabáni Kakas I, Attila út 27 ☎1/375-7165. Popular old place specializing in poultry – it does an excellent *sült libacomb* (goose leg with mashed potatoes and cabbage) – but also serves good fish dishes, such as *paprikás harcsa* (catfish paprika). Main courses 1700–3200Ft, with a lunch menu of three courses and a drink for 2400Ft. Daily noon–midnight.

Tabáni Terasz I, Aprod utca 10 ☎1/201-1086. An excellent setting, on a terrace with views up to the Buda Palace. The interior is cosy in winter, with no-smoking rooms – still quite rare in Budapest. Refreshingly different variations on traditional dishes characterize the menu, such as duck steak with pink peppercorns (2800Ft). Daily noon–midnight.

Óbuda

For the locations of the places reviewed, see the maps on p.117 and p.118.

57 II, Pusztaszeri út 57 ☎1/325-6078, ⊛www .cafe57.hu. Sleek new neighbourhood restaurant with a very laid-back feel. Service is friendly and the cooking excellent, with a "fusion" feel – with steeper than average prices that reflect its air of exclusivity. Mains, such as the breast of duck marinated in honey and ginger, range from 2100Ft to 4600Ft. This is one of a number of places in the city offering spicy chocolate desserts – here, they serve chilli choc soufflé with ginger. Daily noon–1am.

Kerék III, Bécsi út 103 ☎1/250-4261. A small place serving traditional Hungarian food at very reasonable prices (1000–1700Ft for mains). *Srámli* (accordion) music is provided by a couple of old musicians (Mon–Sat from 6pm), and there's outside seating in summer. Daily noon–11pm.

Kéhli III, Mókus utca 22 ☎1/368-0613. One hundred years ago this was the favourite haunt of one of Hungary's great gourmands, the turn-of-the-century writer Gyula Krúdy, and today the *Kéhli* still serves the dishes he loved, such as beef soup served with bone marrow on garlic toast (a starter, for 1800Ft). The restaurant is set in one of the few old buildings in Óbuda to survive the Sixties planning blitz. Most main courses are around 3000Ft, and portions are generous. You can eat your fill to the accompaniment of a lively Hungarian gypsy band (from 8pm), though you'll need to book early to get a table close to the music. Daily noon–midnight.

Kisbuda Gyöngye III, Kenyeres utca 34 ☎1/368-6402. Good Hungarian food in the elegant surroundings of the "Pearl of Little Buda", which is filled with furniture from a fine *fin-de-siècle* well-to-do Budapest home. Gentle piano music and small courtyard at the back. Booking essential. Daily noon–midnight.

Sandwich bars, cafeterias and fast-food diners

Budapest has taken to fast food in a big way, and you'll have little trouble finding a *McDonald's*, *Pizza Hut* or *Burger King* if you want one. For a quick bite in a less commercial setting, try one of the excellent Chinese stand-up joints (*gyors büfé*), which can be found all over town. A Hungarian pecurality is the *étkezde* – a small, lunchtime diner where customers sit at shared tables and eat hearty home-cooked food.

Pest

Duran Sandwich Bar V, Október 6 utca 15 & XII, Retek utca 18. See maps, pp.56 & 93. A sandwich and coffee chain – filling a surprising gap in Budapest. Mon–Fri 8am–6pm, Sat 9am–1pm.

Falafel VI, Paulay Ede utca 53. See map, p.66. Budapest's most popular falafel joint, where you stuff your own pitta breads. Seating upstairs. Mon–Fri 10am–8pm, Sat 10am–6pm.

Három Testvér VI, Teréz körút 62 and XIII, Szent István körút 22. See maps, pp.56 & 66. Chain of Turkish kebab bars offering quick, cheap fare, with a good range of salady bits. Many other branches all over Pest. Daily 9am–3am.

Marie Kristensen Sandwich Bar IX, Ráday utca 7. See map, p.84. The Danish flavour the name implies is hard to spot – this is just a decent, regular sandwich bar. Mon–Fri 8am–9pm, Sat 11am–8pm.

Tower Restaurant Tenth floor of the Central European University, V, Nádor utca 9. See map, p.56. Inexpensive university cafétéria that serves excellent lunches and tasty snacks, and is open to all. Mon–Fri 10am–8pm (university members get priority noon–2pm).

Buda

Lánchíd I, Fő utca 4. See map, p.93. Atmospheric small bar serving hot and cold sandwiches, handily placed at the Buda end of the Chain Bridge. Daily 10am–midnight.

(13)

EATING | Sandwich bars, cafeterias and fast-food diners

Coffee houses and patisseries

D aily life in Budapest is still punctuated by the consumption of black coffee drunk from little glasses, though cappuccinos and white coffee are becoming ever more popular. These quintessentially Central European coffee breaks are less prolonged these days than before the war, when the **coffee house** (*kávéház*) was the social club, home and haven for its clientele. Free newspapers were available to the regulars – writers, journalists and lawyers (for whom the cafés were effectively "offices") or posing revolutionaries – with sympathy drinks or credit to those down on their luck. Today's coffee houses and **patisseries** (*cukrászda*) are less romantic but still full of character, whether fabulously opulent, with silver service, or homely and idiosyncratic.

The Belváros

The locations of places reviewed below are on the map on p.48.

Astoria Kávéház V, Kossuth utca 19. The *Astoria* hotel's coffee house/bar dates from the turn of the last century and is still popular with the locals, though sadly the management have removed the comfy armchairs. Daily 7am–11pm.

Central Kávéház V, Károlyi Mihály utca 9. In its heyday, the decades around World War I, this large coffee house was a popular venue in Budapest's literary scene. After many years as a dowdy university club, it has now been restored to its former grandeur. Also serves a wide range of food throughout the day, from cheap favourites such as creamed spinach to more expensive dishes. Daily 8am–midnight or 1am.

Gerbeaud V, Vörösmarty tér 7. A Budapest institution with a gilded salon and terrace, and good service; always packed with tourists. Around the corner is the Kis Gerbeaud ("Little Gerbeaud"), where you can get the same cakes far cheaper and without the scrum. Daily 9am–9pm.

Gerlóczy V Gerlóczy utca 1. Atmospheric corner café that serves some good snacks. Daily 8am–11pm.

Lipótváros

See the map on p.56 for the locations of places reviewed here.

Café Picard V, Falk Miksa utca 10. Elegant small French café near Parliament, serving good breakfasts (fresh croissants and excellent coffee) and lunches. They also serve up tapas-style dishes – you choose from a series on the menu – and have a good wine list. Mon–Fri 7am–11pm, Sat 9am–10pm.

Europa V, Szent Istv´án körút 7. Excellent cakes at this popular coffee house near the Margit híd.

Sport V, Bank utca 5. Seventies furniture and service and good cakes in this fine exam-

ple of an *ancien-régime* café.

🏃 **Szalai V, Balassi Bálint utca 4.** Old-style cake shop, one of the few remaining in Budapest, serving very good cakes near Parliament. Beneath its large gilt-framed mirrors are a few tables where the regulars watch the world passing. Daily except Tues 9am–7pm.

Terézváros and Erzsébetvaros

See the map on p.66 for the locations of places reviewed below.

Eckermann VI, Andrássy út 24. Attached to the Goethe Institute right by the Opera House, this is popular with young artists and writers (and also with bag thieves, take note). Internet access may be available (free for 30min), though this service has been known to come and go. Mon–Fri 8am–10pm, Sat 9am–10pm.

🏃 **Fröhlich VII, Dob utca 22.** Excellent kosher patisserie five minutes' walk from the Dohány utca synagogue, and a great people-watching place. Specialities include *flodni* (apple, walnut and poppy-seed cake), and the Fröhlich does the best in the city. Mon–Thurs 9am–6pm, Fri 7.30am–3pm, Sun 10am–4pm; closed Sat & Jewish holidays.

Godot VII, Madách út 8. Lively café serving snacks at lunchtimes, with a comedy theatre upstairs. Mon–Fri 9am–midnight, Sat–Sun 4pm–midnight

🏃 **Király V, Király utca 19.** Small patisserie serving excellent cakes and ice

cream, with a very cosy café upstairs. Daily 10am–midnight.

Lukács VI, Andrássy út 70. One of the old coffee houses, restored to its full grandeur by a bank, so you get one cake called "the banker" (bankár), and have to walk in through the bank's main entrance. Mon–Fri 8am–8pm, Sat 10am–8pm.

Művész VI, Andrássy út 29. There's an air of faded grandeur in this coffee house that's noted more for its decor – chandeliers and gilt – than its rather standard cakes. In summer the inside room gets very stuffy, with no air-conditioning. Still, the presence of elderly ladies in fur hats bears witness to the venue's success in retaining a loyal clientele over the years. Daily 8am–midnight.

Napos oldal VI, Jókai utca 7. On the corner of Zichy Jenő utca, this eco-café has a range of herbal teas and other drinks, and serves good salads and snacks. Not all the food here is organic – for that, you'll need to pop over to their organic shop across the road.

Józsefváros

🏃 **Múzeum Cukrászda VIII, Múzeum körút 10. See map, p.84.** Friendly hangout

near the National Museum. Fresh pastries arrive early in the morning. Open daily 24hr.

Buda

See the maps on pp.93, 94 and 118 for the locations of places reviewed below.

🏃 **Ági Rétes II, Retek utca 19.** Best *rétes* in town, all baked on the cosy premises of this patisserie near Moszkva tér. Mon–Fri 10am–6pm, Sat 10am–2pm.

Angelika I, Batthyány tér 7. Quiet but smoky coffee house in a former convent, with comfy seats under its vaulted ceilings. Also has a lively terrace. Daily 10am–midnight.

🏃 **Artigiana Gelati XII, Csaba utca. 8** Exotic flavours and the best quality ice cream in town, just up the road from Moszkva tér. Mon noon-8.30pm, Tues–Sun 10.30am–8.30pm

Daubner III, Szépvölgyi út 29. In spite of the rumours that its profits help fund right-wing groups, this patisserie in Óbuda is always crowded, especially at weekends, when people will patiently queue up for its admittedly delicious cakes, such as the plum slipper (*szilvás papucs*) or pumpkin seed scone (*tökmagos pogácsa*).

Ruszwurm I, Szentháromság tér 7. Near the Mátyás Church in the Castle District, this diminutive Baroque coffee house can be so packed that it's almost impossible to get a seat in summer. Delicious cakes and ices. Daily 10am–8pm.

Bars and clubs

B udapest's nightlife scene is small – spend a few evenings drinking and clubbing and you'll be spotting familiar faces. The scene centres on three main areas: **Liszt Ferenc tér** (the place to see and be seen); semi-pedestrianized **Ráday utca**, running down from Kalvin tér, which, with its innumerable cafés and terraces, styles itself the Budapest Soho; and **Krudy Gyula utca**, between the National Museum and the Nagykörút. Another concentration of bars is in the VII district. These are set up in condemned buildings: most of them move from year to year, but they have become an established feature. The gay and lesbian scene is covered separately in chapter 16.

Bars

Budapest's bars can be divided into three kinds: the *borozó* (wine bar), the *söröző* (beer bar) and the newer, more lively bars that don't bother with such distinctions. The majority of **wine bars** are nothing like their counterparts in the West, being mainly working men's watering holes offering such humble snacks as *zsíros kenyér* (bread and pork dripping with onion and paprika). Conversely, **beer halls** (*söröző*) are often quite upmarket, striving to resemble an English pub or a German *bierkeller*, and serving full meals. The new bars aim at a younger generation and have live music or DJs, table football and other attractions. These bars will sell whatever people are drinking – and all bars sell *pálinka*, the powerful Hungarian schnapps. A big growth area has been **summer outdoor bars**: big open-air ones such as *Sark kert* and *Zöld Pardon*, and the more interesting venues that are squeezed – often temporarily – into abandoned buildings (and their gardens) in the VII District, such as *Szódakert* and *Szimplakert*. The latter group are often run by established bars as summertime ventures, so while they may move from year to year, they retain their name. To find out the latest situation, you can either ask at the bars which run these operations – such as the *Szóda*, *Sark* and *Cha-cha-cha* – or look in the listings magazines (see p.26). Some of these venues also have dance floors and are covered under "Clubs" on p.168.

Most places open around lunchtime and stay open until after midnight, unless otherwise stated, though bars in residential areas have to close their terraces at 10pm. There is a good network of night buses (see p.31) which can help you make your way home after a late night out, though they run only every half-hour or so. See p.39 for warnings about **rip-offs** in restaurants, which apply equally to bars.

The Belváros

Spoon V, on the river by the Inter-Continental hotel Ⓦ www.spooncafe.hu. **See map, p.48.** A bar enjoying a grand setting, looking across to the Lanchíd and the Buda Palace. The toilets have the best views of any toilets in Budapest. There's also a restaurant, which is good but expensive, with cocky waiters. Daily noon–2am.

Lipótváros

Tokaji Borozó V, Falk Miksa utca 32. See map, p.56. Lively, smoky old-style cellar wine bar serving wines from the Tokaj region in northeast Hungary, as well as snacks such as *lapsánka* (potato pancakes) and *zsíros kenyér*. Mon–Fri noon–9pm.

Terézváros and Erzsébetváros

For the locations of the places reviewed here, see the map on p.66.
Brooklyn VI, Jókai utca 4. Smoky cellar bar with excellent music every night from 9pm. One of their regular bands plays excellent jazz with a strong Roma accent. Tues–Sun 7pm–3am.

Kuplung VII, Király utca 46. A new, surprisingly large bar down a narrow alleyway in what was once a police stable and later a moped repair shop (the name means "clutch"). Has table football and regular live music in its highly soundproofed side-room. Daily till late.

Old Man's Music Pub VII, Akácfa utca 13, Ⓦ www.oldmans.hu. Large, popular joint near Blaha Lujza tér, with live local acts and good food. Daily 3pm–dawn.

Picasso Point VI, Hajos utca 31 Ⓦ www.picassopoint.hu. This spacious bar has comfortable chairs upstairs and a disco downstairs (not during summer break). Also serves food. Popular and relaxed. Mon–Fri noon–midnight, Sat 6pm–midnight.

Potkulcs VI, Csengery utca 65b. In a former workshop. Atmospheric and laid-back, it's popular with a youngish crowd. As befits a venue whose name means "spare key", you enter through a small metal door into a shaded yard. The bar is straight ahead, while off to the left is a room with sofas and table football. Some live music. Gets very smoky in winter. Mon–Wed & Sun 5pm–1.30am, Thurs–Sat 5pm–2.30am.

Sark VII, Klauzál tér 14. Small, heaving bar, decorated with massive murals. DJs and good live music (world/klezmer/Roma) downstairs from September to May. From June to September much of the action moves to the Sark kert at the southern tip of the Margit sziget – ask at the bar for directions. Daily 6am–3am.

Szóda VII, Wesselényi utca 18 Ⓦ www.szoda.com. Busy bar behind the main synagogue. Pleasant laid-back music from the DJs, not too expensive and no pretensions. There's free Wi-Fi access too. Check the website for its summertime venture (*Szóda Udvar* or *Szóda Kert*). Mon–Fri 9am–midnight, Sat & Sun 2pm–midnight or later, unless the neighbours are complaining.

Szimplakert VII, Kazinczy utca 14 Ⓦ www.szimpla.hu. Atmospheric bar spilling over from room to room, with good music, regular film showings (600Ft) in the garden and free Wi-Fi access. During school summer holidays it runs the *Kis Szimplakert* in the nearby courtyard of the school at VI, Hegedűs utca 3, which puts on excellent live music. Daily noon–midnight.

Vian VI, Liszt Ferenc tér 11. Less pretentious than others on this posiest of squares, with pleasant staff, a relaxed atmosphere and good food. Free Wi-Fi access. Daily 9am–midnight.

Joszefváros and Ferencváros

For the locations of the places reviewed here, see the map on p.84.

Castro IX, Ráday utca 35. A popular place on the corner with Kinizsi utca, attracting a good mix of locals and expats. The Serb chef rustles up excellent food, such as spinach pies. Internet access too. Daily 10am–midnight/1am.

Csiga VIII, Vásár utca 2. By the Rákóczi tér market hall, this friendly, smoky corner bar is popular with locals and expats. Good food and occasional live music. Mon–Sat 11am–1am.

Darshan Udvar VIII, Krudy Gyula utca 7. This, the largest bar in a growing complex of bars, cafés and shops, with exuberant Gaudíesque decorations, generous and tasty servings of food, and live music. There's an outdoor terrace in the summer. Leisurely service. Mon–Wed 11am–1am, Thurs–Sat 11am–2am, Sun 6pm–midnight.

BARS AND CLUBS | Bars

Ötödik bejaró IX, Pipa utca 6. The "Fifth Entrance" is right by the Great Market Hall. It's a very relaxed place run by the friendly Hans, who sometimes plays his saxophone in the downstairs space (they have excellent jazz a couple of times a week). Mon–Thurs 8am-1am, Fri–Sat 8am-2am, Sun 2pm-1am.

Paris-Texas IX, Ráday utca 22. Stylish café with pool tables and a good atmosphere. Mon–Fri 10am–3am, Sat & Sun 1pm–3am.

Buda

A38 Moored on the Danube just south of the Buda bridgehead of Petőfi híd ☎1/464-3946, Ⓦwww.a38.hu. See map, p.84. This former Ukrainian stone transporter ship (the *Artemovsk 38*, for boat-spotters) is one of the more exciting venues in town, an all-round player. Top international and Hungarian bands play in the concert venue downstairs. There's a very good restaurant, too, where the menu is on a card index.

Bambi I, Frankel Leó utca 2–4. See map, p.93. One of the few surviving socialist-realist bars, with stern waitresses and red plastic-covered seats. They serve breakfast, omelettes, snack lunches, cakes and alcohol all day long. Mon–Fri 7am–9pm, Sat & Sun 9am–8pm.

Café Pierrot I, Fortuna utca 14. See map, p.94. A rare elegant hangout in the Communist era, these days *Pierrot* remains one of the better places in the Castle area, and serves decent food as well, though the easy-listening piano music can be a bit much. Daily 11am–midnight.

Kecskeméti Borozó II, Széna tér. See map, p.93. By Moszkva tér, on the corner of Retek utca, is this crowded, sweaty and smoky stand-up wine bar. A notice on the wall reads "We do not serve drunks", but that would rule out most of the people inside. However, they do serve that staple of Hungarian bar fare, *zsíros kenyér*. Mon–Sat 9am–11pm.

Móri Borozó I, Fiáth János utca 16, just up from Moszkva tér. See map, p.93. Cheap and cheerful neighbourhood venue attracting a young crowd. Darts and bar billiards in the room at the far end. June–Aug daily 4–11pm; Sept–May Mon–Sat 2–11pm, Sun 2–9pm.

Ponyvaregény XI, Bercsényi utca 5. See map, p.111. The books around the walls (the name means "pulp fiction") and the sofas give this spacious cellar bar a very friendly feel. A popular student hangout – the technical university is round the corner. Daily 10am–2am.

Clubs

Budapest is catching up fast in both the quantity and quality of its **clubs**, and is growing in popularity as a destination for young Westerners. The scene is especially varied in the summer, when it expands into several large outdoor venues, and there are also one-off events held in the old Turkish baths or sites further out of town (look out for promotional posters at bus stops).

DJs to look out for include Yonderboi, Keyser and Shuriken (easy listening), Palotai, Titus and Mango (drum 'n' bass) and Superbeat (nujazz); anything run by Tilos Rádió, the former pirate radio, is usually good.

Expect to pay 1000–4000Ft to get into a club, and be warned that it's worth keeping on the right side of the bouncers (a common feature of Budapest nightlife). You'll also find dancing in some of the bars listed above, including the *A38* boat, *Old Man's Music Pub* and *Picasso Point*, as well as in the three big arts centres: the Petőfi Csarnok (see p.173), Almássy téri Szabadidő Központ, and the Trafó (see p.173).

Pest

Cha-cha-cha IX, Kálvin tér subway Ⓦwww.chachacha.hu. See map, p.84. Glam Seventies bar with fake zebra furnishings and a louche feel. Despite its strange location, it attracts a big crowd spilling

out into the concourse, and there are DJs Thurs–Sat eves. Check website for the location of its outdoor summer venture, the *Cha-cha-cha terasz*. Mon–Fri 7am–2am, Sat 10am–2am.

Franklin Trocadero Café V, Szent István körút 15. See map, p.56. Excellent Latin music and dancing just up from Nyugati Station. Daily 9pm–5am.

Petőfi Csarnok XIV, Zichy M. út 14 ☎ 1/363-3730, ⓦ www.petoficsarnok.hu. See map, p.76. Huge purpose-built youth centre near the back of the Városliget, hosting the Madonna Club, the Pet Shop Boys Club and other band-specific DJ nights, concerts by local and big-name foreign bands and contemporary dance performance. There's a very good flea market (Sat & Sun mornings). Call for more details in English.

Piaf VI, Nagymező utca 25. See map, p.66. This old favourite is basically a small ground-floor bar and a cellar graced by the odd Hungarian film star and lots of wannabes, with occasional jazz or rock live sets. Entry costs 800Ft, of which 600Ft is drinkable, but it's free to get in on Sunday, when only the bar is open. Daily from 10pm until well after dawn.

West Balkán IX, Kisfaludy utca 36. See map, p.84. Packed but chilled dance spot which has been known to migrate (check listings magazines for the latest location). The Kisfaludy utca setting is another example of a Pest bar with a sprawling set of rooms and a large garden that also doubles as a dance area (there's another dance floor in the cellar). Attracts good DJs. May–Sept daily 5pm–dawn.

Buda

Zöld Pardon XI, Goldmann György tér ⓦ www .zp.hu. See map, p.84. Large, heaving outdoor bar near the Petőfi bridgehead, where you can dance to drum 'n' bass, deep house and jungle. A great venue, sadly marred by punch-ups and knifings despite heavy security. Daily 9am–6am (kitchen noon–6am).

16

Gay Budapest

Budapest's **gay scene** has taken wing in recent years, with new, overtly gay clubs replacing the old, covert meeting places, and the appearance of a trilingual monthly listings magazine, *Mások* ("Outsiders"). This greater prominence is also reflected in law – the age of consent is 14 for homosexuals and heterosexuals alike, and Parliament is moving towards a legal framework for homosexual couples, though if the conservative Fidesz party gets back into power, expect that to be delayed.

These changes are gradual rather than radical; while Budapest is a cosmopolitan city, Hungarian society at large is socially conservative. Gays must still tread warily and lesbians even more so. The Hungarian word for gay is *meleg* – "warm"; *buzi* is the commonly used pejorative term – it derives from the word *buzeráns*, which has the same roots as "bugger".

The Budapest gay scene is very male-dominated. Perhaps the best spot for lesbians is the *Eklektika* bar (see right), though there is also a women-only lesbian group, Ösztrosokk, that meets at 9.30pm on the last Saturday of the month at the *Living Room*, V, Kossuth utca 17 (next to the *Astoria* hotel). The **website** Ⓦ www.gayguide.net has the latest on gay accommodation, bars, clubs, restaurants, baths and events in the city. The largest gay and lesbian organization in town is **Háttér** (Ⓦ www.hatter.hu), which runs a **helpline** (daily 6–11pm; ☏ 329-3380) that can give advice and information on events – although some of the operators only speak Hungarian.

The major event in the gay calendar is **Gay Pride Budapest**, a well-established four-day festival taking place in late June or early July. Incorporating a varied programme of film festivals, public discussion forums and gay parties, it culminates in the colourful Pride March at the weekend, which wends its way from Dózsa György út along Andrassy út, down to Roosevelt tér, across the Lánchíd and left down to the Tabán.

Bars and restaurants

Most of the bars listed opposite levy an **entry fee** or set a minimum consumption level – being gay in Budapest is an expensive privilege. Some venues give you a card when you enter, on which all your drinks are written down; you pay for your drinks and the entry fee as you leave. Be warned that if you lose the card, you'll have to pay a lot of money.

The Belváros

The places reviewed here appear on the map on p.48.

Action V, Magyar utca 42 Ⓦ www.action.gay.hu. The most hardcore of the gay bars, full of young men looking for one-night stands. The entrance is 15m along from the big "A" sign on the door. Dark room and video room. Minimum consumption 1300Ft. Daily 9pm–4am.

Amstel River Café V, Párisi utca 6. Not on the river but in the middle of the Belváros, this Dutch-style pub-restaurant attracts a large foreign clientele and is popular with gays. Daily noon–midnight.

Capella V, Belgrád rakpart 23 Ⓦ www.extra. hu/capellacafe. Drag queens, jungle music and lots of kitsch, with decor as outrageous as the acts. It's become a well-known haunt, and prices are highish. Popular with straights, though more gays come on Wednesdays (when there is no entry fee). Shows start at 11.30pm and 2am. Entry 1500Ft Fri & Sat, possibly higher on special occasions. Daily 10pm–4am or later.

Club 93 V, Vas utca 2 ☎ 1/338-1119. A cheap pizzeria just off Rákóczi út, popular with gays and lebians. The gallery and window seating make it a good place to people-watch. Daily 11am–midnight.

CoXx (formerly Chaos) V, Dohány utca 38 Ⓦ www.coxxpub.hu. The most cultured of the gay bars, this men-only venue is a friendly place to meet. The ground floor is a gallery and Internet café; downstairs is a recently enlarged dance floor, video rooms and numerous other spaces. Minimum consumption 1000Ft. Daily 9pm–4am.

Darling V, Szép utca 1. A men-only beer-house and gallery that gets "warmer" after 9pm and stays open till late. Attracts a lot of Romanian prostitutes. Free entry. Daily 7pm–3am.

Eklektika V, Semmelweis utca 21. Lesbian and gay-friendly café bar – an inviting space with 1960s furniture, good food and a very relaxed feel. DJs on Tuesdays, jazz on Thursdays and regular dancing lessons. No entry fee. Daily noon–midnight.

Elsewhere in the city

Angyál Bár VII, Dohány utca 28 (entered from Kazinczy utca) Ⓦ www.angyalbar.com. See map, **p.66.** Budapest's premier gay club attracts an interesting crowd. Tranny show 11pm, followed by disco. On Friday it's popular with women, when there's karaoke too. Saturdays are men only. Entry 1300Ft. Fri & Sat 10pm–dawn.

Fenyögyöngye II, Szépvölgyi út 155 t1/325-9783. See map, p.117. This restaurant is gay-owned, not that many who go there know that. It's at the last stop of the #65 bus from Kolosy tér in Óbuda. Good Hungarian food, polite service. Daily noon–11pm.

Mystery Bar V, Nagysándor József utca 3, Ⓦ www.mysterybar.hu. See map, p.56. Very small bar near the Arany József utca metro, for talking rather than dancing – there's no disco. Internet café too. Free entry; happy hours Fri & Sat. Mon–Fri 4pm–4am, Sat & Sun 6pm–4am.

Baths

Budapest's first private gay **bath** is Magnum Sauna & Gym at VIII, Csepreghy utca 2 (Mon–Thurs & Sun 1pm–1am, Fri & Sat 1pm–6am; 1600Ft; ☎ 1/267-2532, Ⓦ www.magnumszauna.hu), near the Ferenc körut metro stop. It opened in 2001 and has a steam room and dry sauna, as well as a gym and numerous smaller spaces. Gay activity in the public steam baths has been dealt a blow by a TV report in early 2005 showing video footage of gay encounters, taken secretly in the Király Baths. At the time of writing, swimming costumes were compulsory at the Király and the baths were patrolled to prevent "untoward behaviour". Locals believe it will be business as usual soon, although there is no saying when that will be; if attitudes swing the other way, compulsory swimming costumes could be introduced at the other male steam baths.

Of the public baths, the Király used to see the most action, while the Rudas Baths were considered gay-friendly, as were the Gellért and the Lukács. The sun terrace at the Palatinus strand and the roof terrace at the Széchenyi remain popular gay meeting places. Note that increased entry fees mean that you see fewer young local men and more tourists in the baths.

Entertainment

ive **music** is one of Budapest's strengths: the country has a huge depth of talent (see the colour insert on music for more), and most evenings you can choose from classical, folk and jazz performances. The city also boasts some stunning **cinemas** and **theatres** that are worth visiting for their architecture alone. If you are undeterred by the language barrier, an evening at the theatre can be a rewarding experience. Language is less of a problem at cinemas, with foreign films often screened in their original language.

Tickets for most big events are available from numerous outlets in the city: Filharmónia, V, Madách utca 3 (Mon–Fri 10am–5pm; ℡1/321-4199); Publika (no credit cards) at VII, Károly körút 9 (℡1/322-2010); the Rózsavölgyi ticket office, in the record shop of the same name at V, Szervita tér 5 (near Deák tér; Mon–Fri 10am–6pm, Sat 10am–3pm); and TicketExpress (credit cards accepted for purchases made through the website only), VI, Andrássy út 18 (Mon Fri 9.30am–6.30pm, Sat 9am–1pm; ℡1/312-0000, ⓦwww.ticketexpress.hu). Ticket prices for major international acts will often have a small handling fee slapped on them.

If you can't get tickets for a performance, it is always worth persevering with the staff at the ticket office or door, as there is often some way in, even if it costs a bit extra – for instance, the Music Academy puts aside tickets each performance for a fire and a police officer, which are often not used, and it also has space on its top balcony.

Arts centres and multi-purpose venues

The venues listed below are used for a variety of concerts and other entertainment events. Bear in mind that many arts centres close for the summer.

A38 XI, Pázmány Péter sétány ℡1/464-3940, ⓦwww.a38.hu. One of the best new venues on a boat moored on the Buda side of the river bank, just below Petőfi Bridge. Attracts top international and Hungarian performers in the worlds of rock, jazz, folk and world music.

Aranytíz V, Arany János utca 10 ℡1/311-2248, ⓦwww.aranytiz.hu. Besides the excellent Saturday folk dance sessions, its programme includes Hungarian and international theatre performances and jazz concerts.

Budapest Convention Centre (Budapest Kongresszusi Központ) XII, Jagelló út 1–3 ℡1 /209-1990. Modern venue behind the Novotel, hosting big concerts; good acoustics but low on atmosphere.

Millenáris Park II, Fény utca 20–22 ⓦwww. millenaris.hu. The Fogadó concert hall regularly hosts good concerts and festivals, some featuring international acts. In summer concerts are held on the park's outdoor stages.

Palace of Arts (Művészetek palotája) IX, Komor Marcell utca 1 Ⓦwww.mupa.hu. This substantial new complex has a top-of-the-range concert hall, theatre and museum, and as the shop-window for the capital's culture scene, it's ensured a superb range of concerts, attracting the top international performers in the classical music, jazz and world music.
Petofi Csarnok XIV, Zichy Mihály út 14. ☎1/363-3730 Ⓦwww.petoficsarnok.hu. On the edge of the Városliget, this big hall is often used by local and international rock and jazz acts – as well as hosting weekend flea markets and occasional craft fairs.
Trafó IX, Liliom utca 41 ☎1/456-2040, Ⓦwww.trafo.hu. A dynamic contemporary arts centre in a former transformer station. It pulls full houses with concerts and theatre and dance performances, by Hungarian and foreign artistes. Good bar downstairs.

Classical music, opera and ballet

The city offers a wide variety of **classical music** performances, with several concerts most nights, especially during the Budapest Spring and Autumn festivals (see p.37 and p.38 respectively).

You can enjoy **opera** and **ballet** in Budapest at a very reasonable price, even treating yourself to several glasses of (Hungarian) champagne in the bar during the interval. Most opera productions are in Hungarian, a custom introduced by Mahler when he was director of the State Opera House. Of the two venues, the grandest is the State Opera House, while the Erkel Theatre is much more modern. The Opera House has its own box office (inside the main doors or, if they are closed, round on the left-hand side of the building in Dalszinház utca, Mon–Sat 11am–5pm, Sun 4–7pm) for events there and in the Erkel Theatre.

Besides the key venues listed below, a few places of worship regularly host concerts, among them the **Kálvín tér church**; the **Lutheran Church** on Deák tér (see p.53; the programme includes free performances of Bach before Easter, details of which are posted by the church entrance); and the **Dohány utca synagogue** (see p.70). The **Mátyás Church** on Várhegy (see p.95) stages choral or organ recitals on Fridays and Saturdays between June and September (from 8pm), and less frequently the rest of the year.

The opera, theatre and concert halls take a **summer break** at the end of May, reopening in mid-September; there is a summer season of concerts at open-air venues, including the outdoor stage on Margit sziget, the **Dominican Yard** of the Hilton hotel in the Castle District, and the **Vajdahunyad Castle** in the Városliget, though the music they offer is fairly mainstream.

A comprehensive listing, in Hungarian, of classical music events can be found at Ⓦwww.koncertkalendarium.hu, in the free monthly Koncert Kalendárium found in ticket offices or in listings magazines (see p.26). Regular concerts are held at the following venues.

Bartók Memorial House (Bartók Emlékház) II, Csalán utca 29. Concerts – not just of the music of Bartók – are held in the villa where the composer used to live, most Fridays at 11am.
Erkel Theatre (Erkel Színház) VIII, Köztársaság tér 30 ☎1/333-0540. A modern venue for operas, ballet and musicals, near Blaha Lujza tér.
Music Academy (Zeneakadémia) VI, Liszt Ferenc tér 8 ☎342-0179. Founded by Liszt in 1875, it hosts nightly concerts and recitals in the magnificent gold-covered Nagyterem (Great Hall) or the smaller Kisterem. The music is excellent and the place has a real buzz.
National Concert Hall (Nemzeti Hangversenyterem) In the Palace of Arts (see above). This concert hall was designed by a top international architect and has superb acoustics. As the shop-window for the capital's culture scene, it's ensured a superb range of concerts, attracting the top international performers, not just in the classical arena.

Old Music Academy (Régi Zeneakadémia) VI, Vörösmarty utca 35. Performances by young musicians every Saturday morning, in the concert hall of the Liszt Memorial Museum.
Opera House (Magyar Állami Operaház) VI, Andrássy út 22 ☎1/353-0170, ⊛www.opera.hu. Budapest's grandest venue, with gilded frescoes and three-tonne chandeliers – a place to dress up for. Tickets 600-900Ft – or up to 15,000Ft for big names.
Operetta Theatre (Operett Színház) VI, Nagymező utca 17 ☎1/332-0535 ⊛www.operettszinhaz.

hu. The stunningly refurbished home of Hungarian operetta. Here you can enjoy works by Lehár and Kálmán, who achieved international fame with their work, as well as modern musicals.
Pesti Vigadó V, Vigadó tér 1. Another fabulously decorated hall, though the acoustics are inferior. Dating from 1865, it is the oldest of the major concert venues and several Liszt premiers were performed here. Closed for restoration at the time of writing.

Pop, rock, jazz and contemporary dance music

Budapest attracts every Hungarian **band** worth its amplifiers and a growing roll-call of international stars, appearances by whom are well publicized in the media. Posters around town – particularly around Deák tér, Ferenciek tere and the Astoria underpass – publicize concerts by local bands. Don't get too excited by flyposters advertising Michael Jackson or the Cure, however, as these usually refer to light shows or themed nights at clubs and discos. Concert ticket prices range from 1000Ft for local bands and up to as much as 15,000Ft for stadium gigs by international superstars. Don't be fooled by the small number of regular **jazz** venues in Budapest – the country boasts some brilliant jazz players, some of them well known abroad. Apart from the venues listed below, performances take place at the venues listed on pp.172–173; at the vast Puskás Ferenc Stadion, the smaller Kisstadion or the Papp László Sportaréna (all in the same complex); and in a number of the venues listed in chapter 15, such as the *Gödör Klub* and *Ötödik bejáró*. There are also occasional jazz concerts in theatres such as *Mu Színház* and *Studio K* (see p.178).

The biggest venue of all is the Óbudai (or Hajógyári) sziget north of Margit sziget, which in mid-August hosts the week-long **Sziget festival** (⊛www.sziget.hu/fesztival), one of the big European music events. In 2005, 170 international stars including Franz Ferdinand, Nick Cave and Youssou N'dour, and 450 Hungarian performers (such as the rock group Korai Öröm), attracted 385,000 people, served by 74 bars and 27 buffets. Day tickets cost €20, weekly tickets €100. Going by foot, you take the HÉV from Batthyány tér to the Filorigát stop and follow the crowds across the bridge to the island. Slightly less crowded is the bus from Deák tér and the boats from Batthyány tér or Jászai Mari tér, at the Pest end of the Margit híd (see the website for more information).

Brooklyn VI, Jókai utca 4. Relaxed bar run by accomplished Roma musicians, whose improvisational jazz is worth catching. Music starts at 9pm – except on Monday, when it's closed, and Thursday, when there's English stand-up comedy.
Fonó Budai Zeneház XI, Sztregova utca 3 ☎1/206-5300, ⊛www.fono.hu. Lively international folk, world music and jazz venue, 2km south of Móricz Zsigmond körtér, four stops on tram #18 or #47.

Jazz Garden V, Veres Pálné utca 44A ☎1/266-7364, ⊛www.jazzgarden.hu. Cellar jazz bar and restaurant. Guests include Hungarian stars Béla Szakcsi Lakatos and Aladár Pege, as well as local resident American blues guitarist Bruce Lewis. Daily noon–1am.
New Orleans Jazz Club VI, Lovas utca 5 ☎06-20/451-7525, ⊛www.neworleans.hu. New modern bar attracting big international names – but ticket prices can be astronomical even by Western standards. Daily noon–2am.

△ Korai Öröm on stage

Folk music and dance

Hungarian **folk music** and **dancing** underwent a revival in the 1970s, drawing inspiration from Hungarian communities in Transylvania, regarded as pure well-springs of Magyar culture. Enthusiasts would form a **táncház** ("dance house"), to play folk music on traditional instruments and teach the old dance steps to young Hungarians. The movement still exists today, and has been extended to other cultures – you'll also see adverts for Greek (görög), Roma and other dance houses. Visitors are welcome to attend the gatherings (350–800Ft admission; see ⓦ www.tanchaz.hu for more) and learn the steps.

Concerts of Hungarian folk music by the likes of Muzsikás, Téka, Ökrös and Kalamajka take place regularly, while there are also performances by groups such as Vujicsics, inspired by South Slav music from Serbia, Croatia and Bulgaria. There has been a sudden growth in **Roma** groups as the local communities discover their own voice, and the old Jewish musical traditions are continued by a number of klezmer performers such as Di Naye Kapelye. Apart from the venues listed below, performances take place at the venues listed on pp.172–173 and in bars and clubs listed in chapter 15.

A38 See p.172. This floating venue attracts top folk and world music international and Hungarian performers.
Aranytíz See p.172. The Kalamajka ensemble plays here to a packed dance floor on Saturday nights from late September through to early June. Dance teaching from 7pm – the children's session begins at 5pm. There is also music in the bar upstairs, and as the evening rolls on a jamming session often develops.
Fonó Budai Zeneház See p.174. Every

Wednesday evening, dance house led by Téka, Méta or Tükrös.
Millenáris Park See p.172. Muzsikás and the top local ethno-jazz group, the Dresch Quartet, perform here.
Műhely VII, Dohány utca 84 (entrance from Almássy utca). Cellar bar with folk and other music and a lively atmosphere.

Potkulcs VI, Csengery utca 65b. Dance house every other Sunday, featuring Téka, and there is regular live music.
Roma Parlament VIII, Tavaszmező 6. Regular concerts by Roma stars such as Ando Drom in the run-down home of the Roma Assembly.

Cinema

Hollywood blockbusters and Euro soft-porn films dominate Budapest's mainstream **cinemas**, though the city has a chain of art-house cinemas that specialize in the latest releases and obscure European films – *angol* indicates a British film, *lengyel* Polish, *német* German, *olasz* Italian, and *orosz* Russian. A host of **multiplex** cinemas showing the latest Hollywood blockbusters and mainstream fare can be found across the city, including the Corvin Film Palace at VIII, Corvin köz 1 (Corvin Filmpalota; ☎1/459-5050, ⓦwww.corvin.hu), and the Palace Westend in the Westend City Center by Nyugati Station (☎1/336-5555).

Cinema listings – including details of which films are dubbed and which subtitled – can be found on the English website ⓦwww.pestiside.hu, and the *Budapest Sun* runs listings of all movies playing in English. The fullest **listings** appear in Hungarian in the free *Pesti Est* (see the *mozi* section). The times of shows are cryptically abbreviated to *n8* or *1/4 8* for 7.15pm; *f8* or *1/2 8* for

Hungary on film

Hungarians have an impressive record in film, and many of the Hollywood greats were **Hungarian emigrés** – Michael Curtiz, Sir Alex Korda, George Cukor, and actors Béla Lugosi, Tony Curtis and Leslie Howard to name but a few. In the Communist years Hungarian films continued to make waves, with Károly Makk, István Szabó, Márta Mészáros and others making films that managed to say much about the oppressive regime in spite of its restrictions. Now the main restriction on film makers is chronic underfunding, but what the Hungarian film industry lacks in money it makes up for in ideas.

Established directors to look out for are **Peter Gothár**, with his absurd humour and love of the fantastic (*Time Stands Still, Let Me Hang Vaska*), **Ildikó Enyedi** (*My Twentieth Century* and *Simon the Magician*), **Béla Tarr** (*Werckmeister Harmonies* and the epic eight-hour *Satan Tango*) and **János Szász**, whose film *The Witman Boys* won the best international film at Cannes. Other rising stars are Kornél Mundroczó, Szabolcs Hajdú, Nimrod Antal, whose first film, the black comedy *Kontroll*, was a big hit abroad, and György Pálfi, whose *Hukkle* similarly won international acclaim.

Budapest has been a popular **location** for films, both for its looks and its cheapness, serving as Buenos Aires in *Evita* and as Paris in the *Maigret* TV series – the view towards the Basilica down Lázár utca behind the Opera House acts as the view of the Sacre Coeur, and in the series Paris developed a hill rising on one bank of the Seine rather like that in Budapest. But it also serves as itself: the American documentary *Divan* by Pearl Gluck captures some of the characters and atmosphere of the old Jewish quarter in its interviews.

DVDs, most of them subtitled, have made Hungarian films much more accessible, making it possible to enjoy classics such as Géza Radványi's *Valahol Európában* (1947) and Zoltán Fábri's *Körhinta* (1955).

Hungarian
music

From the dazzling Gypsy violinists who inspired Brahms' *Hungarian Dances* to Márta Sebestyén's soaring voice in the *The English Patient* film score, Hungarian music has long exerted a fascination over foreigners. Both Sebestyén and Brahms' fiddlers are products of a culture that values music very highly: for the Hungarian people – a Magyar island in a sea of Slavs – music has always been a crucial means of expressing their identity. This being Eastern Europe, there has been a constant exchange with other

musics of the region – Slav, Germanic, Romanian and more – and many of Hungary's best-known musicians have been from Jewish or Gypsy backgrounds. What's more, the various musical traditions within Hungary – classical, folk, pop – have intermingled. This fusion of styles has ensured the magnetism of Hungarian music remains as strong as ever.

Classical music

Hungary's classical music tradition is so strong that the roll call of home-grown icons is out of all proportion to the size of the population: contemporary **composers** such as György Ligeti and György Kurtág, stalwart **conductors** like Sir Georg Solti and George Széll, and of course great **musicians**, from Annie Fischer to Joseph Szigeti and Sándor Végh. Classical music is a thriving entity in Budapest, and if you want to take in a concert you'll be spoilt for choice. The pick of the **orchestras** are the Budapest Festival, conducted by the charismatic Iván Fischer (ⓦwww.bfz.hu), and the National Philharmonic under Zoltán Kocsis (ⓦwww.hunphilharmonic .org.hu). Ever the innovator, Fischer established his orchestra as the first privately funded ensemble in the country and his radical approach has won accolades all around the world. Kócsis made his name as a brilliant pianist via his interpretations of Bartók but as a conductor

Hungary's classical innovators

Béla Bartók

Credited with shaping Hungary's old musical traditions into their modern form, the triumvirate of Liszt, Bartók and Kodály have left a lasting and potent legacy. The finest pianist of his day and a great innovator, **Ferenc (Franz) Liszt** (1811–1886) did a huge service to his homeland by founding Budapest's Music Academy, which has turned out so many great musicians. Two of its students were **Béla Bartók** (1881–1945) and **Zoltán Kodály** (1882–1967), who together pioneered the recording of folk music – not just Hungarian, but also Slovakian, Ruthenian, Romanian and others. Their attempts to promote both contemporary and folk forms met with a hostile reception initially but today, a century after they first met in 1905, audiences in Budapest are remarkably receptive to both genres. Bartók went on to make his name as a composer, while Kodály – no mean composer himself – played a key role in musical education: today, every Hungarian child learns the Kodály version of do-re-mi, with its accompanying hand movements.

has forged distinction out of an ordinary ensemble. Look out also for performances by the Radio and Television Symphony Orchestra (or Budapest Symphony Orchestra, as they are sometimes called), conducted by Ádám Fischer; the Budafók Dohnányi Ernő Symphony Orchestra, under Gábor Hollerung; and three excellent **chamber ensembles**: the Liszt Ferenc Chamber Orchestra, the Budapest Strings (*Budapesti Vónosók*) and the Weiner Száz Orchestra.

Budapest is equally well supplied with excellent **soloists**. You'll be lucky to catch the Hungarian pianist András Schiff (now based in Britain), but other internationally recognised pianists who regularly perform here include Tamás Vasary, Péter Frankl, Desző Ránki and Zoltán Kocsis; emerging star Gábor Csalog is also worth hearing. Two young violinists to look out for are Barnabás Kelemen and József Lendvai, while the cellist Miklós Perényi is an old hand on the classical circuit. Finally, the organist Xavier Varnus deserves a special mention: an inspired musician, he packs churches and concert halls both for his technique and his unusual approach, performing variations on any tune the audience names.

Hungarian State Opera House

Folk music

Far from withering away with the peasant culture that spawned it, **folk music** has proved surprisingly resilient and its survival highlights the centrality of music to Hungarian life. Back in the 1960s, when the Communist party stifled any independent initiatives and when anything national in character smacked of anti-Communism, folk was reduced to sanitized performances by big groups such as the State Folk Dance Ensemble. Come the gentle liberalization of the early 1970s, a group of musicians, led by Béla Halmos and Ferenc Sebő, decided to start a **táncház** or "dance house" in Budapest, modelling it on traditional village barn dances. Halmos and Sebő were inspired by their visits to villages settled by Hungarians in Transylvania and Slovakia, where folk traditions had been kept alive. Following in the footsteps of Bartók and Kodály, they recorded old folk tunes and traditional dance steps and recreated them in the *táncház*, teaching Budapestis the dances rather than just performing them on stage, and so reintroducing a whole generation to their roots. The idea quickly caught on, and the *táncház* movement developed as a kind of counter-culture for city folk.

Folk dancers

The *táncház* band consists of at least two violins, a bass and perhaps a cimbalom (a stringed instrument like an open-topped piano, played with two small hammers) or a hurdy-gurdy. The lead violinist (the *primás*) watches the dancers and times the changes in tempo that are an essential part of *táncház* dances such as the *csárdás* and the *verbunkos*. It makes for enticingly raw and earthy music and the atmosphere is relaxed and unselfconscious – you don't have to dress up, and anyone is welcome to go along and join in. Thirty years on, the *táncház* movement is still going, though the fall of communism has removed its edgy, rebellious image – today's youth are more likely to head for a rave. You can still enjoy the full experience at several regular *táncház* – you'll find Béla Halmos leading his band at the *Aranytíz* club on Saturdays – and the phenomenon has since spread to other cultures with Slav, Greek and even Irish *táncház* staged in Budapest's clubs.

Live folk

One of the best places to hear and learn about folk music is the **National Folk Festival**, held every spring and featuring bands, dancers and craft workers from all over the region. As well as its many *táncház*, Budapest sees regular concerts by groups such as **Téka**, **Tükrös** and **Muzsikás**, the latter one of the best-known names on the circuit, who often perform with their acclaimed partner **Márta Sebestyén**. Two other singers to look out for on the circuit are **Beáta Pálya**, whose repertoire draws on her Hungarian and Roma roots as well as other cultures, and **Ági Szalóki**, who captures the traditional female folk sound – she accompanies bands such as the **Ökrös Ensemble** as well as performing solo.

Beáta Pálya

Roma (Gypsy) rhythms

One major development in Hungary's post-communist music scene has been the emergence of a powerful **Roma music**. Surprisingly, given the Roma's reputation as instrumental virtuosos, their music traditionally used no instruments, relying instead on oral gymnastics and a variety of percussion, and it was played purely in rural Oláh Gypsy communities. It was first performed for a wider public by bands like Kályi Jág (led by Gusztáv Varga) and Ando Drom, with its compelling singer Mitsou. These have since been joined on the circuit by numerous other groups, including Romano Drom, the Szilvási Folk Band, Parno Graszt, the younger band Nomada and the Roma rap group Fekete Vonat. Today, Roma groups have achieved unprecedented prominence on the wider music scene: in 2005, a Roma singer, the 23-year-old Ferenc Molnár (better known as Caramel) won the TV pop contest *Megasztár*, while Kályi Jág's musical *Gypsy Fire* was given a run at the prestigious Erkel Theatre.

Restaurant Gypsy band

There's another more complex strand of Roma music, though, most usually played in Budapest's restaurants and often dismissed as tourist fodder. Its history is a telling example of the region's cultural mix: tell a Hungarian that these schmaltzy tunes are Hungarian folk music and you'll probably be informed, in no uncertain terms, that it's Gypsy music and not to be confused with the *real* Hungarian folk music. However, the rural Roma will say exactly the opposite: that the songs are a Hungarian entity, and quite different to what the Roma play for themselves. In fact, they are merely popularized versions of the old folk songs – **magyar nóta** – composed in the nineteenth century by Hungarian Romungro Gypsy dynasties. In Budapest, the best restaurants to hear this kind of Roma music are the elegant *Rézkakas* in the Belváros, or the *Kéhli* in Óbuda.

The familiar style of this playing – with two violins, a bass and a cimbalom soaring up and down in constant movement – has spawned some brilliant instrumentalists outside the tradition. Two must-see names are the cimbalom player **Kálmán Balogh**, who captivates audiences with everything from Bach onwards; and **Roby Lakatos**, the latest in a dynasty of fiddlers that dates back to the eighteenth century: with his long moustache and flowing coat, he cuts an imposing figure on stage and his playing is nothing short of mesmerising. You'll see why Brahms was fascinated.

7.30pm; and *h8* or *3/4 8* for 7.45pm. *"Mb."* indicates the film is dubbed – as many films are – and *fel.* or *feliratos* means that it has Hungarian subtitles.

Cinema-going is cheap, with tickets costing from 600Ft in the smaller cinemas, 1100Ft or more in the multiplexes. In the summer some of the outdoor bars, such as the Szimplakert (see p.167), show films a couple of times a week; in summer there are also outdoor and drive-in cinemas on the edge of town – for more details of these contact Tourinform.

The three main **film festivals** are the Hungarian Film Festival (ⓦwww .szemle.film.hu), a parade of the year's new films in February (tickets from the Corvin Filmpalota), and two alternative festivals of Hungarian and foreign films, the Titanic Film Festival (ⓦwww.datanet.hu/titanic) in October and the Európa Film Festival in December.

Cirko-gejzir V, Balassi Bálint utca 15–17. One of the best alternative cinemas, with a regular selection of films from around the globe – in any given week they might be showing films by Almodovar, Tarkovsky, Jarmusch, Wenders and Rohmer.

Corvin Budapest Filmpalota VIII, Corvin köz 1, ⓦwww.corvin.hu. The glitzy Film Palace, near the Ferenc körút metro, is a modern jungle of cinemas, popcorn and drinks. It's a good place to catch the latest foreign releases, and in February it hosts the Hungarian Film Festival. Reduced-price tickets on Wednesdays.

Művész VI, Teréz körút 30. Art-house cinema near the Oktogon, with one large and several smaller rooms named after big film personalities.

Puskin V, Kossuth Lajos 18. Complex of three cinemas in the centre of town with a large café attached. The coffered ceiling of the turn-of-the-century main screen is magnificent.

Toldi V, Bajcsy-Zsilinszky út 36–38. Next door to Arany János utca metro station, the Toldi is one of the more dynamic alternative cinemas in town, with a bar and a bookshop where people congregate. One of the venues for the annual Titanic Film Festival.

Uránia National Film Theatre (Uránia Nemzeti Filmszínház) VIII, Rákóczi út 21 ⓦwww.uranianf.hu. With its magnificent Venetian-Moorish decorations, this might seem a strange choice of location for the main showcase for Hungarian films in the city. But it was in this cinema, built in the 1890s as a dance hall, that the first Hungarian feature film was filmed in 1901. While it places special emphasis on local films, its programme is international.

Theatre

Hungarians usually show great taste when it comes to building theatres: take the splendid mass of the **Vígszínház** up the road from Nyugati Station or the **Új Színház** opposite the Opera House. However, if the newly constructed **National Theatre** is anything to go by (see p.90), the theatre world is suffering a lapse in taste that extends to the stage as well. The new showcase for Hungarian theatre is a sad mish-mash of styles, mainstream Hungarian **theatre** is in the doldrums, and its melodramatic and unsubtle productions offer little to tempt the visitor – but look out for those by the provincial theatre company from the town of **Kaposvár**, in southwest Hungary, or by Hungarian companies from outside the borders, such as from Cluj, Romania.

Alternative theatre tends to be more interesting – and since music and dance play a greater part here, language can be less of a barrier. One Hungarian group that has received considerable critical acclaim abroad is the **Mozgó haz** theatre company, whose inventive combination of music and movement under the direction of László Hudi won the top award at the International Theatre Festival in Sarajevo in 1998 and was well received at the London International Festival of Theatre in 2001. Look out for them – they also perform as HUDI – at the Trafó. Other names to keep in mind are the **Krétakör** group, under the young director Árpád Schilling, which was a big hit at the Edinburgh Festival in 2005 with its interpretation of Chekhov's *The Seagull*, and performances by **Péter Halász**, an actor–director who spent many years in New York before returning to Hungary.

To find out what's on, look out for flyers and check out the theatre listings publication Súgó (published in English in July and Aug) or the usual listings magazines.

Besides the venues below, there's the outdoor theatre on Margit sziget, which hosts colourful musicals in summer.

Budapest Bábszínház VI, Andrássy út 69 ⓦ www.budapest-babszinhaz.hu. Budapest Puppet Theatre has a lot of puppet shows for adults – masked grotesqueries or renditions of Bartók's *The Wooden Prince* and *The Miraculous Mandarin*.

Kolibri Színház VI, Jókai tér 10 ☎ 1/353-4633, ⓦ www.szinhaz.hu/kolibri. Puppet shows and live performances for adults as well as children.

Merlin Theatre V, Gerlóczy utca 4 ☎ 1/317-9338, ⓦ www.szinhaz.hu/merlin. In the centre of Pest, this often hosts visiting British theatre companies.

MU Színház XI, Körössy József utca 17 ☎ 1/209 4014, ⓦ www.mu.hu. Alternative venue that also hosts jazz concerts.

National Theatre (Nemzeti Színház) IX, Bajor Gizi park 1 ☎ 1/476-6800, ⓦ www.nemzetiszinhaz .hu. The proud new flagship of Hungarian theatre. Some shows are in English, put on by local troupes.

Radnoti Színház VI, Nagymező utca 11 ☎ 1/321-0600. Established theatre with major Hun-

garian actors in its company, performing Hungarian and foreign plays – in Hungarian.

Studio K IX, Mátyás utca 9 ☎ 1/216-7170, ⓦ www.szinhaz.hu/studiok. Like the MU, this venue hosts alternative theatre and jazz.

Szkéné Színház XI, Műegyetem rakpart 3 ☎ 1/463-2451, ⓦ www.szkene.hu. A small theatre housed in the main building of the Technical University near the Gellért Hotel, this has been an alternative venue for many years, dating back to the bad old days of Communism.

Új Színház VI, Paulay Ede utca 35 ☎ 1/351-1406. This stunning Art Nouveau building across the road from the Opera House is one of the better mainstream theatres, offering reliably polished performances.

Vígszínház XIII, Szent István krt 14 ☎ 1/329 2340. Great place for people-watching, as the locals dress up in their finest to attend performances, which are very much in the mainstream Hungarian style. Visiting companies also perform here.

18

Sports

Hungarians are passionate about sport. **Spectator sports** such as Grand Prix racing, soccer and horse-racing are very popular, though years of underfunding and mismanagement have brought the last two nearly to their knees. Hungary's strongest showing on an international level is in kayaking, shooting, water polo and fencing – for its size it performs very well in the Olympic medal charts. Sports **facilities** have suffered similarly from a lack of funding, but you can find a reasonable range of sports and activities to choose from around the capital. Information about the city's extensive bath and swimming facilities is given in chapter 19, while information about bike rental is in the Directory on p.195.

One activity (rather than a sport) which you can easily join in is **chess**: Hungary has a long tradition of great chess players, and you can see the game being keenly played in many parks.

Soccer

Hungary's great footballing days are long past – the golden team of the 1950s that beat England 6–3 with stars such as Ferenc Puskás and József Bozsik is a world away from today's national team, struggling to qualify for big tournaments. The club scene is also in deep crisis, with teams floundering in a financial desert.

While **international matches** are held at the Puskás Ferenc Stadion – generally filling just a third of its 76,000 seats – club football revolves around the turf of three **premier league teams** listed below; see the daily paper *Nemzeti Sport* for details of fixtures. The **season** runs from late July to late November and late February to mid-June. Matches are played on Saturday afternoons, with tickets costing around Ft2000.

Ferencváros (aka FTC or Fradi) IX, Üllői út 129, ⓦ www.ftc.hu. By the Népliget metro, Fradi is the biggest club in the country and almost a national institution; its supporters, dressed in the club's colours of green and white, are the loudest presence at international matches too. The club has long had right-wing ties – this was the fascists' team before the war, and in recent years it has attracted a strong skinhead – and anti-Semitic – element. Their local rivals are **MTK** (VIII, Salgótarján utca 12–14, ⓦ www .mtkhungaria.hu, tram #37 from Blaha Lujza tér), which has strong support among the Jewish community, and was also the setting for scenes in the film *Escape to Victory*; and **Újpest** (IV, Megyeri út 13, ⓦ www.ujpestfc.hu, four stops on bus #30 from Újpest Központ metro station), which used to be the police team.

Horse-racing

Horse-racing was introduced from England by Count Széchenyi in 1827 and flourished until 1949, when flat racing (*galopp*) was banned by the Communists. For many years punters could only enjoy trotting races, but in the mid-1980s flat racing resumed at **Kincsem Park**, X, Albertirsai út 2–6 (Pillangó utca on the red metro, and then either walk or catch #100 bus). Flat racing takes place here on Sundays from spring to autumn; trotting is all year round, on Wednesdays and Saturdays (on Wednesdays and Sundays in winter when the flat racing stops). Races are advertised in *Fortuna* magazine. The atmosphere at the tracks is informal, but photographing the racegoers is frowned upon, since many attend unbeknownst to their spouses or employers.

Betting operates on a tote system, where your returns are affected by how the odds stood at the close of betting. The different types of bet comprise *tét*, placing money on the winner; *hely*, on a horse coming in the first three; and the popular *befutó*, a bet on two horses to come in either first and second or first and third. Winnings are paid out about fifteen minutes after the end of the race.

Grand Prix racing

The **Hungarian Grand Prix** takes place in summer – usually mid-August – at the purpose-built Formula One racing track, the **Hungaroring**, at **Mogyoród**, 20km northeast of Budapest. The event was first held in 1986, but every year financial uncertainties surrounding the event spark rumours concerning its future. Assuming it's going ahead as normal, you can get details from Tourinform, any listings magazine or the website ⓦ www.hungaroring.hu.

Tickets are available from Ostermann Forma 1, V, Apáczai Csere János utca 11, third floor (☎ 1/266-2040), online at the address above; or from booths in Ferenciek tér. Prices range from €35–90 for the first day to €100–290 for the final day, and €110–400 for a three-day pass – the price being partly determined by the location, and whether you book in advance or (risking disappointment) on the day. You can reach the track by special buses from the Árpád híd bus station; trains from Keleti Station to Fót, and then a bus from there; or by HÉV train from Örs vezér tere to the Szilasliget stop, which is 1800m northeast of Gate C.

Participatory sports

Caving The Hungarian Association of Speleologists, at the Szemlőhegyi Cave (see p.121; ☎ 1/346-0494) can put you in touch with groups exploring caves in the Buda Hills and elsewhere in Hungary.

Fitness centres and gyms Most of the larger hotels and some of the shopping malls (see p.189) have them – they are properly regulated, unlike some of the backstreet ones, and are open to non-residents as well.

Horse-riding The Hungarian Equestrian Tourism Association at IX, Ráday utca 8 (☎ 1/456-0444, ⓦ www.equi.hu), can put you in touch with their members close to the city or further afield.

Ice-skating There's an ice rink by Hősök tere in the Városliget (Nov–March Mon–Fri 9am–1pm, 4–8pm, Sat–Sun 10am–2pm; 600Ft); skates can be rented out.

Skiing If it's a snowy winter, you can ski at Normafa in the Buda Hills, best reached on bus #21 from Moszkva tér. Equipment can be rented from Bikebase (VI, Podmaniczky utca 19 ☎ 1/269-5983 ⓦ www.bikebase .hu, open daily 9am–7pm), where the friendly staff can advise you on other places to ski; or Suli Sí in the Komjádi swimming complex at II, Árpád Fejedelem utca 8 (☎ 1/212-0330).

Squash City Squash Club, II, Marcibányi tér 13 (☎1/325-0082). Courts five minutes' walk from Moszkva tér open to the public and reasonably priced. The *Marriott Hotel* in central Pest also has squash courts, though these cost a bit more.

Tennis Courts can be booked all year round at the Városmajor Tennis Academy in Város- major Park, near Moszkva tér (☎1/202-5337); at Margitszigeti Teniszpalyak at the the southern end of the Margit sziget (☎1/340-4484); and at the *Thermal Hotel Helia* in Angyalföld, XIII, Kárpát utca 62 (☎1/452-5800). Racquets are available for rent.

Baths and pools

B
udapest has a long **bathing tradition** going back to Roman times or even earlier, and a visit to the city's baths should not be missed. There are three types of bath: *gyógyfürdő*, a thermal bath in its original Turkish form, as at the Rudas and Király, or the magnificent nineteenth-century settings of the Gellért and Széchenyi; *uszoda*, a proper swimming pool like the Sport; and *strand*, a summer pool in a verdant setting, like the Palatinus. Most baths are divided into a **swimming** area and a separate section for **steam baths** (*gőzfürdő* or the *göz*, as they are popularly known). For information on bathing etiquette and the history of Budapest's baths, see the Bathing insert.

The website for the Budapest Baths Directorate is Ⓦ www.spasbudapest.com, which has general information on all the main baths.

Császár Komjádi Uszoda II, Árpád fejedelem útja 8. A large modern pool complex whose entrance is on the embankment side of the building. The large outdoor swimming pool is covered over in winter. The complex is one of the major water-polo venues in Budapest, which means some of its pools may be given over to sportsmen. There's also an old Turkish bath hall, but this is closed indefinitely. Mon–Sat 6am–9pm, Sun 6am–7pm; 800Ft; bathing caps compulsory in the pool.

Gellért Gyógyfürdő XI, Kelenhegyi út 4. The most popular of the city's baths, and also one of the oldest – although nothing remains of the medieval buildings – the Gellért has it all: a magnificent main pool for swimming, hot pools for sitting around in both inside and outside on the terrace, fabulous Art Nouveau steam baths, and a large outdoor area, including a wave machine in the main pool and shaded terraces. Of course there's also a restaurant where you can get your daily dose of meat fried in breadcrumbs. The baths attract a lot of foreigners, and some of the attendants speak German or English. To enjoy the waters you must first reach the changing rooms by a labyrinth of passages; staff are

usually helpful with directions. At the far end of the pool are steps leading down to the separate thermal baths (daily 6am–6pm), with segregated areas and ornate plunge pools for men and women. Tickets cover both sections; towels, bathrobes and swimsuits can be rented, though you can get free blue plastic bathing caps at the exit from the changing-rooms. May–Sept daily 6am–7pm (July & Aug also Fri & Sat 8pm–midnight); Oct–April Mon–Fri 6am–7pm, Sat & Sun 6am 5pm; thermal baths daily 6am–6pm. Tickets cost 2500ft with locker, 3000Ft with cubicle, with 700Ft refunded if you leave within 2hr, 400Ft in 3hr, 200Ft in 4hr.

Hajós Alfred Sport Uszoda XIII, southern part of of Margit sziget. One of the nicest places for proper swimming – a beautiful 1930s lido renovated for the 2001 European water-polo championships. There's a small sauna, and two large outdoor pools against a backdrop of trees; one is normally given over to water polo. In the winter you can swim out along a channel to the larger of the pools without walking outside. The buffets on the terrace and in the entrance hall serve excellent pastries. Daily 6am–6pm; 900Ft.

Király Gyógyfürdő II, Fő utca 84. Fabulous Turkish baths, easy to spot thanks to the

△ Király baths

four copper cupolas. This was the most popular of the steam baths with the gay community until February 2005, when a television reporter secretly filmed the goings-on in the pool among the naked bathers. When the scenes were broadcast on national news, the bath authorities immediately imposed a compulsory swimming trunks order on bathers and patrol the bathing areas, severely cramping gay bathers' style. The main pool under the cupola is surrounded by smaller – hotter and cooler – pools, with doors leading off to the steam massage rooms. Unlike at the Rudas baths, there are separate days for the sexes: women Mon, Wed & Fri 7am–6pm; men Tues, Thurs & Sat 9am–8pm. Tickets cost 1100Ft (last tickets 1hr before closing); the maximum stay is 1hr 30min Mon–Fri, 1hr Sat.

Lukács Fürdő II, Frankl Leó út 25–29. This spa complex has four small but delightful open-air pools, as well as mud baths and a medical treatment section – its waters are good for rheumatism and arthritis and other complaints. The open-air facilities, including a thermal pool, a cooler small swimming pool and a Jacuzzi pool with whirling currents, are in two intimate courtyards. The ticket hall by the road, which looks like a mansion-garden folly, sells tickets for the steam baths only – for the main baths and ticket office go into the courtyard and head

round to the left, past plaques of gratitude in different languages from those who have benefited from the medicinal waters. Follow the signs for the "uszoda" (pool) and go through the doors at the far end. All parts of the baths are mixed. Mon–Sat 6am–7pm, Sun 6am–5pm; 1500Ft for a locker, 1700Ft for a cabin, with a refund of 500Ft if you leave within 2hr, 300Ft within 3hr, 100Ft within 4hr.

Palatinus Strand Margit sziget. Halfway up the island on the west side, the Palatinus has a large outdoor set of pools, including a wave pool and children's pools, all set in a big expanse of grass. The sunroof above the changing rooms is something of a gay centre. May Mon–Fri 10am–6pm, Sat & Sun 9am–7pm; June–August daily 9am–7pm; 1500Ft.

Rác Gyógyfürdo I, Hadnagy utca 8–10. One of the oldest baths – the medieval King Mátyás is said to have used the baths on this site – but nothing remains from those times. Closed for redevelopment at time of writing, due to reopen as part of a luxury spa hotel complex.

Rudas Gyógyfürdő I, Döbrentei tér 9. One of the original Turkish baths in the city, this is at its best when the sun shines through the holes in the dome to light up the beautiful interior. The steam baths have been for men only since 1937 – women can only get a look if raves are held in the baths (look out for adverts in listings magazines). It still operates the apron system in the steam section, though you might find that swimming togs have been introduced after the Király's experience (see p.183). There is also a nineteenth-century swimming pool, open to both sexes, to the left of the main entrance – normal swimwear here. Mon–Fri 6am–7pm, Sat & Sun 6am–1pm; the maximum stay is 1hr 30min Mon–Fri, 1hr Sat. 1100Ft.

Széchenyi Fürdő XIV, Állatkerti körút 11. A magnificent nineteenth-century complex in the Városliget with sixteen pools in all, including the various medicinal sections. The entrance is opposite the entrance to the Budapest Circus. You'll probably use just the three outdoor pools – the hot one with people playing chess that appears in so many photos of the city, a pool for swimming (bathing cap compulsory), and a Jacuzzi/whirling pool. Bring your own chess set if you want to play. Across the far side of the hot pool from the changing rooms is a mixed sauna with a maze of hot and cold pools. There are also separate steam baths which are men-only on Mondays, Wednesdays and Fridays, women-only on Tuesdays, Thursdays and Saturdays. Daily 6am–7pm (summer till 10pm); 2000Ft for locker, 2300Ft for cabin, with a refund of 800Ft if you leave within 2hr, 500Ft within 3hr, 200Ft within 4hr.

Kids' Budapest

Budapest offers a healthy range of activities for kids, from state-of-the-art playgrounds to roller-skating parks, with concessions on most entry tickets for under-14s. Don't expect anything especially high-tech, however, as a lack of cash dogs the facilities, but at least many of the city's playgrounds have been refurbished in recent years, and plenty of places have activities specifically for children, from the **Palace of Arts**, which has events most weekends, to restaurants such as *Trattoria Toscana*, which has a clown to entertain children at weekends.

It also helps that people are child-friendly: they will talk to children on buses and give up their seats for parents carrying small babies (it also means old ladies will loudly berate parents for not dressing their babies adequately, which for Hungarians means not putting a hat on in the mildest of weather); and if you are pushing a baby buggy, help is usually quickly forthcoming when you're trying to negotiate stairs.

Budapest's **public transport** can be a source of amusement, with children under 6 travelling free. **Trams** are an endless source of fun, the best ride being along the embankment in tram #2. Across the water, the **Sikló** (see p.105) is a great experience, running up from the Lánchíd to the Royal Palace, with the view of Pest suddenly appearing before your eyes. A popular way for families to spend an afternoon in the Buda Hills is to go on the "**railway circuit**" – the Cogwheel Railway, the Children's Railway and the chairlift (see p.123). From April to October there's the added thrill of **boat rides** on the Danube – either short tours of the city up to Margit sziget and back, or further afield to Szentendre and on to Esztergom – though the shorter rides are perhaps more suited to young children, as they might get bored. Another summertime source of delight are the **steam trains** that run from Nyugati Station up to Visegrád and Esztergom.

Parks and outdoor activities

Since Budapest is still very much lived in and offices have not yet taken over the centre of town, there are a lot of **playgrounds** in squares and parks, such as in Klauzál tér and the Károlyi kert near Astoria. The best of the adventure playgrounds are in the **Millenaris Park** (p.108) and in the **Zoo** (p.81). There are **trampolines** in big cages at the Buda end of the Margit híd and in the Városliget, south of the Széchenyi baths, for a small fee. More expensive are the indoor play areas in some malls, such as the **Kölyökpark** (Kids' park) in Mammut 2 (shop 328), II, Lövőház utca 1–5, where you pay 700Ft for half an hour and can go on slides, climbing walls and more.

The **caves** in Buda are good fun for children as long as they aren't scared of the dark. The **Buda Castle Labyrinth** under the Várhegy (see p.99) offers some exciting exploration, while the Pálvölgyi Stalactite Caves and the Szemlőhegyi Caves (pp.120–121) display dramatic geological formations.

Görzenál Skatepark III, Árpád fejedelem útja wwww.gorzenal.hu. Space to rollerblade, skateboard and cycle, with ramps and jumps, all to your heart's content. You can get here by taking the Szentendre HÉV to Timár utca. Mon & Thurs–Sun 9am–6pm, Fri & Sat 9am–7pm; Mon–Thurs 400Ft, Fri–Sun 600Ft.

Margit sziget See p.121. A great open space where you can rent bikes and four-person trikes, or take a trip round the island on the train on wheels, leaving from the strange sculpture at the southern end of the island. The Palatinus open-air baths (see p.183) have a wave machine and lots of small pools for kids. The low point of the island is the zoo across on the east – a smelly and sorry-looking place. Otherwise the island's varied scenery and big open spaces for frisbee and ball games all create a very pleasant atmosphere.

Városliget and the Zoo See p.80. This is where you'll find the largest concentration of activities and attractions for children, including a circus and a fairground; the last of these has a summertime section for younger kids (Kisvidám Park) with suitably tame rides. Recent improvements to the zoo have made it a great place to visit; kids can feed the camels and giraffes, tickle the rhinos, stroke the farm animals and explore the new Palm House. The adventure playground is excellent too. The Széchenyi Baths (see p.184) are popular with children – especially the large outdoor hot pool and the Jacuzzi/ whirlpool. For those who prefer to stay above water level, there's rowing in summer and ice-skating in winter (Nov–March Mon–Fri 9am–1pm & 4–8pm, Sat & Sun 10am–2pm & 4–8pm, depending on the weather) on the lake by Hősök tere.

Museums

Natural History Museum See p.89. Full of colour and activity, with interactive games and lots to look at, plenty of it at child height. Well thought out, it certainly grabs children's attention.

Underground Railway Museum See p.54. The small Földalattivasút Múzeum still preserves some of the original track the trains first ran on, as well as the original wooden carriages, decorated with old advertisements.

Palace of Miracles See p.64. An interactive playhouse with loads of things to do – a back door way of explaining scientific principles to kids.

Railway History Park See p.127. Strong child appeal here: lots of big old engines and carriages, and in summer you can even drive an engine yourself.

Szentendre Village Museum See p.134. Children's programmes every weekend, a playground and frequent folk-craft and folk-dancing displays in this museum outside Szentendre, north of the city.

Telephone Museum See p.99. A hands-on museum, which is a rarity in Budapest; children enjoy sending faxes and calling one another on vintage phones.

Transport Museum Városliget; see p.80. Vehicles, trams, ships and trains of all kinds and sizes, and a model train set that runs on the hour every hour until 5pm. Across the way, on the first floor of the Petőfi Csarnok, is an Aviation and Space Flight display.

Theatre, dance and other activities

Budapest has a strong tradition in **puppetry**, and many big Hungarian writers have contributed to its children's repertoire. There are some English-language performances, but puppets can be enjoyable without the language. Morning and matinée performances are for kids. Tickets are available from the puppet theatres (*bábszínház*) or the ticket offices on p.172, and children can also take their first steps in Hungarian folk dances.

Aranytíz See p.172. The same top musicians who play for the adults play for the children too at the Kalamajka táncház event (Sat 5–6pm).
Budapest Bábszínház VI, Andrássy út 69 Ⓦ www.budapest-babszinhaz.hu. Budapest Puppet Theatre (see p.178).
Kolibri Színház VI, Jókai tér 10 Ⓦ www.szinhaz .hu/kolibri. Puppets and live performances (see p.178).

Kölyökvár ("Kidstown") VII, Almássy tér Leisure Centre, Almássy tér 6 Ⓣ 1/267-8709. A play centre offering all sorts of activities from face-painting to model-building – plus films, music and drama. Mid-Oct to April Sun 10am–1pm.
Millenáris Park See p.172. Regular children's programmes are put on here, including puppet shows, craft workshops and more.

Shopping

B udapest's shopping scene has been transformed in recent years by the mushrooming of international stores such as Benetton, Mango and Mexx and the opening of modern **shopping malls** across the city. The malls have brought in long opening hours and a bright new style that sets the pace for other shops – not that many locals can afford to shop in the malls, where prices are high by Hungarian standards. Holding their own, however, against the international brands are numerous small backstreet shops, which continue to preserve **local crafts** and traditions. Budapest also has a set of distinguished **market halls** (*vásárcsarnok*) dating from the late nineteenth century, some of which still function as food markets; others have been turned into supermarkets, though you can still admire their structure. There are also some outdoor markets (*piac*), which are a more lively proposition, with smallholders coming into town to sell their produce. Most of the markets are busy, crowded places, so you should mind your pockets and bags at all times. And all of them sell some kind of refreshment – usually fried or alcoholic.

The main shopping **areas** are located to the south of Vörösmarty tér in central Pest, in particular in and around pedestrianized Váci utca, which has the biggest concentration of glamorous and expensive shops, as well as branches of popular Western stores including H&M, Mango, Springfield, Esprit and Zara. The main streets radiating out from the centre – Bajcsy-Zsilinszky, Andrássy and Rákóczi – are other major shopping focuses, as are the Nagykörut (especially from Margit Bridge to Blaha Lujza tér) and the Kiskörút. Some of the old craftsmen and workshops are still operating in the backstreets inside the Nagykörút. Shops in the Várhegy are almost exclusively given over to providing foreign tourists with folksy souvenirs such as embroidered tablecloths, hussar pots and fancy bottles of Tokaj wine.

Most shops are **open** Monday to Friday between 10am and 6pm, and Saturday until 1pm, with food stores generally operating from 8am to 6pm or 7pm. Some shops in the centre of the city stay open later on Saturdays, while the malls are open roughly 10am-8pm every day, but closing around 6pm on Sunday. You can usually find a 24-hour outlet selling alcohol, cigarettes and some food in the centre of town, eg at V, Október 6 utca 11 and at XIII, Pozsonyi út 18. It's useful to recognize that "Azonnal jövök" or "Rögtön jövök" signs on shop doors both mean "I am back shortly".

Malls

**Mammut and Mammut 2 II, Széna tér ⓦwww
.mammut.hu.** This has doubled in size with
the opening of Mammut II. Amid the 320
shops there are also a fitness centre,
squash courts and a cinema, as well as an
excellent market at the back.

**Mom Park XII, Alkotás utca 53 ⓦwww.mompark
.hu.** One of the newest malls, up the road
from Deli Station, with more than seventy
shops, a cinema and a fitness centre.

**West End City Center VI, Váci út 1–3 (next to
Nyugati Station) ⓦwww.westend.hu.** Past the
grand indoor waterfall cascading down at
the southern entrance, you'll find brands
such as Mango, Mexx and Springfield, as
well as M&S.

Markets and market halls

**Fény utca XII, at the back of the Mammut mall,
by Moszkva tér.** Popular market that has
survived a transfer to a modern setting.
There's an excellent cheese shop on the top
floor, which is where you'll also find what is
perhaps the best *lángos* in town – a popular stand-up snack of fried dough eaten
with garlic, sour cream, cheese or all three
together. Mon–Fri 6am–4pm, Sat 6am–1pm.

Hold utca V, Hold utca 13. Right behind the
American Embassy, this is one of the city's
fine nineteenth-century market halls and still
has some smaller holders selling their produce. Mon–Fri 6am–5pm, Sat 6am–1pm.

Hunyadi tér VI. Another of the old market
halls, free of any modernization. Stalls spill
out into the square in front.

István tér IV. Large market in the square
behind the town hall in the northern suburb of Újpest, at the northern end of the
blue metro line.
It attracts a large
number of farmers
from the country-
side, making it one
of the most atmos-
pheric markets in
the city. Mon–Fri
7am–5pm, Sat
7am–1pm.

Klauzál tér VII. In
the heart of the old
Jewish quarter. A
supermarket has
squeezed the fruit
and veg stands out
into the entrance
passage. Mon–Fri
6am–5pm, Sat
6am–1pm.

**Lehel Csarnok XIII,
Lehel tér.** Large,
popular market housed in a whacky new
market hall designed by the former dis-
sident László Rajk – whatever you think of
the outside, it's a lively place inside with
lots of small stalls. Mon–Fri 6am–5pm, Sat
6am–1pm, Sun 6am–noon.

Mom Ökopiac XII, Csörsz utca 18. Organic
farmers' market housed in the Mom Cultural
Centre (Mom Művelődési Központ) up the
road from the Mom Park Mall – Mom was
the now demolished Hungarian Optical
Works – Saturday 6.30am–noon.

**Nagycsarnok (Great Market Hall) IX, Vámház körút
2.** By the Szabadság híd at the bottom end of
Váci utca, the Nagycsarnok is the largest and
finest market hall of them all, as well as being
the most expensive. It also has good stalls
upstairs, selling knives and wood craft, amid
the touristy embroideries and tat. Mon 6am–
4pm, Tues–Fri 6am–6pm, Sat 6am–2pm.

△ Vásárcsarnok exterior

Flea markets

Ecseri piac XIX, Nagykörösi út. On the southeast edge of the city, this has become a well-known spot for tourists – and for ripping them off (you'll need to bargain hard). Stalls sell everything from bike parts and jackboots to nineteenth-century peasant clothing and hand-carved pipes, with a few genuine antiques in among the tat. You can get here on bus #54 (red) from the Határ út metro stop on the blue line, or bus #54 (black) from Boráros tér by Petőfi híd. Mon–Fri 8am–4pm, Sat 8am–noon.

Nowák piac VII, Dózsa Gy. utca 1–3. The newest and smallest of the flea markets, a 10min walk from Keleti Station up Verseny utca. Excellent bargains and some pretty shifty characters, although surprisingly for Budapest it's weak in the snack department.

Petőfi Csarnok XIV, Zichy Mihály utca 14. A weekend flea market in and around the ugly cultural centre in the Városliget, it's smaller than Ecseri, and less established. Lots of the wares are junk, but there are some good bargains too. Small entry fee. Sat & Sun 8am–2pm.

Antiques

Falk Miksa utca, running south off Szent István körút, near the Pest end of the Margit híd, is known as Budapest's "Street of Antiques", and is where you'll find the biggest collection of **antique stores** and galleries. Kossuth Lajos utca between Ferenciek tere and the *Astoria Hotel* also has a couple of outlets.

Most antique specialists should be able to advise on what you can export from the country and how to go about it. Several shops organize **auctions**; the best months for these are April, May, September and December – check the free hotel magazine *Where Budapest* for dates. Another good source of antiques are the flea markets listed above, though you'll need to be wary about parting with large sums of money, as stallholders can charge hugely inflated prices.

BÁV V, Bécsi utca 1–3; VI, Andrássy út 27; V, Ferenciek tere 10. There are numerous BÁV outlets, including the three above specializing in paintings, *objets d'art* and carpets respectively. They hold regular auctions at Lonyay utca 30–32. Mon–Fri 10am–6pm, Sat 9am–1pm.

Grand Bazár VII, Klauzál tér 14. Ádám Breier's minute hole of a shop is just off the square next to the *Sark* bar. He's got some fantastic stuff here: old signs, military insignia, medals, documents – old Communist and pre-Communist bits that deserve a lot of browsing. Mon–Fri 9am–6pm.

Judaica VII, Wesselényi utca 13. Jewish books, pictures and artefacts down the road behind the Dohány utca synagogue. Mon–Thur 10am–6pm, Fri 10am–3pm.

Pless & Fox XIII, Szent István körút 18. Old jewellery and rare metals, just down the road from the Margit híd. Mon–Fri 10am–6pm, Sat 10am–1pm

Sóos V, József Attila utca 22. An excellent place to pick up some fine junk and secondhand photographic goods. Mon–Fri 9am–5pm, Sat 10am–1pm.

Art and photography galleries

ACB VI, Király utca 76 ☎1/413-7608, ⓦwww.acbgaleria.hu. Contemporary fine arts with a friendly, well-informed management, up the road from the Music Academy. Tues–Fri 2–6pm or by appointment.

Dovin Galéria V, Galamb utca 6 ☎1/318-3673. Elegant gallery in central Pest selling contemporary Hungarian art. Tues–Fri noon–6pm, Sat 11am–2pm.

Godot Studio VII, Madach Imre út 8 ☎1/322-5272. Contemporary art gallery next to a lively café.

Tues–Fri 10am–6pm, Sat 10am–3pm.

Mai Manó VI, Nagymező utca 20 ☎1/302-4398. Contemporary and old Hungarian photographs. The gallery above it is covered on p.67. Mon–Fri 2–7pm, Sat & Sun 11am–7pm.

Várfok Galéria I, Várfok utca 14 ☎1/213-5155. One of three small galleries just off Moszkva tér, this displays work by the younger generation of Hungarian artists. Tues–Sat 11am–6pm.

Books and maps

Hungarians love their books and their flats are crammed with literature – one of the much awaited events each June is the Book Week. Bookshops stock a good range of photographic albums, books about the city and foreign-language books. If it's old books and prints you want, one of the best places to head for is Múzeum körút, where there are several **secondhand bookshops** (*antikvárium*) clustered opposite the Hungarian National Museum – they have quite a selection of English and German books.

Alexandra V, Nyugati tér 7 ☎ 1/428-7077, ⓦ www.alexandrakonyveshaz.hu. A vast new bookshop on five floors across from Nyugati Station, with very long opening hours. There are regular, free literary and music events on its stage. Daily 10am–midnight.

Bestsellers V, Október 6 utca 11 ☎ 1/312-1295. Excellent range of English books, with English and Hungarian literature, travel and reference books, and newspapers too. Staff are friendly and can order books in. Mon–Fri 9am–6.30pm, Sat 10am–5pm, Sun 10am–4pm.

Book Station VII, Thököly út 18 ☎ 1/413-1158, ⓦ www.bookstation.hu. Tucked inside the Thököly Udvar shopping yard across the road from Keleti Station, this has a good range of English, German and some French books, mainly secondhand and remaindered. Tues–Sat 10am–7pm.

Cártográfia VI, Bajcsy-Zsilinszky út 37. A well-stocked map shop, but you have to ask the stern staff for the maps you want, which makes browsing difficult. Mon–Wed 9am–5pm, Thurs 9am–6.30pm, Fri 9am–3.30pm.

Forgács Kempinski Corvinus Hotel, V, Erzsébet tér 7–8 ☎ 1/266-1000 ext 898. A good range of old books and prints from a friendly dealer. Mon–Fri 2–6pm.

Honterus V, Múzeum körút 35 ☎ 1/317-3270. Engravings, postcards and secondhand books. Mon–Fri 10am–6pm, Sat 10am–2pm.

Írók Boltja VI, Andrássy út 45. On the premises of the prewar *Japán* coffee house, the "Writers' Bookshop" has a wide range of English-language books at the back, and a good selection of photography, art and architecture books in the main part of the shop. You can drink coffee and read at the tables in the front. Mon–Fri 10am–6pm, Sat 10am–1pm (July & Aug closed Sat).

Központi Antikvárium V, Múzeum körút 17 ☎ 1/317-3781. Large secondhand bookshop with some antiquarian books and prints too. Mon–Fri 10am–6.30pm, Sat 10am–2pm.

Libri V, Váci utca 22 and Rákoczi út 12. The *Studium* branch in Váci utca is a foreign language specialist store, and has a good stock of books on Hungary. English-language and travel books are upstairs at Rákoczi út 12, where you'll also find a small Internet café. Mon–Fri 10am–7pm, Sat 10am–3pm, Sun 10am–3pm.

Litea I, Hess András tér 4. This well-lit shop has a good stock of English books on Hungary, some CDs and cassettes, and a coffee bar with tables. Daily 10am–6pm.

Párisi könyvesbolt V, Párisi Udvar, Petőfi Sándor utca 2. Inside the gloomy interior of this Moorish building is a small foreign-language outlet stocking English travel books but also fiction and coffee-table books. Mon–Fri 10am–6pm, Sat 10am–1pm

Pendragon XIII, Pozsonyi út 21-23 ☎ 1/340-4426. New English-language bookshop up near the Margít híd with a good range of fiction, children's books and more.

Red Bus V, Semmelweis utca 14 ☎ 1/337-7453, ⓦ www.redbusbudapest.hu. Up the road from Astoria, this is one of the best places in Budapest to pick up secondhand English paperbacks for your holiday reading. Mon–Fri 10am–6pm, Sat 10am–2pm.

Térképkirály VI, Bajcsy-Zsilinszky út 23. Range of maps and guidebooks across the road from Arany János utca metro station. Mon–Fri 9am–5.30pm.

Records and CDs

CD Bar VIII, Krúdy Gyula utca 6. Classical and jazz records in this basement shop in an increasingly fashionable backstreet a couple of streets behind the

Hungarian National Museum. Mon–Fri 10am–8pm, Sat 10am–4pm.

Fonó XI, Sztregova utca 3. It's a 20min tram ride from Deák tér on #47 to get to the shop in the bar of this folk club, but it's worth the effort for the range of jazz, ethno-jazz blues and world music, and, above all, Hungarian folk music CDs. Mon–Fri & Sun 10am–11pm, Sat 6–11pm.

Indiego VIII, Krudy Gyula utca 7. Inside the Darshan udvar to the right, an excellent range of CDs, including world music, house and more. Mon–Fri 10am–6pm, Sat 10am–1pm.

Kodály Zoltán Zeneműbolt V, Múzeum körút 21. Scores of secondhand Hungarian clas-

sical records, tapes and CDs, opposite the Hungarian National Museum. Mon–Fri 10am–6pm, Sat 10am–1pm.

Lemezdokk VIII, Horánszky utca 27. Another music shop in the cluster around Krudy Gyula utca. Lots of old vinyl as well as some CDs; they have blues, rock and some jazz. Mon–Fri noon–6pm.

Rózsavölgyi Zeneműbolt V, Szervita tér 5. Established record shop with a know-ledgeable staff, near Vörösmarty tér. Classical music on the ground floor, rock and folk downstairs. Good for sheet music as well. Mon–Fri 9.30am–7pm, Wed 10am–7pm, Sat 10am–5pm.

Clothes and shoes

Ciankáli IX, Ráday utca 20. A good stock of secondhand clothes are sold in this basement shop – the entrance is round the corner in Mátyás utca.

Emilia Anda V, Váci utca 16/b and Galamb utca 4. Classy, well-designed day and evening wear for women, and a range of jewellery including chunky rings and beautiful pendants.

Fleischer Shirts V, Paulay Ede utca 53. Old-fashioned shirt-maker selling handmade garments at good prices. On the corner of Nagymező utca, five minutes' walk from the Opera House.

Manier V, Váci utca 68 ⓦwww.manier.hu. Zany but appealing clothes from young fashion designer Ágnes Németh.

Marácz Kalapbolt VII, Wesselényi utca 41. An old-fashioned hat shop with steamers and

other old equipment in the back room. They sell beautiful fedoras in black and grey. Mon–Fri 11am–6pm.

Náray Tamás V, Károlyi Mihály utca 12. Housed in an old block designed by the great Ybl Miklós (he of Opera fame), this is the place for haute couture of a fancy and colourful variety.

Paroka bolt VII, Kazinczy utca 46. Wig-makers in the heart of the old Jewish quarter. Wigs don't come much cheaper between here and Brooklyn.

Vass V, Haris köz 2. A traditional shoemaker, just behind Ferenciek tere, producing hand-made shoes to order and ready-to-wear.

V50 V, Váci utca 50. Just south of Ferenciek tere, a small shop with hats and smart clothes designed by Valéria Fazekas.

Crafts and curios

Hephaistos V, Molnár utca 27. Sells all kinds of wrought-iron objects from candlesticks to bookshelves – the smaller items aren't that heavy and make great gifts. The shop is also moving increasingly into glassware, abandoning its more appealing base. All goods are made in their Szentendre premises. Mon–Fri 11am–6pm, Sat 10am–2pm.

Holló Folk Art Gallery V, Vitkovics Mihály utca 10. This beautiful early nine-

teenth-century shop near the Astoria is a very pleasant place in which to browse wares such as wooden furniture, boxes, eggs and candlesticks, all hand-painted with bird, tulip and heart folk motifs, and intricately iced gingerbread figures.

Vulcano VI, Andrássy út 55. Some very appealing wrought-iron work here of the kind that made Hephaistos's name a few years back. Mon–Fri 10am–7pm.

Household goods

Brush shop VII, Dob utca 3. A wonderful little place: every kind of brush you can think off in this very traditional artisan's shop. Mon–Fri 10am–6pm, Sat 10am–1pm.
Kátay VI, Teréz körút 28. Amid the fantastic range of plates, bowls, saucepans and electrical goods you can find excellent presents such as a wooden spoon stand and wooden bowls. Mon–Fri 10am–6pm, Sat 10am–1pm.

Pottery and jewellery

Haas & Czjzek VI, Bajcsy-Zsilinszky út 23, ⓦ www.porcelan.hu. Full selection of Hungarian porcelain, including Hollóháza, Alföld and Zsolnay, and some glassware. The shop dates back to 1792, as the small display at the back documents. Mon–Fri 10am–7pm, Sat 10am–3pm.

Herend V, József nádor tér 11, ⓦ www.herend. com. Very fancy – some would say twee – and expensive porcelain from the Herend factory in western Hungary, collected by the likes of Queen Victoria.

Intuita V, Váci utca 67. Amid the tourist tat at the main market hall end of Váci utca, this shop stands out for its quality Hungarian pottery and jewellery. Mon–Fri 10am–6pm, Sat 10am–1pm.

Ómama Bizsúja V, Szent István körút 1. A tiny treasure trove of a shop - its entrance is tucked in to the left as you walk down the passageway that leads in from the street. Absolutely crammed full of jewellery. It's worth perservering, as there are some stunning Deco-style pieces and good-quality paste in amongst the more glitzy costume jewellery. Mon–Fri 10am–6pm, Sat 10am–1pm.

Porcelánház V, Váci utca 46 ⓦ www.porcelan-haz.hu. Chunky and cheerful modern pottery at a reasonable price. Mon–Fri 10am–6pm, Sat 10am–1pm.

Zsolnay V, Váci utca 19–21 ⓦ www.zsolnay. hu. Art Nouveau-style porcelain, less kitsch than some other Hungarian porcelains. The merchandise is made at the factory in Pécs in southern Hungary, which made its name designing the tiles on Art Nouveau buildings such as the Applied Arts Museum. Mon–Fri 10am–6pm, Sat 10am–1pm.

Photos

Fotólabor VIII, Gyulai Pál utca 14. Good black and white prints done very cheaply, and photos developed and enlarged. Mon–Fri 8am–6pm.

Fotolux VII, Károly körút 21. Good-quality photographic developing and printing, and professional films. Mon–Fri 9am–9pm, Sat 9am–7pm.

Toys

Fakopáncs VIII, Baross utca 50 and József körút 50. A massive array of wooden puzzles and toys are crammed into the two "Woodpecker" shops, both at the junction of Baross utca and the Nagykörút. Mon–Fri 9am–7pm, Sat 9am–4pm, Sun 9am–2pm.

Játékszerek anno VI, Teréz körút 54 ⓦ www .kelle.hu. Beautifully made reproductions of toys and games from the turn of the last century, including wooden tops, kaleidoscopes, and a spectacular wind-up duck on a bicycle. Mon–Fri 10am–6pm, Sat 9am–1pm.

Food

Azték V, on a long courtyard running between Károly körút 22 and Semmelweis utca 19 ⓦ www.choxolat.hu. Perhaps the best place for chocolate gourmands in the city, they sell home-made chocolate as well as imported products, all made with a minimum of sugar, and some fabulous hot chocolate – ask for the extra thick variety, which will warm you up on a winter's day. You can sit at the tables inside, or outside in summer in the courtyard. Mon–Fri 7am–7pm, Sat 9am–2pm.

🏃 **Bio ABC V, Múzeum körút 19.** Natural oils, organic fruits, juices, cheeses and snacks. Opposite the Hungarian National Museum. Mon–Fri 10am–7pm, Sat 10am–2pm.

Culinaris VI, Hunyadi tér 3 ☎1/341-7001, ⓦwww.culinaris.hu. A couple of doors along from the Hunyadi tér market hall, Culinaris has a good stock of quality produce, some of it organic, from both Hungary and further afield. Mon noon–7pm, Tues–Sat 9am–7pm.

🏃 **Lekvárium VII, Dohány utca 39.** Hungarians have a strong tradition of pickling and preserving, with most families laying up jars of plum and apricot jam (*lekvár*), pickled cucumbers and peppers for the winter. This shop also sells some more interesting varieties, like quince compote and tobacco flower honey. Mon–Fri 10am–6pm.

Napos Oldal VI, Jókai utca 8. One of the few organic fruit and veg shops in town, near the Oktogon and just across from the Napos Oldal café. Mon–Fri 10am–6pm, Sat 10am–1pm.

Rothschild VII, Dob utca 12. On the edge of the Jewish quarter, a couple of minutes' walk from the Dohány utca synagogue, this is one of the few shops in Budapest selling kosher Hungarian and imported wines and foods. Mon–Thurs 8.30am–6pm, Fri 8.30am–2pm.

Wine

🏃 **Budapest Wine Society V, Batthyány utca 59** ☎1/212-2569. In a basement just up the street from Moszkva tér, they offer some of Hungary's best wines from producers across the country, and good advice in English. They also have an outlet at Ráday utca 7, near Kálvin tér. Mon–Fri 10am–8pm, Sat 10am–6pm.

In Vino Veritas VII, Dohány utca 58-62 ☎1/341-0464, ⓦwww.borkereskedes.hu. Friendly store just off the Nagykörút with an excellent range of wines as well as other produce. Mon–Fri 9am–8pm, Sat 10am–6pm.

La Boutique des Vins V, József Attila utca 12 ☎1/266-4397, ⓦwww.malatinszky.hu. Founded by the former *sommelier* of the *Gundel* restaurant, who now has a vineyard of his own. Strongest in wines from Villány and Tokaj. Mon–Fri 10am–6pm, Sept–May also Sat 10am–3pm.

Monarchia IX, Kinizsi utca 30–36 ☎1/456.9898, ⓦwww.magyarborok.hu. One of the new outlets and distributors in the city, it's earning a strong reputation in wine circles. Opposite the Applied Arts Museum. Mon–Fri noon–7pm, Sat 10am–6pm.

Directory

Airlines Air France, V, Váci utca 19 ☎1/483-8800; British Airways/Qantas, V, East-West Business Centre, VIII, Rákóczi út 1–3 ☎1/777-4747; KLM, VIII, Rákóczi út 1–3 ☎1/373-7737; Lufthansa, V, Váci utca 19 ☎1/266-4511; Malév, V, Dorottya utca 2 ☎1/235-3565.

Airport information Flight arrivals and departures available on ☎1/296-7000 or from ⓦwww.bud.hu.

Banks and exchange Cash dispensers can be found across the city. The best places for changing money are the larger banks such as the Magyar Külkereskedelmí Bank at Türr István utca 9, by the top of Váci utca; avoid many of the exchange offices around Vörösmarty tér and Váci utca which giver poor rates. The Magyar Külkereskedelmi Bank has safe-deposit boxes for storing valuables.

Bike rental and repairs Bikebase, VI, Podmaniczky utca 19 (☎1/269-5983 ⓦwww.bikebase.hu; daily 9am–7pm), is a basement operation near Nyugati Station, with very friendly staff who can give out maps and advise on cycling routes. They have a service session every afternoon at 3pm. Yellow Zebra, in the courtyard at Sütő utca 2 by Deak tér (☎1/266-8777, ⓦwww.yellowzebrabikes.com; daily 9.30am–6.30pm) offers a friendly service and good information. Budapest Bike, in the *Szóda* bar, VII, Wesselényi utca 18 (☎06-30/944-5533 ⓦwww.budapestbike.hu; daily 9am–midnight) rents out bicycles and mopeds, and also organizes moped tours. Bike shops include Nella Bikes off Bajcsy-Zsilinszky út at V, Kálmán Imre utca 23 (☎1/331-3184); the Bike Store, VI, Nagymező utca 43 (☎1/312-5073); and Kerékvár, I, Hunyadi János utca 4, at the Buda end of the Lánchíd (☎1/214-8814).

British Council With a library (containing newspapers) and a useful noticeboard, the British Council is at VI, Benczúr utca 26 (☎1/478-4700, ⓦwww.britishcouncil.hu; Mon–Thurs 11am–6pm, Fri 11am–5pm; closed Aug).

Car breakdown The Magyar Autóklub has 24hr breakdown assistance (☎188).

Car rental Avis, V, Szervita tér 8 (by the Jet petrol station under the multistorey car park) ☎1/318-4240, ⓦwww.avis.hu; Budget, *Hotel Mercure Buda*, I, Krisztina körút 41–43 ☎ & ⓕ1/214-0420, ⓦwww.budget.hu; Europcar V, Deák Ferenc tér 3 ☎1/328-6464, ⓦwww.europcar.hu; Hertz, V, Apáczai Csere János utca 4 (beside the *Marriott Hotel*) ☎1/296-0999, ⓦwww.hertz.hu. All these companies also have offices at the airport.

Electricity 220 volts. Round two-pin plugs are used.

Embassies Australia, XII, Királyhágó tér 8–9 ☎1/457-9777, ⓦwww.ausembbp.hu; Canada, XII, Budakeszi út 32 ☎1/392-3360, ⓦwww.kanada.hu; France, VI, 27 Lendvay utca ☎1/374-1100, ⓦwww.ambafrance.hu; Germany, I, Úri utca 64 ☎1/488-3500, ⓦwww.deutschebotschaft-budapest.hu; Ireland, V, Szabadság tér 7, Bank Center, seventh floor ☎1/302-9600; UK, V, Harmincad utca 6 ☎1/266-2888, ⓦwww.britishembassy.hu; USA, V, Szabadság tér 12 ☎1/475-4400, ⓦwww.usembassy.hu.

Danube boats Mahart (☎1/484-4013 ⓦwww.mahartpassnave.hu) operates other services within the city, all from Vigadó tér, including a boat to Margit sziget four times a day and boat sightseeing trips with a drink, a meal or music and dance. They also operate boats to Szentendre and the Danube Bend; see p.140 for details. Mahart's website has information about times and prices. Other companies offer similar sightseeing trips at similar prices from the piers to the south, between Vigadó tér and Erzsébet híd, such as Legenda (☎1/317-2203, ⓦwww.legenda.hu) and Dunayacht (☎1/268-9020, ⓦwww.dunayacht.com). The main differences are in the number of languages offered and whether commentaries are by earphone or over a loudspeaker.

Emergencies Ambulance ☎104; police ☎107; fire service ☎105.

Hospitals and dentistry There are 24hr casualty departments at V, Hold utca 19 (☎1/311-6816), behind the US embassy; and at II, Ganz utca 13–15 (☎1/202-1370). Profident, VII, Károly korut 1, is a round-the-clock dentist where they speak English. A private clinic with English-speaking personnel is the IMS (International Medical Services) at XIII, Váci út 202 (☎1/329-8423; Mon–Fri 7.30am–7pm) and at III, Vihar utca 29 ☎1/388-8257 (24-hour).

International buses and trains Bookings are required on all international train routes. Buy your tickets 24–36 hours in advance at the MÁV booking office, VI, Andrássy út 35 (Mon–Fri 9am–5pm, until 6pm April–Sept; ☎1/461-5500, ⓦwww.mav.hu, booking service and timetables on ⓦwww.elvira.hu).The Vienna-bound *Wiener Waltzer* often runs late, so reserve sleepers in Budapest. Also bring drinks, as the buffet staff overcharge shamelessly. International bus services depart from Népliget Bus Station, where you can buy tickets (Mon–Fri 6am–6pm, till 9pm mid-June to mid-Sept, Sat–Sun 6am–4pm; English information on ☎1/219-8021).

Laundry Házimosoda, V, Galamb utca 9 (Mon–Fri 8am–7.30pm, Sat 9am–1pm), offers laundry and dry cleaning; Irisz Szalon, V, Városház utca 3–5 (Mon–Fri 7am–7pm, Sat 7am–1pm), is one of the few self-service launderettes left in the city.

Lost property For items left on public transport go to the BKV office at VII, Akácfa utca 18 (☎1/267-5299; Mon, Tues &

Thurs 7.30am–3pm, Wed 7.30am–7pm, Fri 7.30am–2pm). Lost or stolen passports should be reported to the police station in the district where they were lost.

Names Surnames precede forenames in Hungary, to the confusion of foreigners. In this book, the names of historical personages are rendered in the Western fashion, for instance, Lajos Kossuth rather than Kossuth Lajos (Hungarian-style), except when referring to the names of buildings, streets, etc.

Pharmacies Details of each district's 24hr pharmacy are posted in every pharmacy's window. Central 24hr pharmacies include those at Alkotás utca 2, opposite Déli Station, and at Teréz körút 41, near Oktogon. For herbal remedies try Herbária, VIII, Rákóczi út 49, and V, Bajcsy-Zsilinszky út 58.

Religious services in English Anglican: Sun 11am (call the rectory on ☎06-23/452-023 for the location); Baptist: Sun 10.30am, International Baptist Church, II, Törökvész út 48–54 (Móricz Zsigmond Gimnázium) ☎1/319-8525; Roman Catholic: Sat 5pm, Pesti Jézus Szíve Templom, VIII, Mária utca 25 ☎1/318-3479.

Time Hungary is one hour ahead of GMT, six hours ahead of Eastern Standard Time and nine ahead of Pacific Standard Time in North America. A word of caution: Hungarians express time in a way that might confuse the anglophone traveller. For example, 10.30am is expressed as "half eleven" (written 1/2 11 or f11), 10.45am is "three-quarter-eleven" (3/4 11 or h11), and 10.15am is "a quarter of eleven" (1/4 11 or n11).

Tipping It's standard practice to add a tip of around 10 percent when paying for meals, drinks in bars and taxi fares. In some newer restaurants this may have quietly been added for you. If you expect change back, don't say *köszönöm* (thank you) when handing over payment, as it will be assumed that you want them to keep the change.

Contexts

Contexts

History

Although Budapest has only formally existed since 1873, when the twin cities of Buda and Pest were united in a single municipality together with the smaller Óbuda, the locality has been settled since **prehistory**. *Homo sapiens* appeared here around 8000 BC, and a succession of peoples overran the region during the first Age of Migrations, the most important of whom were the Celtic Eravisci who settled on Gellért-Hegy in about 400 BC.

In 35 BC the Danube Basin was conquered by the **Romans** and subsequently incorporated within their empire as the province of Pannonia, whose northern half was governed from the town of **Aquincum** on the west bank of the Danube. Ruins of a camp, villas, baths and an amphitheatre can still be seen today in Óbuda and Rómaifürdő. Roman rule lasted until 430 AD, when Pannonia was ceded to **Attila the Hun**. Attila's planned assault on Rome was averted by his death on his wedding night, and thereafter Pannonia was carved up by Germanic tribes until they were ousted by the Turkic-speaking Avars, who were in turn assailed by the Bulgars, another warlike race from the Eurasian steppes.

The coming of the Magyars

The most significant of the invaders from the east were the **Magyars**, who stamped their language and identity on Hungary. Their origins lie in the Finno-Ugric peoples who dwelt in the snowy forests between the Volga and the Urals, where today two Siberian peoples still speak languages that are the closest linguistic relatives to Hungarian; along with Finnish, Turkish and Mongolian, these languages make up the Altaic family. Many of these Magyars migrated south, where they eventually became vassals of the Khazar empire and mingled with the Bulgars as both peoples moved westwards to escape the marauding Petchenegs.

In 895 or 896 AD, seven Magyar tribes led by Árpád entered the Carpathian Basin and spread out across the plain, in what Hungarians call the "**landtaking**" (*honfoglalás*). They settled here, though they remained raiders for the next seventy years, striking terror as far afield as France (where people thought them to be Huns), until a series of defeats persuaded them to settle for assimilating their gains. According to the medieval chronicler, known today simply as Anonymous, the clan of Árpád settled on Csepel sziget, and it was Árpád's brother, Buda, who purportedly gave his name to the west bank of the new settlement.

The Árpád dynasty

Civilization developed gradually after Árpád's great-grandson **Prince Géza** established links with Bavaria and invited Catholic missionaries to Hungary. His son **Stephen** took the decisive step of applying to Pope Sylvester for recognition, and on Christmas Day in the year 1000 AD was crowned as a Christian king.

With the help of the Italian Bishop Gellért, he then set about converting his pagan subjects. Stephen was subsequently credited with the **foundation of Hungary** and canonized after his death in 1038. His mummified hand and the crown of St Stephen have since been revered as both holy and national relics, and are today some of Budapest's most popular tourist attractions.

Despite succession struggles after Stephen's death, a lack of external threats during the eleventh and twelfth centuries enabled the **development of Buda and Pest** to begin in earnest, largely thanks to French, Walloon and German settlers who worked and traded here under royal protection. However, the growth in royal power caused tribal leaders to rebel in 1222 AD, and Andrew II was forced to recognize the noble status and rights of the **natio** – landed freemen exempt from taxation – in the Golden Bull, a kind of Hungarian Magna Carta.

Andrew's son **Béla IV** tried to restore royal authority, but the **Mongol invasion** of 1241 devastated the country and left even the royal palace of Esztergom in ruins. Only the timely death of Ghengis Khan spared Hungary from further ravages. Mindful of a return visit, Béla selected **Várhegy** as a more defensible seat and encouraged foreign artisans to rebuild Buda, which German colonists called "*Ofen*" after its numerous lime-kilns (the name Pest, which is of Slav origin, also means "oven").

Renaissance and decline

After the Árpád dynasty expired in 1301, foreign powers advanced their own claims to the throne and for a while there were three competing kings, all duly crowned. Eventually **Charles Robert** of the French Angevin (or Anjou) dynasty triumphed. Peacetime gave him the opportunity to develop the gold mines of Transylvania and northern Hungary – the richest in Europe – and Charles bequeathed a robust exchequer to his son **Louis the Great**, whose reign saw the population of Hungary rise to three million, and the crown territories expand to include much of what are now Croatia and Poland. The oldest extant strata of the Buda Palace on Várhegy date from this time.

After Louis's demise, the throne was claimed by **Sigismund of Luxembourg**, Prince of Bohemia, whom the nobility despised as the "Czech swine". His failure to check the advance of the Turks through the Balkans was only redeemed by the Transylvanian warlord **János Hunyadi**, whose lifting of the siege of Belgrade caused rejoicing throughout Christendom. Vajdahunyad Castle in the Városliget is a romantic nineteenth-century replica of Hunyadi's ancestral seat in Transylvania.

Hunyadi's nephew, **Mátyás Corvinus**, is remembered as the **Renaissance king**, who, together with his second wife Beatrice of Naples, lured humanists and artists from Italy to their court. Mátyás was an enlightened despot, renowned for his fairness, but when he died in 1490, leaving no legitimate heir, the nobles took control, choosing a pliable successor and exploiting the peasantry. However, in 1514 the peasants, led by **György Dózsa**, rebelled against the oppression. The savage repression of this **revolt** (over 70,000 peasants were killed and Dózsa was roasted alive) and subsequent laws imposing "perpetual serfdom" alienated the mass of the population – a situation hardly improved by the coronation of the 9-year-old **Louis II**, who was barely 16 when he had to face the full might of the Turks under Sultan Süleyman "the Magnificent".

The Turkish conquest: Hungary divided

The battle of **Mohács** in 1526 was a shattering defeat for the Hungarians. After sacking Buda, the Turks withdrew to muster forces for their real objective, Vienna. To forestall this, Ferdinand of Habsburg proclaimed himself king of Hungary and occupied the western part of the country, while in Buda the nobles put János Zápolyai on the throne. Following Zápolyai's death in 1541, Ferdinand claimed full sovereignty, but the Sultan occupied Buda and central Hungary and made Zápolyai's son ruler of Transylvania, which henceforth became a semi-autonomous principality – a **tripartite division** formally recognized in 1568. Despite various truces, warfare became a fact of life for the next 150 years, and national independence was not to be recovered for centuries afterwards.

Turkish-occupied Hungary was ruled by a Pasha in Buda, with much of the land either deeded to the Sultan's soldiers and officials, or run directly as a state fief. The towns, however, enjoyed some rights and were encouraged to trade, and the Turks were largely indifferent to the sectarian bigotry practised in Habsburg-ruled Hungary. The Habsburg **liberation of Buda** in 1686 was actually a disaster for its inhabitants, as the victors massacred Jews, pillaged at will and reduced Buda and Pest to rubble. The city's Turkish baths and the tomb of Gül Baba were among the few surviving buildings.

Habsburg rule

Habsburg rule was a bitter pill, which the Hungarians attempted to reject in the **War of Independence** of 1703–11, led by **Ferenc Rákóczi II**. Though it was unsuccessful, the Habsburgs began to soften their autocracy with paternalism as a result. The revival of towns and villages during this time owed much to settlers from all over the empire, hence the Serb and Greek churches that remain in Pest and Szentendre. Yet while the aristocracy commissioned over two hundred palaces, and Baroque town centres and orchestras flourished, the masses remained all but serfs, mired in isolated villages.

Such contradictions impelled the Reform movement led by **Count István Széchenyi**. His vision of progress was embodied in the construction of the Lánchíd (Chain Bridge) between Buda and Pest, which proved an enormous spur to the development of the two districts. The National Museum, the Academy of Sciences and many other institutions were founded at this time, while the coffee houses of Pest became a hotbed of radical politics. Széchenyi's arch-rival was **Lajos Kossuth**, small-town lawyer turned Member of Parliament and editor of the radical *Pesti Hírlap*, which scandalized and delighted citizens. Kossuth detested the Habsburgs, revered "universal liberty", and demanded an end to serfdom and censorship. Magyar chauvinism was his blind spot, however, and the law of 1840, his greatest pre-revolutionary achievement, inflamed dormant nationalist feelings among Croats, Slovaks and Romanians by making Magyar the sole official language.

When the empire was shaken by revolutions that broke out across Europe in **March 1848**, local radicals seized the moment. Kossuth dominated Parliament, while **Sándor Petőfi** mobilized crowds on the streets of Pest. A second war of independence followed, which again ended in defeat and Habsburg repression, epitomized by the execution of Prime Minister Batthyány in 1849, and the Citadella atop Gellért-Hegy, built to intimidate citizens with its guns.

Budapest's Belle Époque

Gradually, brute force was replaced by a **policy of compromise**, by which Hungary was economically integrated with Austria and, as Austrian power waned, was given a major shareholding in the Habsburg empire, henceforth known as the "Dual Monarchy". The compromise (*Ausgleich*) of 1867, engineered by **Ferenc Deák**, brought Hungary prosperity and status, but tied the country inextricably to the empire's fortunes. Buda and Pest underwent rapid expansion and formally merged. Pest was extensively remodelled, acquiring the Nagykörút (Great Boulevard) and Andrássy út, a grand approach to the Városliget, where Hungary's millennial anniversary celebrations were staged in 1896 – marking a thousand years since the arrival of the Hungarian tribes in the Carpathian Basin. (In fact they arrived in 895 but preparations were late, so the official date was adjusted to 896.) New suburbs were created to house the burgeoning population, which was by now predominantly Magyar, though there were still large German and Jewish communities. Both elegance and squalor abounded, café society reached its apogee, and Budapest experienced a **cultural efflorescence** in the early years of the twentieth century to rival that of Vienna. Today, the most tangible reminders are the remarkable buildings by Ödön Lechner, Béla Lajta and other masters of Art Nouveau and National Romanticism – the styles that characterized the era.

The Horthy years

Dragged into **World War I** by its allegiance to the Central Powers, Hungary was facing defeat by the autumn of 1918. The Western or Entente powers decided to dismantle the Habsburg empire in favour of the "**Successor States**" – Romania, Czechoslovakia and Yugoslavia – which would acquire much of their territory at Hungary's expense. In Budapest, the October 30 "Michaelmas Daisy Revolution" put the Social Democratic party of **Mihály Károlyi** in power, but his government avoided the issue of land reform, attempted unsuccessfully to negotiate peace with the Entente and finally resigned when France backed further demands by the Successor States.

On March 21, 1919, a **Republic of Councils** (Tanácsköztársaság) was proclaimed led by **Béla Kun**, which ruled through local Soviets. Hoping for radical change and believing that "Russia will save us", many initially supported the new regime, but enforced nationalization of land and capital and attacks on religion, soon alienated the majority. After 134 days, the regime collapsed before the advancing Romanian army, which occupied Budapest.

Then came the **White Terror**, as right-wing gangs moved up from the south killing "Reds" and Jews, who were made scapegoats for the earlier Communist "Red Terror", especially in Budapest, the Bolshevik capital. **Admiral Miklós Horthy**, self-appointed regent for Karl IV, who had been exiled by the Western allies ("the Admiral without a fleet, for the king without a kingdom") entered the "sinful city", as he called it, on a white horse, and ordered a return to "traditional values". Meanwhile, at the Paris Conference, Hungary was obliged to sign the **Treaty of Trianon** (July 4, 1920), surrendering two-thirds of its historic territory and three-fifths of its total population (three million in all) to the Successor States. The bitterest loss was **Transylvania** – a devastating blow to national pride. Horthy's regency was characterized by gala balls and hunger marches, revanchism and growing anti-Semitism. Yet Horthy was a moderate compared to the **Arrow Cross** Fascists waiting in the wings, whose power grew as **World War II** raged.

Anticipating Horthy's defection from the Axis in October 1944, Nazi Germany staged a coup, installing an Arrow Cross government, which enabled them to begin the massacre of the **Jews** of Budapest. It was only thanks to the valiant efforts of foreign diplomats like Wallenberg and Lutz that half of them survived, when ninety percent of Hungary's provincial Jews perished. In the same year, the five-month-long **siege of Budapest** was a time of awful hardships for the city's inhabitants, who had to endure endless shelling amidst a very bitter winter. In the course of the siege the Danube bridges were blown up and Várhegy reduced to rubble, as the Red Army battered the *Wehrmacht* into submission.

The Communist takeover and the 1956 Uprising

As Budapestis struggled to rebuild their lives after the war, the Soviet-backed **Communists** took control bit by bit – stealthily reducing the power of other forces in society, and using the threat of the Red Army and the ÁVO secret police, who took over the former Arrow Cross torture chambers on Andrássy út. By 1948 their hold on Hungary was total, symbolized by the red stars that everywhere replaced the crown of St Stephen, and a huge statue of Stalin beside the Városliget, where citizens were obliged to parade before Hungary's "Little Stalin", **Mátyás Rákosi**.

The power struggles in the Moscow Communist Party leadership that followed the death of Stalin in 1953 were replicated in the other eastern European capitals, and in Hungary Rákosi was replaced by **Imre Nagy**. Nagy's "New Course" allowed Hungarians an easier life before Rákosi struck back by expelling him from the Party for "deviationism". However, society had taken heart from the respite and intellectuals held increasingly outspoken public debates during the summer of 1956. The mood came to a head in October, when 200,000 people attended the funeral of László Rajk, a victim of the show trials in 1949, in Kerepesi Cemetery, and Budapest's students decided to march to the General Bem statue near the Margit híd.

On October 23, demonstrators chanting anti-Rákosi slogans crossed the Danube to mass outside Parliament. As dusk fell, students demanding access to the Radio Building were fired upon by the ÁVO, and a spontaneous **1956 Uprising** began that rapidly took hold throughout Budapest and spread across Hungary. The newly restored Nagy found himself in a maelstrom, as popular demands were irreconcilable with realpolitik. It was Hungary's misfortune that the UN was preoccupied with the Suez Crisis when the Soviets reinvaded and crushed the Uprising, causing 200,000 Hungarians to flee abroad.

"Goulash socialism" and the end of Communism

After Soviet power had been bloodily restored, **János Kádár** gradually normalized conditions, embarking on cautious reforms to create a "**goulash socialism**" that made Hungary the envy of its Warsaw Pact neighbours and the West's favourite Communist state in the late 1970s. Though everyone knew the limits of the "Hungarian condition", there was enough freedom and consumer goods to keep the majority content. During the 1980s, however, it became apparent that the attempt to reconcile a command economy and one-party rule with market forces was unsustainable. Dissidents tested the limits of criticism, and even within the Party there were those who realized that changes were needed. Happily, this coincided with the advent of Gorbachev, which made it much easier for the reform Communists to shunt Kádár aside in 1988.

The **end of Communism** was heralded by two events the following summer: the ceremonial reburial of Imre Nagy, and the dismantling of the barbed wire along the border with Austria, which enabled thousands of East Germans to escape to the west while "on holiday". In October 1989, the government announced the legalization of other parties as a prelude to free elections, and the People's Republic was renamed the Republic of Hungary in a ceremony broadcast live on national television. Two weeks later this was eclipsed by the fall of the Berlin Wall, closely followed by the Velvet Revolution in Czechoslovakia and the overthrow of Ceaucescu in Romania.

Budapest today: the post-Communist era

Hungary's first **free elections** in the spring of 1990 resulted in a rejection of the Hungarian Socialist Party (MSzP – reform Communists), and the installation of a centre-right coalition dominated by the **Hungarian Democratic Forum (MDF)** under Premier **József Antall**. The MDF aimed to restore the traditions and hierarchies of prewar Hungary. However, not everyone wanted the Catholic Church to regain its former power, and the MDF's desire to restore the Hungarian nation to its former position sounded to Hungary's neighbours like a revanchist claim on the lost lands of Trianon.

After Antall's death in 1993, his successor was unable to turn the economy around, and the 1994 elections saw the **Socialists return to power**. To guard against accusations of totalitarianism such as those levelled at predecessors, they included the **Free Democrats (SzDSz)** in government and reassured Hungary's creditors with austerity measures that disillusioned voters who had hoped that the Socialists would reverse the growing inequalities in society. The emergence of a brash new entrepreneurial class and consumer culture, rising crime, unemployment and homelessness were deeply unsettling to many, especially the older generation. Widespread corruption among the Socialists led to their defeat in the 1998 election, which was narrowly won by the Fidesz–Hungarian Civic Party of **Viktor Orbán**. The youngest premier in Hungarian history, Orbán managed to reposition his party to the right by talking about the need to revive national culture and using the buzz-word **polgári** (meaning "civic", but redolent of bourgeois middle-class values) to appeal to a broad constituency. Once in government, Orbán and his young cabinet vehemently promoted their conservative and Christian agenda, showing an acute understanding of national and religious symbolism. Like Horthy before him, Orbán viewed the capital with suspicion, and he waged a continuing war with its mayor, Gábor Demszky of the SzDSz party. In an effort to undermine Demszky's position, Orbán halted the building of the National Theatre, whose foundations had already been laid at vast expense (see p.90), and cancelled the city's planned fourth metro line.

With an upwardly mobile economy, steadily falling inflation and low unemployment levels, as well as the achievement of steering Hungary into Nato, Orbán expected to triumph in the **2002 parliamentary elections**. However, in what was the most spitefully contested election since the end of Communism, the Orbán-led Fidesz-MDF coalition was ousted. Rejecting Orbán's media-savvy, aggressive style and attendant nationalist overtures, the Hungarian electorate instead opted for a return to the same centre-left coalition – the Hungarian Socialist Party (MSzP) ruling with the Alliance of Free Democrats (SzDSz) – that had governed, albeit largely ineffectively, between 1994 and 1998. The new premier was **Péter Medgyessy**, a former banker and an altogether less charismatic figure than Orbán. Medgyessy reaped the benefits of Orbán's tough negotiations when Hungary, alongside nine other former Eastern bloc countries, was **admitted to the EU** on May 1, 2004. While most Hungarians remain fervently committed to membership, believing that they will benefit under Europe's protective mantle, there are several areas of deep concern, such as the desire of most Hungarians to limit foreign ownership, which goes against EU directives, and apprehension over the distribution of agricultural subsidies.

General dissatisfaction at Medgyessy's bumbling performance resulted in his resignation in August 2004, and replacement by the sports minister and millionaire businessman, **Ferenc Gyurcsány**. Gyurcsány brought a welcome air of youth to the ageing Socialist team, and in spite of a series of gaffes has been moderately successful. He may lack Orbán's sharp political instinct, but he benefits in the public eye from being a more humane, less divisive character. His cabinet of Socialist millionaires who struck rich in the sell-off of state assets – one exception is the popular environment minister, Miklós Persányi, who came to fame as the director of Budapest Zoo – has once again brought allegations of corruption. However, growing voter apathy reflects the popular perception that politicians on all sides are just lining their pockets, with little interest in helping the many people for whom the new democracy has been a more mixed blessing.

While governments have come and gone since the historic 1990 elections, Budapest's administration has remained in the hands of the mayor, **Gábor Demszky**, who is now working with his fifth prime minister. People have voted for him partly because he is neither a Communist nor a nationalist, and his dour image invites a sense of reliability, perhaps fitting in well with the cynicism of the city dwellers. Under Demszky, Budapest has progressed gently without any major upsets, but his star may now be waning; he has recently been tainted by scandal, with talk of a villa built in dubious circumstances in Croatia, and various tax questions hanging over him.

Books

There is quite a range of books on Budapest available in the city, particularly books on architecture and translations of Hungarian literature. Publishers are detailed below in the form of British publisher/American publisher, where both exist. Where books are published in one country only, UK or US follows the publisher's name. Out of print books are designated o/p; University Press is abbreviated UP. Books tagged with the ✠ symbol are particularly recommended. For a gentle introduction to current affairs and literature, look for the Budapest-published *The Hungarian Quarterly* (ⓦwww .hungarianquarterly.com). Most of Budapest's better bookshops have a good range of books and can take orders (see Budapest "Listings").

See p.191 for details of bookshops in Budapest.

Art, architecture and photography

Our Budapest (Budapest City Hall). A very informative series of pocket-size books. Written in Hungarian and English by experts in their fields, they cover the city's architecture, baths, and parks, and are very cheap, though unfortunately the standard of English varies.

✠ **Irén Ács** *Hungary at Home* (Jövendő, Hungary). Excellent collection of photos covering all walks of life in postwar Hungary. Her other books, including *Rendezvous* (Interart), are also worth looking out for in bookshops.

✠ **Bruno Bourel & Lajos Parti Nagy** *Lightscapes*. One of the most interesting collections of photos available. Taken around the city by Bourel, a sharp-eyed French photographer who has lived there for many years, they are accompanied by words from a leading contemporary Hungarian writer.

Györgyi Éri et al *A Golden Age: Art and Society in Hungary 1896– 1914* (Corvina). Hungary's Art Nouveau age captured in a beautifully illustrated coffee-table volume.

János Gerle et al *Budapest: An Architectural Guide* (6 BT, Budapest). The best of the small new guides to the city's twentieth-century architec-

ture, covering almost 300 buildings, with brief descriptions in Hungarian and English.

Ruth Gruber *Jewish Heritage Travel: A Guide to Central and Eastern Europe* (John Wiley o/p). The most comprehensive guide to Jewish sights in Budapest and elsewhere.

Edwin Heathcote *Budapest: A Guide to Twentieth-Century Architecture* (Ellipsis, UK). A useful and informative pocket guide to the city, though with some curious omissions.

Tamás Hofer et al *Hungarian Peasant Art* (Constable/International Publications Service o/p). An excellently produced examination of Hungarian folk art, with lots of good photos.

Imre Móra *Budapest Then and Now* (New World Publishing, Budapest). A personal and very informative set of accounts of life in the capital, past and present.

Tamás Révész *Budapest: A City before the Millennium* (Herald, Budapest). Excellent collection of black and white photographs of the city, though the text can be irritating.

Dora Wieberson et al *The Architecture of Historic Hungary* (MIT Press, US). Comprehensive illustrated survey of Hungarian architecture through the ages.

History, politics and society

Robert Bideleux, Ian Jeffries *A History of Eastern Europe: Crisis and Change* (Routledge, UK). An excellent and wide-ranging history of the region.

Judit Frigyesi *Béla Bartók and Turn-of-the-century Budapest* (University of California Press). Placing Bartók in his cultural milieu, this is an excellent account of the Hungarian intellectual world at the beginning of the century.

Jörg K Hoensch *A History of Modern Hungary 1867–1994* (Longman/Addison-Wesley). An authoritative history of the country.

László Kontler *Millenium in Central Europe: A History of Hungary* (Atlantisz). Another very thorough and reliable history of the country, although its archaic style lets it down somewhat.

Paul Lendvai *The Hungarians: 1000 Years of Victory in Defeat* (Hurst & Co). Refreshing and authoritative book on Hungary's complex and often tragic history, with particularly stimulating accounts of the Treaty of Trianon and the subsequent Nazi and Communist tyrannies – there are some fascinating pictures, too.

Bill Lomax *Hungary 1956* (Allison & Busby/St Martin's Press o/p). Still probably the best – and shortest – book on the Uprising, by an acknowledged expert on modern Hungary. Lomax also edited *Eyewitness in Hungary* (Spokesman, UK), an anthology of accounts by foreign Communists (most of whom were sympathetic to the Uprising) that vividly depicts the elation, confusion and tragedy of the events of October 1956.

John Lukács *Budapest 1900* (Weidenfeld/Grove Press). Excellent and very readable account of the politics and society of Budapest at the turn of the century, during a golden age that was shortly to come to an end.

George Schöpflin *Politics in Eastern Europe 1945–92* (Blackwell). An excellent overview of the region in the last fifty years by one of the acknowledged experts: interestingly, as poacher turned gamekeeper, Schöpflin has now become an MEP for Fidesz.

Michael Stewart *The Time of the Gypsies* (Westview Press). This superb book on gypsy culture is based on anthropological research in a gypsy community in Hungary.

Peter Sugar (ed) *A History of Hungary* (I B Tauris). A useful, not too academic, survey of Hungarian history from pre-Conquest times to the close of the Kádár era, with a brief epilogue on the transition to democracy.

Nigel Swain *Hungary: The Rise and Fall of Feasible Socialism* (Verso/Routledge Chapman & Hall). Analyses the "Hungarian model" of socialism in decline, and the prospects for a market economy in the 1990s, now that capitalism is showing little sign of delivering prosperity and social justice.

Biography and travel writing

Magda Dénes *Castles Burning: A Child's Life in War* (Anchor/Touchstone Books). A moving biographical account of the Budapest ghetto and postwar escape to France, Cuba, and the United States, seen through the eyes of a Jewish girl. The author died in December 1966, shortly before the book she always wanted to write was published.

Ray Keenoy *Eminent Hungarians* (Boulevard). Everything you always wanted to know about Hungary's most renowned historical and contemporary figures – from Lajos Kossuth and Attila József, to Harry Houdini and Ernő Rubik, creator of the Rubik's cube.

Patrick Leigh Fermor *A Time of Gifts* (Penguin); *Between the Woods and the Water* (Penguin). In 1934 the young Leigh Fermor started walking from Holland to Turkey, reaching Hungary in the closing chapter of *A Time of Gifts*. In *Between the Woods and the Water* the inhabitants of the Great Plain and Transylvania – both gypsies and aristocrats – are superbly evoked. Lyrical and erudite.

Edward Fox *The Hungarian Who Walked to Heaven* (Short Books). A brief account of the life of Sándor Kőrösi Csoma, the Hungarian who went in search of the roots of the ancient Hungarians and got sidetracked into making the first Tibetan dictionary.

George Mikes *Any Souvenirs?* (Penguin/Harvard Common Press o/p). Born in Siklós in southern Hungary, Mikes fled the country in 1956 and made a new life in Britain as a humorist. This wry account relates his first visit home in fifteen years.

John Paget *Hungary and Transylvania* (Ayer, US). Paget's massive book attempted to explain nineteenth-century Hungary to the English middle class, and, within its aristocratic limitations, succeeded. Occasionally found in secondhand bookshops.

Giorgio and Nicola Pressburger *Homage to the Eighth District* (Readers International). Evocative short stories about Jewish life in Budapest, before, during and after World War II, by twin brothers who fled Hungary in 1956.

Walter Starkie *Raggle-Taggle* (John Murray o/p/Transatlantic Arts o/p). The wanderings of a Dublin professor with a fiddle, who bummed around Budapest and the Plain in search of gypsy music in the 1920s. First published in 1933 and last issued in 1964; a secondhand bookshop perennial.

Ernoo Szép *The Smell of Humans* (Central European University Press, Budapest/Arrow, UK). A superb and harrowing memoir of the Holocaust in Hungary.

Rogan Taylor & Klára Jamrich (eds) *Puskás on Puskás* (Robson Books Ltd). Not only does this marvellous book depict the life of Hungary's, and one of the world's, greatest footballers, it also provides an intriguing insight into postwar Communist Hungary.

Literature

Hungary has a fabulously rich literary heritage, and approach to the genre has greatly improved in recent years, thanks in no small part to the success of authors such as Sándor Márai and the Nobel-prize-winning Imre Kertész. A useful starting point is *Hungarian Literature* (Babel Guides), an informative guide to the best Hungarian fiction, drama and poetry in translation, with selected excerpts. There are also numerous collections of short stories published in Budapest, though the quality of translations varies from the sublime to the ridiculous. Works by nineteenth-century authors such as Mór Jókai are most likely to be found in secondhand bookshops (see p.191).

Anthologies

Loránt Czigány (ed) *The Oxford History of Hungarian Literature from the Earliest Times to the Present* (Oxford University Press). Probably the most comprehensive collection in print to date. In chronological order, with good coverage of the political and social background.
György Gömöri (ed) *Colonnade of Teeth* (Bloodaxe/Dufour). In spite of its strange title, this is a good introduction to the work of young Hungarian poets.

Michael March (ed) *Description of a Struggle* (Picador/Vintage). A collection of contemporary Eastern European prose, featuring four pieces by Hungarian writers including Nádas and Esterházy.
George Szirtes (ed) *Leopard V: An Island of Sound* (Harvill). Superbly compiled anthology featuring the cream of Hungarian prose and poetry from the end of World War II through to 1989.

Poetry

Endre Ady *Poems of Endre Ady* (University Press of America). Regarded by many as the finest Hungarian poet of the twentieth century, Ady's allusive verses are notoriously difficult to translate.
George Faludy *Selected Poems 1933–80* (McClelland & Stewart/ University of Georgia Press o/p). Fiery, lyrical poetry by a victim of both Nazi and Soviet repression. Themes of political defiance, the nobility of the human spirit, and the struggle to preserve human values in the face of oppression predominate.

Miklós Radnóti *Under Gemini: the Selected Poems of Miklós Radnóti, with a Prose Memoir* (Ohio University Press, US); *Foamy Sky: the Major Poems* (Princeton University Press, US). The two best collections of Radnóti's sparse, anguished poetry. His final poems, found in his coat pocket after he had been shot on a forced march to a labour camp, are especially moving.
Zsuzsa Rákovsky *New Life* (Oxford UP, UK). Well-received volume translated by the Hungarian-born English poet George Szirtes.

Fiction

Chico Barque *Budapest* (Bloomsbury). Not Hungarian fiction but Brazilian, about a ghost-writer's romance with a Hungarian and her language. An intriguing play on storytelling that captures the atmosphere of the city very well – all the more remarkable since the author has never been to Budapest.
Géza Csáth *The Magician's Garden and Other Stories* (Penguin/Columbia University Press o/p); *Opium and Other Stories* (Penguin o/p). Disturbing short stories written in the magic realist genre. The author was tormented by insanity and opium

addiction, killing his wife and then himself in 1918.
Tibor Déry *The Portuguese Princess* (Calder/Northwestern University Press o/p). Short stories by a once-committed Communist, who was jailed for three years after the Uprising and died in 1977.
Péter Esterházy *Celestial Harmonies* (Flamingo). This most recent novel, by a descendant of the famous aristocratic family, is dense and demanding, chronicling the rise of the Esterházys during the Austro-Hungarian empire, and their subsequent downfall under Communism.

Tibor Fischer *Under the Frog, A Black Comedy* (Penguin/New Press). A fictional account of the 1956 revolution by the son of Hungarian survivor emigrés. Witty and enjoyable.

Jenő Rejtő *The Blonde Hurricane* (Corvina). Like Antal Szerb and Miklós Radnoti, Rejtő was a great Hungarian writer who was killed in the Holocaust for his Jewish descent: they could have escaped but they thought it would never happen in Budapest. He wrote a series of excellent romps – this translation succeeds far better than *Quarantine at the Grand Hotel*.

Imre Kertész *Fateless* (Northwestern). Drawing from his own experiences as an Auschwitz survivor, this Nobel-prize winning book tells the tale of a young boy's deportation to, and survival in, a concentration camp. A brilliant translation by Tim Wilkinson.

Dezső Kosztolányi *Skylark* (Central European University Press, Budapest). A short and tragic story of an old couple and their beloved child by one of Hungary's top writers of the twentieth century, in a masterly translation by Richard Aczél.

Gyula Krúdy *Adventures of Sinbad* (Central European University Press, Budapest/Random House). Stories about a gourmand and womanizer by a popular Hungarian author with similar interests to his hero.

Sándor Márai *Embers* (Penguin). Atmospheric and moving tale about friendship, love and betrayal by one of Hungary's most respected pre-World War II writers; a beautiful read. His *Conversations in Bolzano* (Penguin – US title *Casanova in Bolzano*) has also been very well received.

Zsigmond Móricz *Be Faithful Unto Death* (Penguin). This novel by a major late nineteenth-century Hungarian author sheds light on how Hungarians see themselves – both then and now.

Péter Nádas *A Book of Memories* (Vintage/Overlook Press). This translation of a novel about a novelist writing about a novel caused a sensation when it appeared in 1998. A Proustian account of bisexual relationships, Stalinist repression, and modern-day Hungary in a brilliant translation by Iván Sanders.

Antal Szerb *Journey by Moonlight* (Pushkin Press). This recently translated Hungarian classic, written in 1937, tells the story of a Hungarian businessman on honeymoon in Italy who embarks upon a mystical and dazzling journey through the country. The superb translation by Len Rix ensures that the atmosphere of the original is beautifully retained. Szerb's *Martians' Guide to Budapest* is a delightful introduction to the city.

Food and wine and miscellaneous

Lesley Chamberlain *The Food and Cooking of Eastern Europe* (Penguin o/p). A great compendium of recipes, nostrums and gastronomical history, guaranteed to have you experimenting in the kitchen.

Susan Derecskey *The Hungarian Cookbook* (HarperCollins, US). A good, easy-to-follow selection of traditional and modern recipes.

Gerald Gorman *Birds of Hungary* (C Helm, UK). The best book available on the ornithological world of the country by a resident expert.

Stephen Kirkland *The Wine and Vines of Hungary* (New World Publishing, Budapest). Authoritative and accessible guide with tips on what to order. Covers the different wines of the country's regions, and their wine-makers too.

George Lang *The Cuisine of Hun-gary* (Penguin/Random House). A well-written and beautifully illus-trated work, telling you everything you need to know about Hungarian cooking, its history and how to do it yourself.

Glossary of Hungarian terms

ÁFA Goods tax, equivalent to VAT.
Állatkert Zoo.
Arrow Cross see Nyilas.
Áruház Department store.
ÁVO The dreaded secret police of the Rákosi era, renamed the ÁVH in 1949.
Barlang Cave.
Biedermeier Heavy nineteenth-century style of Viennese furniture that became very popular in Budapest homes.
Borkostoló Wine tasting.
Borozó Wine bar.
Botanikuskert Botanical garden.
Büfé Snack bar.
Cigány Gypsy/Roma (can be abusive).
Cigánytelep Gypsy settlement.
Cigányzene Gypsy music.
Csárda Inn; nowadays, a restaurant with rustic decor.
Csárdás Traditional wild dance to violin music.
Cukrászda Cake shop.
Diszterem Ceremonial hall.
Domb Hill.
Duna River Danube.
Egyetem University.
Erdély The Hungarian word for Transylvania, the region of Romania where a large Hungarian minority lives.
Erdő Forest, wood.
Étterem Restaurant.
Fasor Avenue.
Fogadó Inn.
Folyó River.
Forrás Natural spring.
Fürdő Public baths.
Gözfürdő Steam bath.
Gyógyfürdő Mineral baths fed by thermal springs with therapeutic properties.

Hajó Boat.
Hajóállomás Boat landing stage.
Halászcsárda/halászkert Fish restaurant.
Ház House.
Hegy Hill or low mountain.
HÉV Commuter trains running from Budapest
Híd Bridge.
Honvéd Hungarian army.
Ifjúsági szálló Youth hostel.
Iskola School.
Kápolna Chapel.
Kapu Gate.
Kert Garden, park.
Kerület (*ker.*) District.
Kiállítás Exhibition.
Kincstár Treasury.
Kirakodó vásár Fair, craft or flea market.
Kollégium Student hostel.
Komp Ferry.
Korzó Promenade.
Körö.nd Circus (road junction, as in Piccadilly Circus).
Körút (*krt.*) Literally, ring road, but in Budapest refers to the main boulevards surrounding the Belváros.
Körtér Circus (see *körönd*).
Köz Alley, lane; also used to define narrow geographical regions.
Kulcs Key.
Kút Well or fountain.
Lakótelep High-rise housing estate.
Lépcső Flight of steps.
Liget Park, grove or wood.
Lovarda Riding school.
Magyar Hungarian (pronounced "*mod*-yor").
Magyarország Hungary.
Malév Hungarian national airline.
MÁV Hungarian national railways.
Megálló Railway station or tram or bus stop.

Megye County; the county system was originally established by King Stephen to extend his authority over the Magyar tribes.

Mozi Cinema.

Műemlék Historic monument, protected building.

Művelődési ház/központ Arts centre.

Nádor Palatine, highest administrative office in Hungary in the Habsburg empire pre-1848.

Nyilas "Arrow Cross"; Hungarian Fascist movement.

Palota Palace; *püspök-palota*, a bishop's residence.

Pályaudvar (*pu.*) Rail terminus.

Panzió Pension.

Patak Stream.

Pénz Money.

Piac Outdoor market.

Pince Cellar.

Rakpart Embankment or quay.

Református The reformed church, which in Hungary means the Calvinist faith.

Rendőrség Police.

Repülőtér Airport.

Rév Ferry.

Rom Ruined building; sometimes set in a *romkert*, a garden with stonework finds.

Roma The romany word for gypsy, preferred by many Roma in Hungary.

Sétány "Walk" or promenade.

Skanzen Outdoor ethnographic museum.

Sor Row, as in *fasor*, row of trees, ie avenue.

Söröző Beer hall.

Strand Beach, open-air baths or any area for sunbathing or swimming.

Szabadtér Open-air.

Szálló or **szálloda** Hotel.

Szent Saint.

Sziget Island.

Szoba kiadó Room to let.

Tájház Old peasant house turned into a museum, often illustrating the folk traditions of a region or ethnic group.

Táncház Venue for Hungarian folk music and dance.

Temető Cemetery.

Templom Church.

Tér Square; *tere* in the possessive case.

Terem Hall.

Tilos Forbidden; *tilos a dohányzás* means "smoking is forbidden".

Tó Lake.

Torony Tower.

Türbe Tomb or mausoleum of a Muslim dignitary.

Turista térkép Hiking map.

Uszoda Swimming pool.

Udvar Courtyard.

Út Road; in the possessive case, *útja*.

Utca (*u.*) Street.

Vár Castle.

Város Town.

Városháza Town hall.

Vásár Market.

Vásárcsarnok Market hall.

Vasútállomás Railway station.

Vendéglő Restaurant.

Verbunkos Folk dance, originally a recruiting dance.

Völgy Valley.

Zsidó Jew or Jewish.

Zsinagóga Synagogue.

Language

Language

Hungarian

Hungarian is a unique, complex and subtle tongue, classified as belonging to the Finno-Ugric linguistic group, which includes Finnish and Estonian. If you happen to know those languages, however, don't expect it to be a help: there are some structural similarities, but lexically they are totally different. In fact, some scholars think the connection is completely bogus and have linked Hungarian to the Siberian Chuvash language and a whole host of other fairly obscure tongues. Basically the origins of Hungarian remain a mystery and, although a few words from Turkish have crept in, together with some German, English and (a few) Russian neologisms, there is not much that the beginner will recognize.

Consequently, foreigners aren't really expected to speak Hungarian, and natives are used to being addressed in **German**, the lingua franca of Hungarian tourism. However, **English** is gaining ground rapidly, and is increasingly widely understood. That said, a few basic Magyar phrases can make all the difference. Hungarians are intensely proud of their language, and as a nation are surprisingly bad at learning anyone else's.

The Rough Guides' *Hungarian for Travellers* is a useful **phrasebook** and, if you're prepared to study the language seriously, the best available book is *Colloquial Hungarian* (Routledge). As a supplement, invest in the handy little *Angol–Magyar/Magyar–Angol Kisszótár* dictionaries, available from bookshops in Hungary.

Basic grammar

Although its rules are complicated, it's worth describing a few features of **Hungarian grammar**, albeit imperfectly. Hungarian is an agglutinative language, in other words, its vocabulary is built upon **root-words**, which are modified in various ways to express different ideas and nuances. Instead of prepositions "to", "from", "in", etc, Hungarian uses **suffixes**, or tags added to the ends of genderless **nouns**. The change in suffix is largely determined by the noun's context: for example the noun "book" (*könyv*) will take a final "*et*" in the accusative (*könyvet*); "in the book" = *könyvben*; "from the book" = *könyvből*. It is also affected by the rules of vowel harmony (which take a while to get used to, but don't alter meaning, so don't worry about getting them wrong!). Most of the nouns in the vocabulary section below are in the nominative or subject form, that is, without suffixes. In Hungarian, "**the**" is *a* (before a word beginning with a consonant) or *az* (preceding a vowel); the word for "**a/an**" is *egy* (which also means "one").

Plurals are indicated by adding a final "k", with a link vowel if necessary, giving -*ek*, -*ok* or -*ak*. Nouns preceded by a number or other indication of quantity (eg, many, several) do *not* appear as plural: eg *könyvek* means "books", but "two books" is *két könyv* (using the singular form of the noun).

Adjectives precede the noun (*a piros ház* = the red house), adopting suffixes to form the comparative (*jó* = good; *jobb* = better), plus the prefix *leg* to signify the superlative (*legjobb* = the best).

Negatives are usually formed by placing the word *nem* before the verb or adjective. *Ez* (this), *ezek* (these), *az* (that) and *azok* (those) are the **demonstratives**.

Pronunciation

Achieving passably good **pronunciation**, rather than grammar, is the first priority (see below for general guidelines). **Stress** almost invariably falls on the first syllable of a word and all letters are spoken, although in sentences the tendency is to slur words together. Vowel sounds are greatly affected by the bristling **accents** (that actually distinguish separate letters) which, together with the "double letters" *cs*, *gy*, *ly*, *ny*, *sz*, *ty*, and *zs*, give the Hungarian **alphabet** its formidable appearance.

a o as in hot
á a as in father
b b as in best
c ts as in bats
cs ch as in church
d d as in dust
e e as in yet
é ay as in say
f f as in fed
g g as in go
gy a soft dy as in due
h h as in hat
i i as in bit, but slightly longer
í ee as in see
j y as in yes
k k as in sick
l l as in leap
ly y as in yes
m m as in mud
n n as in not
ny ny as in onion

o aw as in saw, with the tongue kept high
ó aw as in saw, as above but longer
ö ur as in fur, with the lips tightly rounded but without any "r" sound
ő ur as in fur, as above but longer
p p as in sip
r r pronounced with the tip of the tongue like a Scottish "r"
s sh as in shop
sz s as in so
t t as in sit
ty ty as in Tuesday or prettier, said quickly
u u as in pull
ú oo as in food
ü u as in the German "über" with the lips tightly rounded
ű u as above, but longer
v v as in vat
w v as in "Valkman," "vhiskey" or "WC" (vait-say)
z z as in zero
zs zh as in measure

Words and phrases

Basics

Do you speak . . .	beszél . . .	no/not	nem
English	angolul	I (don't) understand	(nem) értem
German	németül	please	kérem
French	franciául	excuse me (apology)	bocsánat, *or* elnézést
yes	igen	excuse me (to attract attention)	legyen szives
OK	jó		

two beers, please	két sört kérek	what do you call this?	mi a neve ennek?
thank you (very much)	köszönöm (szépen)		
you're welcome	szívesen	please write it down	kérem, írja le
hello/goodbye	szia (informal)	today	ma
good morning	jó reggelt	tomorrow	holnap
good day	jó napot	the day after tomorrow	holnapután
good evening	jó estét		
good night	jó éjszakát	yesterday	tegnap
goodbye	viszontlátásra	the day before yesterday	tegnapelőtt
see you later	viszlát (informal)		
how are you?	hogy vagy? (informal)	in the morning	reggel
how are you?	hogy van? (more formal)	in the evening	este
		at noon	délben
could you speak more slowly?	elmondaná lassabban?	at midnight	éjfélkor

Questions and requests

Hungarian has numerous interrogative modes whose subtleties elude foreigners, so it's best to use the simple *van?* ("is there?"), to which the reply might be *nincs* or *nincsen* ("there isn't"/"there aren't any"). In shops or restaurants you will immediately be addressed with the one-word *tessék,* meaning "Can I help you?", "What would you like?" or "Next!". To order in restaurants, shops and markets, use *kérek* ("I'd like. . .") plus accusative noun; *Kérem, adjon azt* ("Please give me that"); *Egy ilyet kérek* ("I'll have one of those").

I'd like/we'd like	Szeretnék/szeretnénk	Do you have a student discount?	van diák kedvezmény?
Where is/are . . . ?	Hol van/vannak . . ?		
Hurry up!	Siessen!	Is everything included?	Ebben minden szerepel?
How much is it?	Mennyibe kerül?		
per night	egy éjszakára	I asked for . . .	Én . . . .-t rendeltem
per week	egy hétre	The bill please	Fizetni szeretnék
a single room	egyágyas szoba	We're paying separately	Külön-külön fizetünk
a double room	kétágyas szoba		
hot (cold) water	meleg (hideg) víz	what?	mi?
a shower	egy zuhany	why?	miert?
It's very expensive	Ez nagyon drága	when?	mikor?
Do you have anything cheaper?	Van valami olcsóbb?	who?	ki?

Some signs

entrance	bejárat	free admission	szabad belépés
exit	kijárat	women's toilet	női (or WC – "Vait-say")
arrival	érkezés	men's toilet	férfi mosdó (or WC – "Vait-say")
departure	indulás	shop	bolt
open	nyitva	market	piac
closed	zárva	room for rent	szoba kiadó or Zimmer frei

L

hospital	kórház	no smoking	tilos a dohányzás/dohányozni tilos
pharmacy	gyógyszertár		
(local) police	(kerületi) Rendőrség	no bathing	tilos a fürdés/füredni tilos
caution/beware	vigyázat!/vigyázz!		

Directions

Where's the . . . ?	Hol van a . . . ?	towards	felé
campsite	kemping	on the right (left)	jobbra (balra)
hotel	szálloda/ hotel	straight ahead	egyenesen előre
railway station	vasútállomás	(over) there/here	ott/itt
bus station	buszállomás	Where are you going?	Hova megy?
bus-stand	kocsiállás	Is that on the way	Az a . . . úton?
(bus or train) stop	megálló	to . . . ?	
inland	belföldi	I want to get out at . . .	Le akarok szállni . . .-on/en
international	külföldi		
Is it near (far)?	Közel (messze) van?	please stop here	itt álljon meg
Which bus goes	Melyik busz	I'm lost	eltévedtem
to . . . ?	megy . . .-ra/re	arrivals	érkező járatok (or érkezés)
a one-way ticket to . . . please	egy jegyet kérek . . .-ra/re csak oda	departures	induló járatok (or indulás)
a return ticket to . . .	egy retur jegyet . . .-ra/re	to/from	hova/honnan
Do I have to change trains?	Át kell szállnom?	change	átszállás
		via	át

Descriptions and reactions

and	és	small	kicsi
or	vagy	quick	gyors
nothing	semmi	slow	lassú
perhaps	talán	now	most
very	nagyon	later	később
good	jó	beautiful	szép
bad	rossz	ugly	csúnya
better	jobb	Help!	Segítség!
big	nagy	I'm ill	beteg vagyok

Numbers

1	egy	10	tíz
2	kettő	11	tizenegy
3	három	12	tizenkettő
4	négy	13	tizenhárom
5	öt	14	tizennégy
6	hat	15	tizenöt
7	hét	16	tizenhat
8	nyolc	17	tizenhét
9	kilenc	18	tizennyolc

19	tizenkilenc	200	kettőszáz
20	húsz	300	háromszáz
21	huszonegy	400	négyszáz
30	harminc	500	ötszáz
40	negyven	600	hatszáz
50	ötven	700	hétszáz
60	hatvan	800	nyolcszáz
70	hetven	900	kilencszáz
80	nyolcvan	1000	egyezer
90	kilencven	half	fél
100	száz	a quarter	negyed
101	százegy	each/piece	darab
150	százötven		

Time, days and dates

Luckily, the 24-hour clock is used for timetables, but on cinema programmes you may see notations like 1/4, 3/4, etc. These derive from the spoken expression of time which, as in German, makes reference to the hour approaching completion. For example 3:30 is expressed as *fél négy* – "half (on the way to) four"; 3:45 – *háromnegyed négy* ("three quarters on the way to four"); 6:15 – "*negyed hét*" ("one quarter towards seven"), etc. However, ". . . o'clock" is . . . *óra*, rather than referring to the hour ahead. Duration is expressed by the suffixes *-től* ("from") and *-ig* ("to"); minutes are *perc*; to ask the time, say "*Hány óra?*"

Sunday	vasárnap	on Monday	hetfő
Monday	hétfő	on Tuesday	kedden etc.
Tuesday	kedd	day	nap
Wednesday	szerda	week	hét
Thursday	csütörtök	month	hónap
Friday	péntek	year	év
Saturday	szombat		

Hungarian food and drink terms

The food categories opposite refer to the general divisions used in menus. In cheaper places you will also find a further division of meat dishes: ready-made dishes like stews (*készételek*) and freshly cooked (in theory) dishes such as those cooked in breadcrumbs or grilled (*frissensültek*).

Tészták is a rogue pasta-doughy category that can include savoury dishes such as *turoscsusza* (pasta served with cottage cheese and a sprinkling of bacon), as well as sweet ones like *somlói galuska* (cream and chocolate covered sponge). Two popular **snacks** which are nicer than they sound are: *zsíros kenyér* (bread spread with lard and sprinkled with paprika; often sold in older wine bars) and *lángos* (fried dough served with soured cream or a variety of other toppings available in markets).

Basics

bors	pepper	mustár	mustard
cukor	sugar	rizs	rice
ecet	vinegar	só	salt
egészségedre!	Cheers!	tejföl	sour cream
jó étvágyat!	Bon appétit!	tejszín	cream
kenyér	bread	vaj	butter
kifli	croissant-shaped roll	zsemle or péksütemeny	bread rolls
méz	honey		

Cooking terms

comb	leg	jól megfőzve	well done (boiled)
mell	breast	pörkölt	stewed slowly
angolosan	(English-style) underdone/rare	rántott	deep fried in breadcrumbs
főtt	boiled	roston sütve	grilled
főzelék	basic vegetable stews	sülve	roasted
jól megsütve	well done (fried)	sült/sütve	fried

Soups (levesek)

bakonyi betyárleves	"Outlaw soup" of chicken, beef, noodles and vegetables, richly spiced	húsleves	meat consommé
		jókai bableves	bean soup flavoured with smoked meat
csirke-aprólék leves	mixed vegetable and giblet soup	kunsági pandúrleves	chicken soup seasoned with nutmeg, paprika and garlic
erőleves	meat consommé often served with noodles (*tésztával* or *metélttel*), liver dumplings (*májgombóccal*), or an egg placed raw into the soup (*tojással*)	lencseleves	lentil soup
		hideg meggyleves	delicious chilled sour cherry soup
		palócleves	mutton, bean and sour cream soup
gombaleves	mushroom soup	paradicsomleves	tomato soup
gulyásleves	goulash in its original Hungarian form as a soup, sometimes served in a small kettle pot (*bográcsgulyás*)	tarkonyos borjúraguleves	lamb soup flavoured with tarragon
		ujházi tyúkleves	chicken soup with noodles, vegetables and meat
halászlé	a rich paprika fish soup often served with hot paprika	zöldségleves	vegetable soup

Appetizers (előételek)

These can be served cold (*hideg*) or hot (*meleg*).

füstölt csülök tormával	smoked knuckle of pork with horseradish	libamáj	goose liver
		rakott krumpli	layered potato casserole with sausage and eggs
hortobágyi palacsinta	pancake stuffed with minced meat and served with creamy paprika sauce	rántott gomba	mushrooms fried in breadcrumbs, sometimes stuffed with sheep's cheese (*juhtúróval töltött*)
körözött	a paprika-flavoured spread made with sheep's cheese and served with toast		

rántott sajt,	Camembert or cauliflower		paprika and mustard and
Camembert,	fried in breadcrumbs		spread on toast
karfiol		velfőcsont	bone marrow spread on toast
tatárbeefsteak	raw mince that you mix with	fokhagymás	rubbed with garlic, a special
	an egg, salt, pepper, butter,	pirítóssal	delicacy associated with the
			gourmet Gyula Krúdy

Salads (saláták)

Salads are not Hungary's strong point; they are usually simple, and are often served in a vinegary dressing, although other dressings include blue cheese (*rokfortos*), yogurt (*joghurtos*) or French (*francia*).

csalamádé	mixed pickled salad	paradicsom saláta	tomato salad
fejes saláta	lettuce	uborka saláta	cucumber which can
idénysaláta	fresh salad of what		be gherkins (*cse*
	ever is in season		*mege* or *kovászos*) or
jércesaláta	chicken salad		the fresh variety (friss)

Fish dishes (halételek)

csuka tejfölben	fried pike with sour	ponty	carp
sütve	cream	ponty filé	carp fillet in mushroom
fogas	a local fish of the pike-	gombával	sauce
	perch family	rántott pontyfilé	carp fillet fried in
fogasszeletek	breaded fillet of *fogas*		breadcrumbs
Gundel modra		rostélyos töltött	carp stuffed with bread,
harcsa	catfish	ponty	egg, herbs and fish liver
kecsege	sterlet (small sturgeon)		or roe
nyelvhal	sole	süllő	another pike-perch relative
paprikás ponty	carp in paprika sauce	sült hal	fried fish
pisztráng	trout	tonhal	tuna
pisztráng tejszínes	trout baked in cream		
mártásban			

Meat dishes (húsételek)

baromfi	poultry	őz	venison
bécsi szelet	Wiener schnitzel	pulyka	turkey
bélszin	sirloin	sertés	pork
bélszinjava	tenderloin	sonka	ham
csirke	chicken	vaddisznó	wild boar
fácán	pheasant	vadételek	game
fasírt	meatballs	virsli	frankfurter
hátszin	rumpsteak	borjúpörkölt	closer to what foreigners
kacsa	duck		mean by "goulash", veal
kolbász	spicy sausage		stew seasoned with garlic
liba	goose	cigányrostélyos	"gypsy-style" steak with
máj	liver		brown sauce
marha	beef	csikós tokány	strips of beef braised in
nyúl	rabbit		bacon, onion rings, sour
			cream and tomato sauce

csülök Pékné módra	knuckle of pork	sült libacomb tört burgonyával és párolt káposztával	grilled goose leg with potatoes, onions and steamed cabbage
erdélyi rakott-káposzta	layers of cabbage, rice and ground pork baked in sour cream (a Transylvanian speciality)	töltött káposzta	cabbage stuffed with meat and rice, in a tomato sauce
hagymás rostélyos	braised steak piled high with fried onions	töltött paprika	peppers stuffed with meat and rice, in a tomato sauce
pacal	tripe in a paprika sauce	vaddisznó borókamártással	wild boar in juniper sauce
paprikás csirke	chicken in paprika sauce	vasi pecsenye	fried pork marinated in milk and garlic
rablóhús nyárson	kebab of pork, veal and bacon		
sertésborda	pork chop		

Sauces (mártásban)

bormártásban	in a wine sauce	tejszínes paprikás mártásban	in a cream and paprika sauce
ecetes tormával	with horseradish	vadasmártásban	in a brown sauce (made of mushrooms, almonds, herbs and brandy)
fokhagymás mártásban	in a garlic sauce		
gombamártásban	in a mushroom sauce		
kapormártásban	in a dill sauce		
meggymártásban	in a morello cherry sauce	zöldborsós	in a green pea sauce
paprikás mártásban	in a paprika sauce	zöldborsosmártásba	in a green peppercorn sauce
tárkonyos mártásban	in a tarragon sauce		

Accompaniments (köretek)

galuska	noodles	burgonya	served with parsley
hasábburgonya	chips – french fries	rizs	rice
krokett	potato croquettes	zöldköret	mixed vegetables (often of frozen origin)
petrezselymes	boiled potatoes		

Vegetables (zöldségek)

bab	beans	padlizsán	aubergine/eggplant
borsó	peas	paprika (édes/erős)	peppers (sweet/hot)
burgonya/krumpli	potatoes	paradicsom	tomatoes
fokhagyma	garlic	sárgarépa	carrots
gomba	mushrooms	spárga	asparagus
hagyma	onions	spenót	spinach
káposzta	cabbage	uborka	cucumber
karfiol	cauliflower	zöldbab	green beans
kelkáposzta	savoy cabbage	zöldborsó	peas
kukorica	sweetcorn	zukkini	courgette
lecsó	a tomato-green pepper stew, a popular ingredient in Hungarian cooking		

Fruit (gyümölcs)

alma	apple		mandula	almond
birsalma	quince		meggy	morello cherry
bodza	elderflower		mogyoró	hazelnut
citrom	lemon		narancs	orange
dió	walnut		őszibarack	peach
eper	strawberry		sárgabarack	apricot
füge	fig		szilva	plum
(görög) dinnye	(water) melon		szőlő	grape
körte	pear		tök	marrow or pumpkin/squash
málna	raspberry			

Cheese (sajt)

Cheeses made in Hungary are a rather limited selection, the most interesting being the soft *juhtúró*

füstölt sajt	smoked cheese		márvány	Danish blue cheese
juhtúró	sheep's cheese		trappista	rubbery, Edam-type cheese
kecske sajt	goat's cheese		túró	curd cheese

Desserts (édességek)

aranygaluska	golden dumpling cake		rétes	strudel
gesztenye puré	chestnut purée		szilva gombóc	dumpling stuffed with a plum
palacsinta	pancake			

Travel store

TRAVEL

Africa & Middle East
Cape Town & the Garden Route
Egypt
The Gambia
Jordan
Kenya
Marrakesh DIRECTIONS
Morocco
South Africa, Lesotho & Swaziland
Syria
Tanzania
Tunisia
West Africa
Zanzibar

Travel Theme guides
First-Time Around the World
First-Time Asia
First-Time Europe
First-Time Latin America
Travel Online
Travel Health
Travel Survival
Walks in London & SE England
Women Travel

Maps
Algarve
Amsterdam
Andalucia & Costa del Sol
Argentina
Athens
Australia
Baja California
Barcelona
Berlin
Boston
Brittany
Brussels
California
Chicago
Corsica
Costa Rica & Panama
Crete
Croatia
Cuba
Cyprus
Czech Republic
Dominican Republic
Dubai & UAE
Dublin
Egypt
Florence & Siena
Florida
France
Frankfurt
Germany
Greece
Guatemala & Belize
Hong Kong
Iceland
Ireland
Kenya
Lisbon
London
Los Angeles
Madrid
Mallorca
Marrakesh
Mexico
Miami & Key West
Morocco
New England
New York City
New Zealand
Northern Spain
Paris
Peru
Portugal
Prague
Rome
San Francisco
Sicily
South Africa
South India
Spain & Portugal
Sri Lanka
Tenerife
Thailand
Toronto
Trinidad & Tobago
Tuscany
Venice
Washington DC
Yucatán Peninsula

Dictionary Phrasebooks
Croatian
Czech
Dutch
Egyptian Arabic
French
German
Greek
Hindi & Urdu
Italian
Japanese
Latin American Spanish
Mandarin Chinese
Mexican Spanish
Polish
Portuguese
Russian
Spanish
Swahili
Thai
Turkish
Vietnamese

Computers
Blogging
iPods, iTunes & Music Online
The Internet
Macs & OS X
Music Playlists
PCs and Windows
Website Directory

Film & TV
Comedy Movies
Cult Movies
Cult TV
Gangster Movies
Horror Movies
James Bond
Kids' Movies
Sci–Fi Movies

Lifestyle
Ethical Shopping
Babies
Pregnancy & Birth

Music Guides
The Beatles
Bob Dylan
Cult Pop
Classical Music
Elvis
Frank Sinatra
Heavy Metal
Hip-Hop
Jazz
Opera
Reggae
Rock
World Music (2 vols)

Popular Culture
Books for Teenagers
Children's Books, 0-5
Children's Books, 5-11
Conspiracy Theories
Cult Fiction
The Da Vinci Code
Lord of the Rings
Shakespeare
Superheroes
Unexplained Phenomena

Sport
Arsenal 11s
Celtic 11s
Chelsea 11s
Liverpool 11s
Man United 11s
Newcastle 11s
Rangers 11s
Tottenham 11s
Cult Football
Muhammad Ali
Poker

Science
The Universe
Weather

& MORE

Small print and
Index

A Rough Guide to Rough Guides

Published in 1982, the first Rough Guide – to Greece – was a student scheme that became a publishing phenomenon. Mark Ellingham, a recent graduate in English from Bristol University, had been travelling in Greece the previous summer and couldn't find the right guidebook. With a small group of friends he wrote his own guide, combining a highly contemporary, journalistic style with a thoroughly practical approach to travellers' needs.

The immediate success of the book spawned a series that rapidly covered dozens of destinations. And, in addition to impecunious backpackers, Rough Guides soon acquired a much broader and older readership that relished the guides' wit and inquisitiveness as much as their enthusiastic, critical approach and value-for-money ethos.

These days, Rough Guides include recommendations from shoestring to luxury and cover more than 200 destinations around the globe, including almost every country in the Americas and Europe, more than half of Africa and most of Asia and Australasia. Our ever-growing team of authors and photographers is spread all over the world, particularly in Europe, the USA and Australia.

In the early 1990s, Rough Guides branched out of travel, with the publication of Rough Guides to World Music, Classical Music and the Internet. All three have become benchmark titles in their fields, spearheading the publication of a wide range of books under the Rough Guide name.

Including the travel series, Rough Guides now number more than 350 titles, covering: phrasebooks, waterproof maps, music guides from Opera to Heavy Metal, reference works as diverse as Conspiracy Theories and Shakespeare, and popular culture books from iPods to Poker. Rough Guides also produce a series of more than 120 World Music CDs in partnership with World Music Network.

Visit www.roughguides.com to see our latest publications.

Rough Guide travel images are available for commercial licensing at www.roughguidespictures.com

SMALL PRINT

Rough Guide credits

Text editors: Richard Lim, Sarah Eno, Polly Thomas
Layout: Dan May
Cartography: Jai Prakash Mishra, Maxine Repath
Picture editor: Harriet Mills
Production: Katherine Owers
Proofreader: Wendy Smith
Cover design: Chloë Roberts
Photographer: Eddie Gerald

....

Editorial: London Kate Berens, Claire Saunders, Geoff Howard, Ruth Blackmore, Clifton Wilkinson, Alison Murchie, Karoline Densley, Andy Turner, Ella O'Donnell, Keith Drew, Edward Aves, Nikki Birrell, Helen Marsden, Alice Park, Joe Staines, Duncan Clark, Peter Buckley, Matthew Milton, Tracy Hopkins; **New York** Andrew Rosenberg, Richard Koss, Steven Horak, AnneLise Sorensen, Amy Hegarty, Hunter Slaton, April Isaacs
Design & Pictures: London Simon Bracken, Diana Jarvis, Mark Thomas, Jj Luck, Harriot Mills, Chloë Roberts; **Delhi** Madhulita Mohapatra, Umesh Aggarwal, Ajay Verma, Jessica Subramanian, Amit Verma, Ankur Guha
Production: Julia Bovis, Sophie Hewat, Katherine Owers
Cartography: London Ed Wright, Katie Lloyd-Jones; **Delhi** Manish Chandra, Rajesh Chhibber, Ashutosh Bharti, Rajesh Mishra, Animesh Pathak, Jasbir Sandhu, Karobi Gogoi
Online: New York Jennifer Gold, Suzanne Welles, Kristin Mingrone; **Delhi** Manik Chauhan, Narender Kumar, Shekhar Jha, Rakesh Kumar, Chhandita Chakravarty
Marketing & Publicity: London Richard Trillo, Niki Hanmer, David Wearn, Demelza Dallow, Louise Maher; **New York** Geoff Colquitt, Megan Kennedy, Katy Ball; **Delhi** Reem Khokhar
Custom publishing and foreign rights: Philippa Hopkins
Manager India: Punita Singh
Series editor: Mark Ellingham
Reference Director: Andrew Lockett
PA to Managing and Publishing Directors: Megan McIntyre
Publishing Director: Martin Dunford
Managing Director: Kevin Fitzgerald

Publishing information

This 3rd edition published April 2006 by **Rough Guides Ltd**,
80 Strand, London WC2R 0RL
345 Hudson St, 4th Floor,
New York, NY 10014, USA
14 Local Shopping Centre, Panchsheel Park,
New Delhi 110017, India
Distributed by the Penguin Group
Penguin Books Ltd,
80 Strand, London WC2R 0RL
Penguin Putnam, Inc.
375 Hudson Street, NY 10014, USA
Penguin Group (Australia),
250 Camberwell Road, Camberwell,
Victoria 3124, Australia
Penguin Books Canada Ltd,
10 Alcorn Avenue, Toronto, Ontario,
Canada M4V 1E4
Penguin Group (New Zealand),
Cnr Rosedale and Airborne Roads,
Albany, Auckland, New Zealand

Typeset in Bembo and Helvetica to an original design by Henry Iles.
Printed in China
© Charles Hebbert and Dan Richardson

248pp includes index
A catalogue record for this book is available from the British Library
ISBN 13: 781843536123
ISBN 10: 1-84353-612-9

The publishers and authors have done their best to ensure the accuracy and currency of all the information in **The Rough Guide to Budapest**, however, they can accept no responsibility for any loss, injury, or inconvenience sustained by any traveller as a result of information or advice contained in the guide.

1   3   5   7   9   8   6   4   2

Help us update

We've gone to a lot of effort to ensure that the third edition of **The Rough Guide to Budapest** is accurate and up to date. However, things change – places get "discovered", opening hours are notoriously fickle, restaurants and rooms raise prices or lower standards. If you feel we've got it wrong or left something out, we'd like to know, and if you can remember the address, the price, the time, the phone number, so much the better.

We'll credit all contributions, and send a copy of the next edition (or any other Rough Guide if you prefer) for the best letters. Everyone who writes to us and isn't already a subscriber will receive a copy of our full-colour thrice-yearly newsletter. Please mark letters: **"Rough Guide Budapest Update"** and send to: Rough Guides, 80 Strand, London WC2R 0RL, or Rough Guides, 4th Floor, 345 Hudson St, New York, NY 10014. Or send an email to **mail@roughguides.com**

Have your questions answered and tell others about your trip at **www.roughguides.atinfopop.com**

SMALL PRINT

Acknowledgements

Charles Hebbert would like to thank: firstly Caroline for all her help, Rachel Appleby and Rozgonyi Zoltán for additional research, my editor Richard Lim for his assiduous and patient work and advice, and Polly Thomas, Sarah Eno and Claire Saunders for undertaking last-minute editing, Norm Longley for his extensive permissions, Meriel Beattie and Bill Blanchard, Biber Kriszta, Eileen Brown, Simon Broughton, Yankl Falk, Fazakas Péter, Fenyő Kriszta, Linda Kondor, Kosa Judit, Lázár Julia, Richard and Julia Lock, Lőrincz Anna, Mester Tibor, Nádori Péter, Németh Judit, Craigie and Mark Pearson, Duncan Shiels, Szántó Diana, Svirzsovics Éva and Tamás Amaryllis, amongst many others. Finally, Amy, Grace and Theo for their babysitting assistance. And of course Molly, for not doing too much.

Readers' letters

Thanks to all the readers who have taken the time to write in with comments and suggestions (and apologies if we've inadvertently omitted or misspelt anyone's name):

John and Hilda Allen, R. Barton, Micaela Blitz, Roger Bratseth, Una Cronin, Mike and Tania Herniman, Marion Janner, Mirjam Schiffer, Nick and Nic Wallis, Kate Williams.

SMALL PRINT

Photo credits

All photos © Rough Guides except the following:

Back cover:
Parliament Building © Mark Thomas

Things not to miss:
12 Halászbástya, view from Fishermen's Bastion © Mark Thomas
13 *Taormina* by Tivadar Kosztka Csontváry © Tibor Mester with kind permission of Hungarian National Gallery
14 *Study of a Man* by El Greco, c.1595 © Rough Guides/Eddie Gerald, with kind permission of the Museum of Fine Arts, Budapest
16 Schmidl tomb © Charles Hebbert
20 Iván Fischer conducting the Budapest Festival Orchestra © Peter Mares/Lebrecht Music and Arts Photo Library/Alamy
22 Grapes, Tokaj Region © Peter Wilson
23 Budapest Spring Festival, Chain Bridge © Courtesy of Budapest Spring Festival
25 Mihaály Sipos of Muzsikás © Charles Hebbert

Colour insert: Hungarian Music
Táncház scene © Attila Kleb/www.photogram.hu
Béla Bartók © Bettman/Corbis
Folk dancers, Sárközi lakodalom © Attila Kleb/www.photogram.hu
Beáta Pálya © Orpheia Records

Colour insert: Baths
Rác fürdo (used as background) © Attila Kleb/www.photogram.hu
Király Baths © Adam Woolfit/Alamy
Gellért Baths © Attila Kleb/www.photogram.hu

Black and whites
p.152 Gellért Hotel © Mark Thomas
p.175 Korai Öröm on stage © www.korai.hu

SMALL PRINT

Index

Map entries are in colour.

INDEX

INDEX

Map symbols

Maps are listed in the full index using coloured text.

– – –	Chapter division boundary		◆	Point of interest
▬▬▬▬	International boundary		@	Internet café
▬▬▬	Motorway		ⓘ	Tourist office/information point
═══	Major road		⊠	Post office
═══	Minor road		✈	Airport
▬▬▬	Pedestrianized street		■–■	Gate
▥▥▥	Steps		★	Bus stop
▬▬▬	Railway		✡	Synagogue
– – – –	Footpath		⊙	Statue
··········	Bobsleigh route		🏛	Monument
───	River		♕	Castle
– –	Ferry		⋎	Viewpoint
───	Wall		⊞	Hospital
●–--–●	Chairlift		⬤	Baths / swimming pool
—Ⓗ—	HÉV line and station		ⵜ	Fountain
—Ⓜ—	Metro line and station		⸸	Church (regional maps)
⚠	Campsite		⊞	Church (town maps)
⌒	Cave		▮	Building
∴	Ruin		⬭	Stadium
▲	Mountain peak		⌐	Jewish cemetery
◉	Accommodation		⊞	Christian cemetery
▣	Restaurant		▦	Park
🅿	Parking			

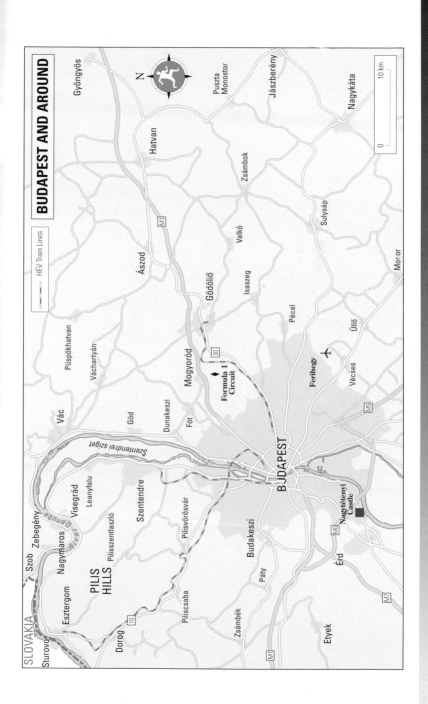

BUDAPEST AND AROUND

BUDAPEST

N

Szentendre

CSILLAGHEGY

Danube

IV

ÚJPEST

Aquincum

Óbudai-
sziget

III

VÁCI ÚT

BÉKE UTCA

TATAI U.

XIV

Rail
History
Park

HŰVÖSVÖLGY

Hármashatár-
hegy

NAGYKOVÁCSI ÚT

RÓBERT KÁROLY KÖRÚT

Bartók
Memorial
House

ÓBUDA

Margit-
sziget

XIII

HŰVÖSVÖLGYI ÚT

II

Városliget

BUDAKESZI ÚT

János-
hegy

Chair
lift

PASARÉT

Nyugati
Station

Puskás
Ferenc
Stadion

VI

THÖKÖLY ÚT

Children's
Railway

MOSZKVA
TÉR

Várhegy

V

VII

Keleti
Station

BUDAKESZI

Cogwheel
Railway

ANDRÁSSY ÚT

ALKOTÁS UTCA

I

Déli
Station

NAGYKÖRÚT

KISKÖRÚT

Kerepesi
Cemetery

KŐBÁNYAI

XII

Budapest
Convention
Centre

VIII

Farkasréti
Cemetery

FTC
Stadium

GAZDAGRÉT

BUDAÖRSI ÚT

Palace of
Arts

KÖNYVES KÁLMÁN KÖRÚT

Népliget
Bus
Station

LÁGYMÁNYOSI
HÍD

IX

Vienna & Lake Balaton

M1/M7

FEHÉRVÁRI ÚT

BUDAFÓKI ÚT

SOROKSÁRI ÚT

BALATONI ÚT

XI

Danube

CSEPEL

M0

Statue
Park

XXI

BUDAFÓK

XXII

Nagytétényi Castle Museum

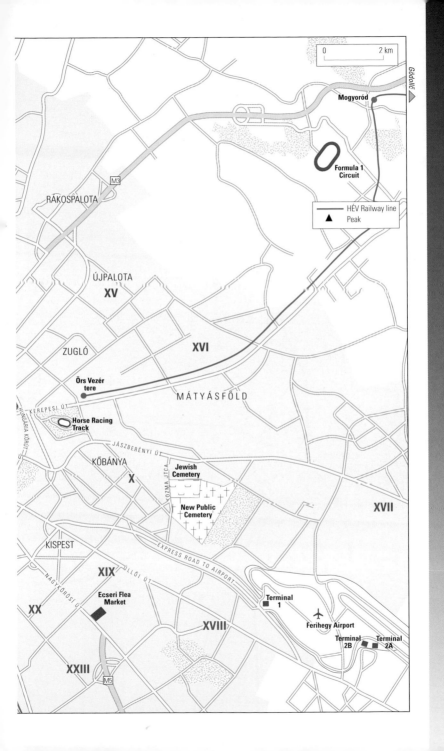

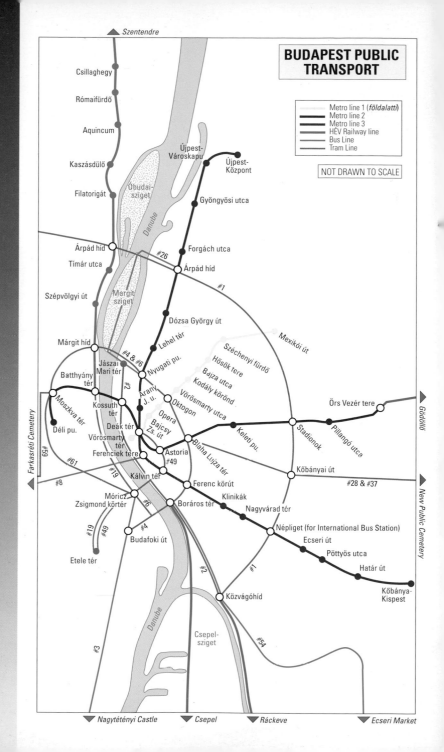